RUSSIA'S WARPLANES, Russian-made Military Aircraft and Helicopters

Piotr Butowski

RUSSIA'S WARPLANES
Volume 2

Russian-made Military Aircraft and Helicopters Today

Piotr Butowski

2803 Sackett Street, Houston, TX 77098-1125, U.S.A.
russias-warplanes@harpia-publishing.com

Consulting and inspiration by Kerstin Berger
Cover artworks by Tom Cooper (front) and Ugo Crisponi (rear)
Drawings by Piotr Butowski
Editorial by Thomas Newdick
Layout by Norbert Novak, www.media-n.at, Vienna
Maps by James Lawrence

Harpia Publishing, L.L.C. is a member of

EUROPEAN MILITARY PRESS ASSOCIATION EMPA

Printed at finidr, Czech Republic

ISBN 978-0-9973092-0-1

Contents

Introduction 7

Acknowledgements 9

Abbreviations 10

Addenda 13

Chapter 1: Long-range Bombers 37

- Tupolev Tu-22M 37
- Tupolev Tu-95MS 49
- Tupolev Tu-160 59
- Future long-range bombers: MARK and Tupolev PAK DA Poslannik 69

Chapter 2: Maritime Aircraft 71

- Beriev Be-12 71
- Beriev Be-200 77
- Ilyushin Il-38 83
- Kamov Ka-27 91
- Mil Mi-14 101
- Tupolev Tu-142 107
- Future maritime patrol aircraft: APK Apatit, Kamov MPVK Minoga, Ilyushin Il-114 maritime patrol variants and Kamov Ka-65 Okovka 113

Chapter 3: Strategic Transport and Tanker Aircraft 119

- Antonov An-22 120
- Antonov An-124 125
- Ilyushin Il-76 139
- Ilyushin Il-78 151
- Future strategic transport and tanker aircraft: Ilyushin Il-96-400TZ and Ilyushin Il-106 157

Chapter 4: Theatre and Special-Purpose Transports 163
Antonov An-12 164
Antonov An-26 169
Antonov An-72 175
Antonov An-140-100 179
Antonov An-148 183
Ilyushin Il-18 187
Ilyushin Il-62M 189
Tupolev Tu-134A Balkany 193
Tupolev Tu-154 197
Future theatre transport aircraft: Ilyushin Il-112V and Ilyushin Il-214 201

Chapter 5: Trainers 207
Aircraft Industries L-410UVP 208
Antonov An-2 211
Kamov Ka-226 213
Kazan Helicopters Ansat-U 217
KB SAT SR-10 223
Mil/PZL Świdnik Mi-2 225
Tupolev Tu-134 trainer versions 227
Yakovlev Yak-52 231
Yakovlev Yak-130 235
Yakovlev Yak-152 245
Future trainer: Tupolev UTK DA 248

Appendix I: Aircraft design and production facilities 249

Introduction

International tensions surrounding Russia have continued to mount since the war with Georgia in 2008 and flared up with the Russian invasion of Ukraine in early 2014. In autumn 2015, as the first volume of this book was going to press, Moscow launched its military intervention in Syria, a campaign conducted primarily by Russian air power. These events have combined to increase interest in Russia's armed forces, including its military aviation, the subject of this book.

This is the second volume in a series that covers the aircraft currently in service or under development for Russian military aviation and for export clients. Volume 2 presents long-range bombers; maritime fixed-wing aircraft and helicopters; transport aircraft of all categories, from strategic to tactical; and fixed-wing training aircraft and training helicopters. The first volume covered tactical combat aircraft, combat and transport helicopters, as well as reconnaissance and special duty aircraft. Separately, a volume covering modern Russian aerial ordnance will appear in the near future, and is understood as being integral to the understanding of the previous two volumes.

As regards the Russian Air Force (formally known as the Vozdushno-Kosmicheskiye Sily, VKS, or Russian Aerospace Forces, but referred to herein as the Russian Air Force, for the sake of consistency), the most important event in recent months has been the aforementioned military intervention in Syria, which commenced in autumn 2015. During this campaign, Russia has exploited a wide range of aircraft in its inventory, and numerous types of aircraft and weapons have made their combat debut. It is too early to discuss the conclusions that the Russian military will draw from this campaign, or the changes it might bring to the Russian armed forces, but they will undoubtedly be significant both for the military and for industry.

Despite the serious recession affecting the Russian economy, Moscow's military expenditure is growing. According to data submitted by Russia to the UN, in 2015 defence spending amounted to 2,900 billion roubles, a 48 per cent increase over 2014 (1,960 billion). (It should be noted that data from different sources, calculated using other methods, may show significant variation.) In Russia's budget for 2016, military expenditure was planned to amount to 3,145 billion roubles. However, in September 2016, Russian media reported that the Ministry of Finance was considering reducing all expenditure within the state budget (with the exception of social expenses) for 2017–19 by six per cent compared to 2016; this was also to include the military budget.

The Russian Air Force began large-scale purchases of new equipment after the war with Georgia in 2008. In December 2010 the National Armament Programme for 2011–20 (Gosudarstvennaya Programma Vooruzheniy, GPV-2020) was approved. According to this document, in this 10-year period the Russian Air Force is to receive more than 600 new fixed-wing aircraft and more than 1,000 helicopters; in the previous decade the total purchases amounted to between 50 and 60 combat aircraft, half of which were MiG-29s that had been returned by Algeria. The GPV-2020 programme is being implemented with almost no delays. Initially, in 2011–12, the deliveries amounted to an average of 30 aircraft per year, with plans for the tempo to increase in the coming years. In 2013 the Russian Air Force received more than 60 aircraft, and around 100 aircraft were delivered in both 2014 and 2015. Helicopter deliveries have remained at a level of around 100 to 140 per year.

Since exact data is hard to obtain, the numbers provided here have been rounded up; most related Russian reports reveal some discrepancies. Sometimes delivery totals include aircraft for testing, and sometimes these are omitted. Furthermore, the Russian figures sometimes include under 'new production' aircraft that have undergone a thorough mid-life upgrade. For example, in January 2016 the commander-in-chief of the Russian Air Force Viktor Bondarev told the Russian press that in 2015 the Air Force had received 190 fixed-wing aircraft and helicopters; a month later he mentioned the figure 243. It is likely that in this latter case Bondarev added aircraft that had undergone upgrade.

The United Aircraft Corporation (UAC) reports that in 2015 it delivered 96 aircraft to the Russian Ministry of Defence (with 105 planned for 2015 and 103 delivered in 2014); a further 34 military aircraft were delivered by UAC to export customers. New orders placed by the Russian Ministry of Defence during the last 12 months amount to 50 Su-35S fighters, 28 Mi-28UB and two Mi-26 helicopters; an order for MiG-35S fighters is still expected. Signature of some of the previously expected contracts – for example, for 31 Il-78M-90A tankers or 48 Il-112V light transport aircraft – has been postponed until later years. The peak output of the years 2014–15 is not likely to be repeated, although Russia still hopes that its economic crisis will be resolved in the next year or two. In a report from June 2016 UAC forecasts that after two lean years, in 2016 and 2017, during which it will deliver 74 aircraft each year to the Russian Ministry of Defence, this total will increase to 95 aircraft in 2018, followed by 102 in 2019 and 104 in 2020.

The Russian Helicopters Corporation is a structure that exists in parallel to the UAC but which deals with rotary-wing aircraft. The corporation reported that in 2015 helicopter production in Russia dropped to 212 units, equivalent to a 22 per cent reduction compared to 2014 (271 helicopters) and a 30 per cent per cent reduction on the peak output in 2013 (303 helicopters); at the same time, the income from the sales increased from 141.5 to 177 billion roubles thanks to export contracts. Sales to foreign customers are nominated in dollars, which after conversion to devalued roubles turn out to be very profitable. The company's CEO Alexander Mikheyev claimed the company would produce 'about 200' helicopters in 2016. The most serious effect of the reduction in output has been felt by the primary product of Russian helicopter industry, the Mi-8 transport helicopter. In the case of this aircraft, the large orders placed in previous years by the Russian Ministry of Defence have already been or will soon be completed; a similar situation is seen as regards several foreign contacts for the type placed by China, India and the United States, while new contracts are much smaller.

The increase in military expenditure currently concerns on-going support for the armed forces and funding for the Syrian campaign, while funds for research and development are being reduced. In UAC's report for 2015, published in June 2016, there are several occasions in which a task is described as not having been carried out due to a 'reduction of funding from the national budget'. Within a large-scale technology development programme for the national defence industry, implemented simultaneously with the GPV-2020 procurement programme, as many as 54 from a total of 178 assignments concerning the aircraft industry were cancelled in 2015. Sixteen new assignments were added, all concerning one programme – the resumption of production of the Tu-160M2 strategic bomber (see Chapter 1).

A meaningful interview was granted to the *Wall Street Journal* (10 March 2016) by Sergei Chemezov, head of the Rostec arms holding that controls, among others, Russian Helicopters and the United Engine Corporation. Chemezov told the newspaper that owing to the crisis in the Russian economy, government defence orders would 'be reduced by about 10 per cent' in 2016. According to Chemezov, only those research and development projects that are already at an advanced stage will be continued, while 'things that we're only just starting, we'll stop'. Chemezov also confirmed that after 2020 the Russian Ministry of Defence will not purchase arms in large numbers. 'Our rearmament programme is designed to go until 2020. It will end, and then these order volumes won't be there.' It should be noted that this reality had become obvious previously, even without the current crisis. Indeed, Russia has scheduled the purchase of such a large quantity of arms by 2020 that they will be sufficient for many years to come.

As with the first volume in this series, this book describes aircraft that are currently in service or under development for Russian military aviation and export clients. Certain older aircraft, which are no longer operated by the Russian armed forces, but continue to fly elsewhere, such as the MiG-21, MiG-27 and Su-22, are excluded.

Acknowledgements

This book, the second volume in the series, is the result of my long-term interest and study of Russian aviation. Information has been collected piece by piece from various sources 'in the field', and not from other publications. Since 1989, when possible, I have visited all significant airshows and defence exhibitions in Russia and those in which the Russians presented themselves abroad. I have visited most Russian aircraft design bureaus, many production plants and some military air bases. I collect all papers, presentations and pictures I can find.

Over the years I have benefited greatly from conversations with Russian aviation specialists, the designers of aircraft and systems. I thank and greet them all heartily. Sadly, I cannot mention their names; not only are there very many of them, but most would also prefer anonymity.

As a rule, the only magazine I read is the monthly *Vzlyot*, published in Moscow by Andrei Fomin, and in my opinion the most valuable aviation magazine in Russia. Trustworthiness is Andrei's advantage. If he knows something, he knows it for sure.

I also want to thank two friends: Viktor Drushlyakov in Russia is my companion at aviation events and in conversations about the history of aviation. Jerzy Gruszczyński in Poland has been my friend for 30 years, since he was a young Su-20 pilot. Now he is the editor-in-chief of the Polish monthly *Lotnictwo*. In simple, soldier's words, Jerzy explains to me, a rotten pacifist, why the military needs aircraft.

I have many reasons to thank my wife Irina – but not on the occasion of this book. She claims that I needlessly work too much and earn too much for the tax office. Finally, a kiss to my children, Joanna, Mark and Filip.

Piotr Butowski, August 2016

Abbreviations

AAM	air-to-air missile
AESA	active electronically scanned array
APK	Aviatsionnyi Patrulnyji Kompleks, Airborne Patrol Complex
APSZ	Aviatsionnyi Polk Samolotov-Zapravshchikov, Tanker Aviation Regiment
APU	auxiliary power unit
ASW	anti-submarine warfare
BAP	Bomber Aviation Regiment
c/n	construction number
CRT	cathode-ray tube
ECM	electronic countermeasures
ELINT	electronic intelligence
EMERCOM	Ministry for Emergency Situations (Russia)
EO	electro-optical
ESM	electronic support measures
FADEC	full-authority digital engine control
FBW	fly-by-wire
FSB	Federalnaya Sluzhba Bezopasnosti, Federal Security Service
FSO	Federalnaya Sluzhba Okhrany, Federal Guard Service
GPS	Global Positioning System
GPV	Gosudarstvennaya Programma Vooruzheniy, National Armament Programme (e.g. GPV-2020 for 2011–20)
HAL	Hindustan Aeronautics Limited
HMS	helmet-mounted sight
HOTAS	hands on throttle and stick
HUD	head-up display
ICAO	International Civil Aviation Organization
ICBM	intercontinental ballistic missile
IFF	identification friend or foe
ILS	instrument landing system
INAS	Indian Naval Air Squadron
INS	Indian Naval Station
INS	inertial navigation system
IR	infrared
IRST	infrared search and track
IRTA	Indian-Russian Transport Aircraft; now called MTA
ISA	International Standard Atmosphere
LCD	liquid-crystal display
LO	Lotnyi Otryad, Flight Detachment
LORAN	long-range navigation
LVTS	Lyogkiy Voyenno-Transportnyi Samolyot, Lightweight Military Transport Aircraft
MAD	magnetic anomaly detector
MAKS	Moscow International Aviation and Space Salon

MChS	Ministerstvo Cherezvychainykh Situatsiy, Ministry of Emergency Situations
MFD	multifunction display
MPVK	Mnogovariantnyi Perspektivnyi Vertoliotnyi Kompleks, Multi-version Future Helicopter Complex
MTA	Multirole Transport Aircraft, a joint project by Ilyushin of Russia and HAL of India; previously IRTA
MTOW	maximum take-off weight
MVD	Ministerstvo Vnutrennikh Del, Ministry of Interior
NATO	North Atlantic Treaty Organization
NVGs	night-vision goggles
OGE	out of ground effect
PAK DA	Perspektivnyi Aviatsionnyi Kompleks Dalney Aviatsii, Future Air Complex of Long-Range Aviation
PMKI	(unconfirmed designation) Perspektivnyi Mnogofunktsyonalnyi Korabelnyi Istrebitel, Future Multirole Shipborne Fighter
PSZ	Perspektyvnyi Samolot Zapravshchik, Future Tanker Aircraft
RATO	rocket-assisted take-off
RWR	radar warning receiver
SALIS	Strategic Airlift Interim Solution (NATO)
SAM	surface-to-air missile
SAR	search and rescue
SSR	Soviet Socialist Republic
SVTS	Sredniy Voyenno-Transportnyi Samolyot, Medium Military Transport Aircraft
TACAN	tactical air navigation system
TBAP	Heavy Bomber Aviation Regiment
TKMV	Tyazholyi Korabelnyi Mnogotselevoi Vertoliot, Heavy Ship-borne Multirole Helicopter
TOW	take-off weight
UAV	unmanned aerial vehicle
UCAV	unmanned combat aerial vehicle
USSR	Union of Soviet Socialist Republics
UAV	unmanned aerial vehicle
UTK DA	Uchebno-Trenirovochnyi Kompleks Dalney Aviatsii, Training Complex of Long-Range Aviation
UTK PNP	Uchebno-Trenirovochnyi Kompleks Pervonachalnoi Podgotovki, Training Complex of Initial Training
VKS	Vozdushno-Kosmicheskiye Sily, Russian Aerospace Forces (referred to herein as the Russian Air Force)
VNE	never-exceed speed
VOR	VHF omnidirectional range
VTA	Voyenno-Transportnaya Aviatsiya, Military Transport Aviation
VTAP	Voyenno-Transportnyi Aviatsionnyi Polk, Military Transport Aviation Regiment
WSO	weapons system operator

ADDENDA

In the light of new developments in the 12 months since the publication of *Russia's Warplanes Volume 1*, the author would like to make the following additions and clarifications. Overall, the developments described represent a continuation of previous tendencies and are therefore to be expected.

Chapter 1: Mikoyan MiG-29, pp13–22

MiG-29 fighters are being gradually withdrawn from the Russian Air Force inventory. Within the Russian Air Force, the final operational regiment is based at Kursk-Khalino, operating examples of the latest MiG-29SMT version that were returned by Algeria. The other regiment at Millerovo has its MiG-29s arranged around the perimeter of the airfield, but these are not used; the regiment has now converted to Su-30SM fighters.

Sixteen new-production MiG-29SMT (izdeliye 9.19R) aircraft that were ordered on 14 April 2014 in order to provide financial support to the RSK MiG Corporation are being delivered to the Russian Air Force training centre at Privolzhskiy airfield near Astrakhan (the initial four examples were delivered in December 2015).

'23 Blue' is one of the first four new-production MiG-29SMT fighters delivered to the Russian Air Force's Privolzhskiy (Astrakhan) training centre in December 2015. (Piotr Butowski)

Chapter 1: Mikoyan MiG-29K (MiG-29M, MiG-35), pp23–30

The RSK MiG Corporation has completed the delivery of 20 MiG-29KR and four MiG-29KUBR fighters ordered as early as February 2012. On 1 December 2015 they constituted a new operational unit, the 100th Independent Ship-borne Fighter Avia-

A MiG-29KUBR belonging to the 100th OKIAP during training at Saki (Crimea) in July 2016, prior to its planned deployment to Syria in autumn 2016. (Viktor Drushlyakov)

tion Regiment (OKIAP) at Yeysk, on the Sea of Azov; the unit was due to move to its permanent location of Monchegorsk at the end of 2016. In October 2016, four or six MiG-29KR/KUBRs were expected to embark on the aircraft carrier *Admiral Kuznetsov*, which was to sail to the Syrian coast. In preparation for that mission, between June and mid-July 2016 five aircraft of the 100th OKIAP (three MiG-29KRs and two two-seat MiG-29KUBRs) trained for the first time at Saki airfield in Crimea. Here, in the early 1980s the Soviet Union constructed a runway with a 'ski-jump' ramp and arresting gear as an imitation of the deck of a future aircraft carrier; it is colloquially known as NITKA (nazemnyi ispytatelno-trenirovochnyi komplex, ground-based research and training complex). However, due to incomplete preparation of the ground facilities, the training was limited to landing approaches with the runway simulating the carrier deck, without ski-jump take-offs, and with only a few arresting landings.

On 8 August 2016 a MiG-29KR piloted by the commander of the 100th OKIAP, Vladimir Kokurin, landed on board the Russian carrier for the first time. After a few weeks of training by the air group, the *Admiral Kuznetsov* was due to return to its dock at Murmansk for the completion of repairs, and was then due to leave Murmansk for the Mediterranean Sea at the end of October. As the MiG-29KR's operational pilots had no prior experience of carrier operations, for the deployment to the Mediterranean the aircraft were to be piloted primarily by test pilots from RSK MiG and the 929th Chkalov State Flight-Test Centre (Gosudarstvennyi lyotno-ispytatelnyi tcentr imeni V. P. Chkalov, GLITs) at Akhtubinsk, who were previously involved in testing MiG-29Ks for India on board the carrier *Vikramaditya*.

The land-based version of this fighter, the MiG-29M, is continuing trials. The subsequent MiG-35 fighter with active electronically scanned array (AESA) radar and uprated RD-33MKM engines is still at the pre-contract announcement stage. Sergey Korotkov, the designer general of the UAC, announced in July 2016 that trials of the MiG-35S in the configuration intended for the Russian Air Force would commence 'by the end of the summer' and would continue until 2017. After the completion of the trials order for 37 MiG-35S aircraft placed by the Russian Ministry of Defence, further orders are expected (reportedly, 28 aircraft plus nine options for the Russian MoD), as well as 46 MiG-35 aircraft to be ordered by Egypt.

Chapter 1: Sukhoi Su-24M, pp39–48

With the partial withdrawal of the Russian Air Force contingent from Syria in 2016, the Russians reportedly handed over eight Su-24M2 bombers to the Syrian Arab Air Force (SyAAF). Since Syria is a previous operator of the Su-24MK2 version, it has existing infrastructure and pilots to support this new acquisition.

Chapter 1: Sukhoi Su-25, pp49–56

Su-25SM prototype '19' launches a Kh-58U anti-radar missile during tests. (Sukhoi)

More details have emerged of various upgrades for the Su-25 attack aircraft. The Su-25SM upgrade, developed for the Russian Air Force under the Izmoroz' (hoarfrost) research and development programme, is currently at the SM3 stage; the pattern for the Su-25SM3 is aircraft '95', belonging to the test centre at Akhtubinsk. In addition to the information provided about the SM3 in Volume 1, details of the full weapons suite of this version have become known. In comparison to the first Su-25SM upgrade, the SM3 version adds Kh-58USh anti-radiation missiles (up to two) and KAB-500S satellite-guided bombs (up to two). The remaining air-to-ground guided ordnance is similar to that of the Su-25SM and includes up to two Kh-29L/T/TD/TE missiles, up to two KAB-500Kr guided bombs and up to four Kh-25ML or S-25L/LD laser-guided missiles. R-73 air-to-air missiles (AAMs) are carried for self-protection. The new SOLT-25 (Sistema Optiko-Laserno-Teplotelevizionnaya, optical-laser-thermo-television system) targeting system, which replaces the simple Klyon-PS laser rangefinder/target designator in the aircraft's nose, will be installed on the SM3 at a later date, after the completion of trials. Two-seat aircraft upgraded according to the Su-25SM3 pattern are designated as the Su-25UBM2 (not UBSM, as was stated in Volume 1).

At the KADEX exhibition held at Astana, Kazakhstan in June 2016, the Belarusian ARZ-558 aircraft repair facility at Baranovichi displayed its variant of the Su-25 upgrade, implemented on aircraft of the Kazakhstan Air Force. In one of the related documents the designation Su-25BM (Belarusian Modernisation) is used, which is somewhat misleading, since the earlier Russian Su-25BM (Buksir Misheney) designation refers to aircraft with added target-towing capability. A cockpit mock-up was displayed at KADEX 2016 where it was announced that the first aircraft was currently being modernised.

The upgraded cockpit of the Belarusian Su-25BM offered to Kazakhstan features two large MFI-10 displays, a small IRP-5 standby display, ILS-31M HUD and PUS-29 data-input panel. (Viktor Drushlyakov)

The Belarusian Su-25BM variant makes use of Russian-made components. The cockpit is retrofitted with the SOI-25 (Sistema Otobrazheniya Informatsii, data presentation system) with an ILS-31M head-up display provided by Elektroavtomatika (the same HUD is used in the Su-27SM(3) fighter). A PUS-29 data-input panel is installed below the ILS-31M, and there are two large MFI-10 displays provided by Ramenskoye RPKB (flight and navigational information is shown on the left-hand display, and targeting information is shown on the right-hand display); a small IRP-5 standby display is installed between them. The new SN-25 navigation suite provides for an accuracy of 5m (16ft) compared to 700m (2,297ft) before upgrade. The new PS-25 stores management and SR-25 radio communication systems are also introduced. The self-defence system is expanded through the introduction of Belarusian Satellit electronic countermeasures pods. The weapons suite is more modest than that of the Russian SM3; only TV-guided Kh-29T air-to-ground missiles (two) and KAB-500Kr bombs (four) have been added, as well as S-13 unguided rockets and R-73 AAMs for self-protection.

On 25 June 2016 the Indian Air Force's Su-30MKI SB200 performed a first flight with the Brahmos-A missile. (Brahmos Aerospace)

Chapter 1: Sukhoi Su-30, Irkutsk line, pp65–70

On 25 June 2016 the long-awaited first flight took place of a Su-30MKI fighter with the Indo-Russian Brahmos-A missile carried on its under-fuselage hardpoint. The flight was made from the Hindustan Aeronautics Limited (HAL) airfield at Nasik. At the time of the flight it was announced that a first launch of the missile by a Su-30MKI would take place 'in the coming months'; it had not occurred by September 2016. The flight trial was observed by 'several other nations in the world in possession of the Su-30 strike fighter who are looking towards acquiring a lethal weapon system.'

At the beginning of 2016 Yuri Belyi, the head of the Tikhomirov NIIP radar company, complained that talks with India regarding the upgrade of the Su-30MKI had come to an end. However, a report in *Defence News* in July, citing Indian sources, stated that 'India has stepped up negotiations with Russia to upgrade its 194 [and eventually the entire fleet of 272] Sukhoi Su-30MKI multirole aircraft to the near fifth-generation level'. The contract was to be signed by the end of the year. The cost of the upgrade is to amount to around USD40 million per aircraft. The upgraded version is apparently to be renamed Super Sukhoi; previously, the designation Super 30 had been published. A major portion of the upgrade involves avionics and sensors, which will be completely renewed.

The Russian Irkut Corporation previously announced that the upgrade is under negotiation and is to include a new computing system as well as new or upgraded sensors, primarily relating to an active electronically scanned array (AESA) radar. The weapons array is to be enhanced; new self-protection systems are expected, as well as new engine compressor blades, wing and empennage leading edges and cockpit canopy coatings to reduce radar cross-section. The AL-31FP engine control system will be upgraded. Following the upgrade, thanks to the similarity of equipment and cockpit, the Super Sukhoi (or perhaps Super 30) will be also be used in India as a combat trainer for the future Fifth-Generation Fighter Aircraft (FGFA), commonly referred to in India as the Prospective Multirole Fighter (PMF). The upgrades will be completed by HAL at its plant in Nasik.

The aforementioned Yuri Belyi also announced that the Russian Air Force plans to order a similar upgrade for its Su-30SMs. In terms of the radar, two separate stages of upgrade are planned: first, the Indian computers will be replaced by indigenous examples, and then the radar performance will be enhanced (longer range, increased jamming resistance, new operational modes). Replacement of the passive electronically scanned array with an active AESA unified with the N036 radar antenna from the T-50 was once considered, but has now been abandoned.

In early 2016, Russia began marketing the Su-30SME version, i.e. the export derivative of the Russian Air Force's Su-30SM, independent from the Indian Su-30MKI version, and without avionics originating from France, Israel or other foreign countries.

Chapter 1: Sukhoi Su-34, pp79–86

In January 2016, Russian media confirmed that Algeria plans to acquire 12 Su-34s, although at the time of writing the contract had not yet been finalised. Production for the Russian Air Force continues at a steady pace; in 2015, 18 aircraft were delivered.

On 31 May 2016 the first four Su-34s arrived with the Khurba bomber regiment located near Komsomolsk-on-Amur.

On 19 August 2016 (precisely marking its 85th anniversary) the Novosibirsk Aircraft Plant ceremonially presented the '100th' Su-34 to the Russian Air Force; in fact, another five or six aircraft were still required to bring the total to 100.

One error appeared in the description of the Su-34 on p82 of Volume 1. Here it is stated that 'eight chaff/flare dispensers, each with eight 50mm (1.9in) rounds, are mounted under the tailboom'. As can be easily seen, there are in fact seven dispensers in this location, each with 14 rounds.

The Su-34 has seven countermeasures launchers, each with 14 50mm (1.9in) decoys, mounted under the tailboom. (Piotr Butowski)

Chapter 1: Sukhoi Su-35, pp87–91

The plant at Komsomolsk-on-Amur produced 14 Su-35S fighters in 2015, completing the first order for 48 aircraft, which had been placed by the Russian Ministry of Defence in August 2009. In December 2015 the Su-35S successfully completed the second stage of state evaluations and all fighters previously delivered to the Air Force have been updated to the ultimate standard. Also in December 2015, the Russian MoD ordered 50 more fighters. In 2016 the Russian MoD was to receive the initial 10 aircraft from this contract and perhaps more; providing there are no export deliveries in the same period, production deliveries for 2016 will amount to 18 aircraft. From 2017 onwards, Su-35S production is set to increase to 24 aircraft per year, in keeping with expected export orders.

A first export contract covering 24 fighters to be delivered to China by 2018 was signed in November 2015. Admittedly, there are still some doubts about this deal. Some reports state that only an 'agreement' has been signed, requiring some further 'ratification'. Nevertheless, it is a genuine contract, since it has been followed by orders placed with subcontractors. For example, the AL-41F1S engines for Chinese Su-35s have already been ordered from the Ufa UMPO engine plant. As of September 2016, Chinese personnel were undergoing training at Sukhoi's facility in Zhukovsky. The initial Su-35s for China will not differ from the Russian version (apart from downgraded radar and IFF mode options); subsequently, specific Chinese systems are to be implemented on the aircraft.

As this volume went to press, another expected export contract with Indonesia was to be signed 'soon' (in fact, contract signature was expected in March 2016, but this did not happen). Indonesia initially wanted to acquire 12 aircraft, later reduced to 10 and then to eight fighters, due to financial reasons. The aforementioned UMPO engine factory reported in June 2016 that it expects (in addition to the Chinese and Indonesian deals) an order for Su-35s from the United Arab Emirates (UAE). It is worth remembering that in November 2003 the Su-35 design was unveiled at the airshow in Dubai in the UAE.

Chapter 1: Sukhoi T-50, pp93–101

On 27 April 2016 the sixth prototype T-50-6-2, '056', made its maiden flight at Komsomolsk-on-Amur. As many as two and a half years have passed since the first flight of

The only new PAK FA prototype to have appeared in the last year is T50-6-2, '056', which first flew on 27 April 2016. (Viktor Drushlyakov)

the fifth prototype T50-5, '055', on 27 October 2013. This is evidence that not everything is going to plane with this programme. The sixth aircraft differs from the previous examples in having a longer aft fuselage section (housing the electronic warfare equipment), different wingtips and a reinforced inner structure of the airframe. Its wingspan is increased from 14.0m (45ft 11in) to 14.1m (46ft 3in), and fuselage length from 19.7m (64ft 7in) to 20.1m (66ft); these are estimated data. The fifth aircraft, T50-5, caught fire on the runway after landing on 10 June 2014, unluckily during a presentation for an Indian delegation. The overhaul at Komsomolsk-on-Amur lasted 16 months; on 16 October 2015 the aircraft, now designated T50-5R, resumed flight tests after repair.

As of September 2016, all six prototypes are under evaluation with the Ministry of Defence's test centre at Akhtubinsk, where they are undergoing an evaluation conducted by military pilots. Vladimir Mikhailov, the former commander-in-chief of the Russian Air Force, told Russian television in March 2016 that the T-50 had launched a weapon from the internal armament compartment for the first time. Unfortunately, this information has not been confirmed by any other source. As this volume went to press, observers were expecting the 1,000th flight by a T-50 prototype (the 500th flight was performed on 14 August 2014).

Previous plans stipulated the launch of series production of the aircraft in its current configuration, followed by development of a 'second stage' aircraft, in which the main new feature was to be the izdeliye 30 engines. Undoubtedly, although it was not discussed, the fighter's targeting systems, avionics and armament were also to undergo modernisation under stage two. However, problems with the T-50 led to an interim stage being introduced to the plans: this aircraft will have an improved and strengthened airframe, but will retain the current AL-41F1 engines; this interim variant is currently (and confusingly) being referred to as the 'second stage' PAK FA. According to current plans, four 'second-stage' prototypes, T-50-8 to T-50-11, are to be procured during 2016–17 and will then be followed by series production. The previous 'second stage' with the new engines has now slipped into the indefinite future. According to rumours, funding for this further modernisation of the fighter has been reduced and some of the most expensive requirements have been abandoned. It is still claimed that a first test example of the izdeliye 30 engine will begin trials on an Il-76LL test-bed aircraft in 2017.

Plans for PAK FA purchases by the Russian Air Force are also being scaled back. Russian media quote a source within the Russian Ministry of Defence stating that the Air Force will order only one squadron with 12 aircraft by 2020, instead of the 60 aircraft provided by the GPV-2020 programme.

In light of this situation, Russia will surely make more concessions to India, which could join the programme and provide a vital injection of money, in the same way that it funded development of the Su-30MKI 20 years earlier. The preliminary design of the Russian-Indian Prospective Multirole Fighter (PMF) or Fifth-Generation Fighter Aircraft (FGFA) programme based on the Russian PAK FA was accepted in June 2013; under this initiative, each party contributed USD295 million. Russia expected the next contract, worth USD6-8 billion, and covering the construction and evaluation of prototypes, to be signed soon after, but it had not happened by September 2016. Indian media quoted an Indian Air Force official saying that 'the FGFA's engine is unreliable, its radar inadequate, its stealth features badly engineered, India's work-share too low, and the fighter's price would be exorbitant by the time it enters service'. India has also complained that its specialists, including pilots, have not been allowed near the aircraft. Nevertheless, the latest Russian documents reveal that the stalemate in the negotiations has been overcome and a contract for the full-scale development of the PMF/FGFA will duly be signed in 2016. A UAC report published in June 2016 stated that 'in the financial matters [the costs of the Indian contribution to research and development work – author's note] a compromise solution has been reached. In the matter of allowing Indian pilots [to fly the PAK FA prototypes] important decisions have been made and they are currently being settled with [the Russian] Ministry of Defence'.

Chapter 1: Future tactical combat aircraft, pp102–104

A small model of a shipborne version of the PAK FA, supposedly designated T-50K, as presented together with a model of the new Russian Project 23000 Logovo (den) aircraft carrier. (Piotr Butowski)

The most significant new development in this chapter is represented by the acronym **PMKI**, which appeared in an article entitled 'Key aspects of military and technological development of the Russian Federation', written by Russian Defence Minister Sergey Shoygu for the directory *National Safety of Russia* in January 2015. Among new aircraft designs for the Russian naval aviation, Shoygu mentioned the 'PMKI carrier-based aircraft'. Judging from the context (alongside the MPVK and Apatit, described in Chapter 2 of this volume), the PMKI is a new carrier-based fighter, which would replace the MiG-29K and Su-33 in the distant future, and the abbreviation may be deciphered as Perspektivnyi Mnogofunktsyonalnyi Korabelnyi Istrebitel, Future Multirole Ship-borne Fighter. There are three options for such a fighter, if it comes into being. The first is a carrier-based version of the Sukhoi PAK FA fighter, in the same way that the Su-33 was developed from the Su-27 some 30 years ago. The second possibility is a MiG fighter, using the design of the LMFI fifth-generation lightweight fighter; of all the Russian design teams, Mikoyan currently has the greatest experience in this field, thanks to its programme for the MiG-29K carrier-based fighter. Finally, the third option, and the least probable, is a short take-off and vertical landing (STOVL) fighter, work on which is continuing slowly within a Yakovlev design team.

As regards unmanned combat aerial vehicles (UCAVs), a little more information has come to light concerning the BAK SD (Bespilotnyi Aviatsionnyi Kompleks Sredney Dalnosti, Medium-Range Unmanned Air Complex) tactical reconnaissance and com-

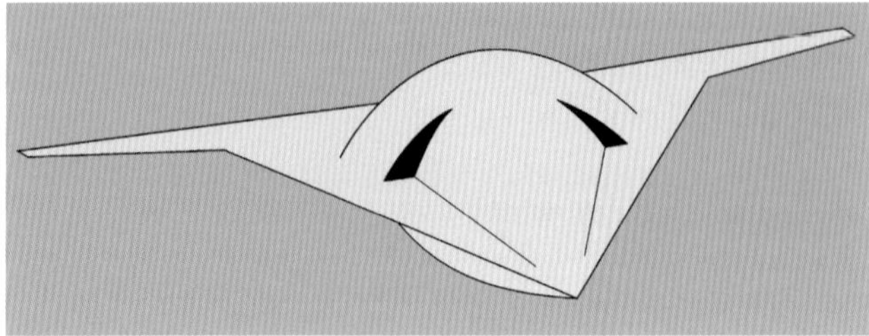

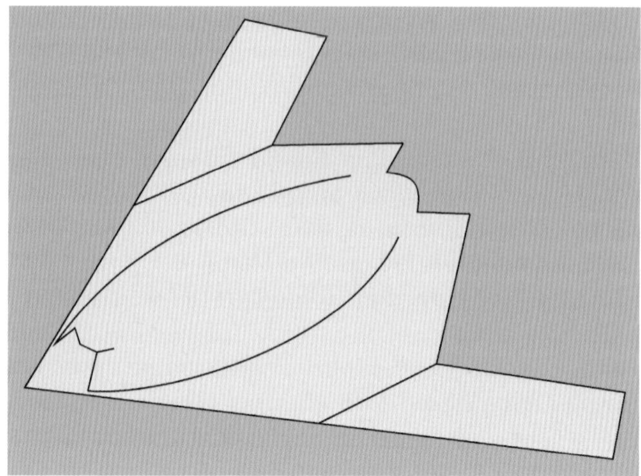

Left: A preliminary impression of the Sukhoi Okhotnik heavy UCAV.
(Piotr Butowski)

Right: A preliminary impression of the MiG Boyets 5-tonne UCAV.
(Piotr Butowski)

bat vehicle produced by RSK MiG, and previously known as the Gonshchik. Its current codename is Boyets (warrior) and it is similar in appearance to the Mikoyan Skat design, and therefore typical for most current UCAVs – it is a fast flying-wing with an internal weapons bay and single turbofan engine.

As for the large Sukhoi Okhotnik UCAV, unconfirmed, but generally trustworthy information has appeared indicating that a demonstrator has already been produced by the Novosibirsk plant belonging to Sukhoi and that a first flight can be expected soon.

Chapter 2: Kamov Ka-52, pp109–116

An Egyptian contract for the Ka-52, reported by the TASS agency in September 2015, has now been confirmed: indeed, Egypt ordered 46 helicopters with deliveries to take place in 2017–19. Russia is holding advanced negotiations regarding the sale of 12 Ka-52s to Algeria; in September 2015 a presentation by a Ka-52 was conducted at Aïn Oussara air base in Algeria, including a display of its combat capabilities. France's refusal to sell the Mistral amphibious assault ships to Russia meant that an expected contract for 32 Ka-52K helicopters for the Russian Navy was not signed; so far, only four helicopters from the pre-production batch have been completed.

In 2015 the Progress Company in Arsenyev completed 16 Ka-52s, all for the Russian Ministry of Defence; the volume of production for 2016 will be similar. At the same time, the plant declared that production output 'in 2017 will increase 3.7 times in comparison with 2016 and in 2018 by 30.8 per cent' – thanks to the export order from Egypt.

Egypt has ordered helicopters equipped with the new OES-52 electro-optical targeting turrets instead of the standard GOES-451. The OES-52 had been developed by the Moscow-based NPK SPP avionics firm using the French Safran STRIX gyrostabilised targeting turret from the Airbus Helicopters Tiger attack helicopter as a prototype. The OES-52 system began trials on a Ka-52 prototype, '062', in January 2015. At the Moscow International Aviation and Space Salon (MAKS) 2015 exhibition the OES-52 system was displayed on the first pre-production Ka-52K maritime helicopters, but the

remaining Ka-52Ks fly with standard GOES-451 systems. In August 2016, Ka-52 '51', the first of three pre-production helicopters used by Kamov for tests, was photographed in flight near Moscow, fitted with the OES-52 system.

Chapter 2: Mil Mi-8, pp117–132

The Mi-8AMTSh-VA is an 'Arctic' version of the Mi-8 produced in Ulan-Ude. Deliveries to the Russian Air Force began on 25 November 2015. (Russian Helicopters)

The Mi-8 helicopter is experiencing tough times; due to a lack of new large orders in 2015, production dropped by around a quarter (from more than 200 to about 150 helicopters) and is going to drop further still. The largest export contract in the order book backlog was placed in May 2015 by Belarus, which ordered 12 Mi-8MTV-5 helicopters from Kazan, to be delivered in 2016–17. Other substantial contracts are under negotiation only. India is considering an order for another batch of 48 helicopters from Kazan. Meanwhile, Pakistan may order 20 helicopters from Ulan-Ude.

The new, thoroughly upgraded Mi-171A2 version, which is destined to be the main production version for years to come, is still undergoing trials and is only expected to receive certification in 2017 (as opposed to 2014, as previously planned). Five Mi-171A2 prototypes are under test, including two used for ground tests (OP-3 and OP-4) and three flying examples. The first, OP-1, '511', made a first hovering flight on 25 August 2014 and a first full circuit flight on 14 November 2014; the second, OP-2, '512', flew in October 2015, while the fifth, OP-5, was completed in April 2016 and was displayed at the Helirussia exhibition in May 2016, but had not yet flown by August 2016.

On 25 November 2015 the Ulan-Ude plant delivered the first of five helicopters in the new Arctic Mi-8AMTSh-VA version to the Russian Ministry of Defence. These aircraft had been ordered in February 2015 (it also included the 1,000th helicopter in the Mi-8AMT/Mi-171 series to be produced at Ulan-Ude). In relation to planned Russian expansion in the Arctic, the plant expected large orders for this modification, but to date has only received this contract for five helicopters. When compared to the standard-production Mi-8AMTSh, the Mi-8AMTSh-VA (V for Vysotnyi, high altitude, A for Arctic) has more powerful Klimov VK-2500-03 engines and TA-14-130-08 auxiliary power unit, additional heating, increased fuel tanks enabling a range of 1,420km (882 miles), and additional navigation and communication equipment.

During the last 12 months, Russian Mi-8 helicopters have begun to be equipped on a large scale with the L370E8 Vitebsk self-protection suite; the system was unveiled on a Mi-8AMTSh-V helicopter during Moscow's International Aviation and Space Salon (MAKS) in August 2015. Since then, several dozen Mi-8 helicopters of the Russian Air Force have been retrofitted with the Vitebsk system, including examples used in Syria (for instance, the Mi-8AMTSh shot down on 1 August 2016 was fitted with Vitebsk).

Ukrainian upgrades of Mi-8 helicopters

The Ukrainian armed forces, which suffer from a lack of equipment and money, are upgrading their old Mi-8T helicopters (aircraft with TV2-117 powerplants, and not the Mi-8MT with TV3-117 engines). The company responsible for these upgrades is a powerplant manufacturer, Motor Sich of Zaporizhzhya, hence the 'Ukrainised' helicopters are designated Mi-8MSB-V, for Motor Sich, Boguslayev (Vyacheslav Boguslayev is the head of the Motor Sich company); V is for viyskovyi, military. The first stage of the upgrade is the replacement of the original engines with the new TV3-117VMA-SBM1V-4E pro-

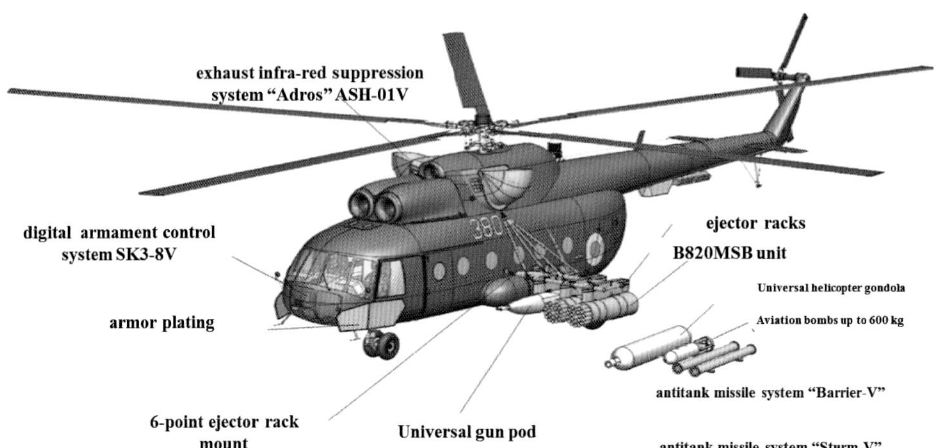

A schematic diagram of the Mi-8MSB-V helicopter with expanded combat capabilities as offered by the Ukrainian Motor Sich plant. (Motor Sich)

duced by Motor Sich, which retains a power rating of 1,119kW (1,500shp) at take-off, but with a longer service life and lower fuel consumption. Mi-8MSB-V helicopters have also been retrofitted with systems providing protection against infrared-guided missiles, made by the Ukrainian Adron company of Kiev: these comprise KT-01AV infrared jammers and KUV 26-50 flare dispensers. Some helicopters have been fitted with fuselage-side racks for carrying unguided weapons. In October 2014 the Ukrainian government ordered 13 Mi-8MSB-V upgrades, 10 for the Ministry of Defence and three for the National Guard; the aircraft were delivered during 2014–15.

Motor Sich offers further upgrades of the helicopters, initially comprising the enhancement of capabilities of the basic Mi-8MSB-V version, and then three special versions, designated V1, V2 and V3, which utilise additional systems of Ukrainian production. The ultimate variant of the Mi-8MSB-V is to be equipped with an SKZ-8V digital armament control system produced by Adron, Baryer-V guided anti-tank missiles made by the GKKB Luch company of Kiev, as well as post-Soviet Shturm-V anti-tank missiles (as used by the Mi-24). Armoured panels are to be fitted to the cockpit sides and the engine exhausts are to be fitted with ASh-01V heat dissipaters made by Adron.

The Mi-8MSB-V1 is to be an assault and attack helicopter, which is also to be fitted with a navigation system made by the Ukrainian Orizon Navigatsiya company, an electro-optical turret from the Belarusian TsiklonBel company, radar and laser warning receivers, anti-aircraft missiles from GKKB Luch, and grenade launcher pods from Adron.

The Mi-8MSB-V2 is a patrol and reconnaissance helicopter, similar to the V1, but not capable of launching guided anti-tank missiles. Instead, it features a control system for reconnaissance drones, which are launched from pods carried on the side pylons.

The Mi-8MSB-V3 is a command and control helicopter with sophisticated communications and radio relay systems, as well as additional armour for the passenger cabin.

In its basic form the Mi-8MSB-V upgrade re-engines existing Mi-8T helicopters. These two Mi-8MSB-V aircraft are among the 10 exampes ordered for the Ukrainian Ministry of Defence in October 2014 and delivered during 2014–15. (Alexander Golz)

Chapter 2: Mil Mi-24 and Mi-35M, pp133–144

The Mi-35M helicopter, which once seemed destined to be an interim aircraft pending large-scale introduction of new-generation Ka-52 and Mi-28N attack helicopters, is still being developed as an entirely independent project. The plans of the Rostvertol plant for 2016 provide for the production of 15 Mi-35M helicopters, only slightly fewer than the number of Ka-52s or Mi-28s.

In spring 2016 (the first photos date from April) the Mi-35M appeared in Syria, equipped with the L370V35 Vitebsk system in a different configuration to that displayed at Moscow's International Aviation and Space Salon (MAKS) in 2015. In particular, it features three L370-5 infrared jammers mounted on the sides and beneath the rear fuselage, rather than a single new-generation jammer as displayed at MAKS 2015. For the time being this is a trial installation, since this system only underwent preliminary tests on the Mi-35M in 2015; the completion of the Vitebsk's tests on the Mi-35M and clearance for regular operation was expected for late 2016. Thereafter, retrofitting of Mi-35M helicopters operated by the Russian Air Force with the Vitebsk system can be expected on mass scale, as is currently the case for the Air Force's Mi-8 helicopters.

It should be remembered that Russia has also begun to diversify the export variants of the Vitebsk. All previous models carried the same designation, President-S. Now the variant for the Mi-35M is the President-S35, for the Mi-28N it is the President-S28, and for the Mi-26T2 it is the President-S26T2.

Due to the breakdown of relations with Ukraine, Russia has had to replace some of the Mi-35M's equipment. Instead of the S17-VG-1M pilot's gunsight, delivered by the Ukrainian Arsenal plant of Kiev, the Russian ILS-28 series 2 head-up display from the Mi-28N is installed. Instead of the 9S477 radio-command datalink for anti-tank missiles made by LORTA of Lvov, the 9S477K-1, production of which was launched by the

Mayak plant of Kirov, Russia, is installed. In the near future Russia plans to abandon radio-command missile guidance (already non-existent on Ka-52 and Mi-28NM helicopters) and replace it with laser beam riding guidance, and this will also apply to the upgraded Mi-35M helicopter. Work on retrofitting the Mi-35M with the new TA14-130-35 auxiliary power unit is in progress (currently the helicopters are equipped with the AI-9V-1 APU).

Information has appeared indicating that work on the mid-life upgrade of Mi-24P helicopters to Mi-24PM standard is now in progress, but nothing is known about it; one may presume that it will be similar to the Mi-35M (which is a new-production helicopter, not a mid-life upgrade). Previously, some operational Mi-24Ps were upgraded to Mi-24PN standard, but this did not prove popular, due to its numerous drawbacks.

Chapter 2: Mil Mi-28, pp153–160

The most important event for the Mi-28 in recent months was the launch of trials for the upgraded Mi-28NM helicopter (izdeliye 296), which made its first hovering flight at Tomilino, near Moscow, on 29 July 2016. According to plans dating from the middle of 2016, the Mi-28NM is to enter production in the second quarter of 2018. As expected, the Mi-28NM has received the upgraded BRLK-28 radar system with the N025M radar and OPS-28M Tor-M electro-optical turret carried in a much bulkier cylindrical housing under the nose. The pilot's TOES-521 ball has been replaced by the new SMS-550 turret. The NPPU-280 gun mount has been reshaped. New Klimov VK-2500P engines with improved 'hot and high' capability as well as a new TA14-130-28 auxiliary power unit provided by Aerosila have been installed. The most obvious external difference in comparison with the Mi-28N is the lack of the distinguishing I-256 datalink antenna for the radio-command guided Ataka missile in the nose. Mil declares that the new main rotor blades that will be installed on the Mi-28NM (see LL PSV below) allow an increase in maximum speed by 10 per cent and an increase in cruise speed by 13 per cent.

The dual-control modification of the Mi-28 has made some progress. It comes in two variants. The version intended for the Russian Air Force is the Mi-28UB (izdeliye 298) and the export version is the 'Mi-28NE with dual controls' (izdeliye 299). The Mi-28UB completed official state evaluations at the end of 2015. In April 2016 the Russian Ministry of Defence placed an order for 24 Mi-28UB helicopters. At the same time, production of the izdeliye 299 export variant of the helicopter began; on 16 March 2016, Rostvertol presented the first two helicopters of this variant at the factory airfield. The significance of this modification for Rostvertol is much greater than it might first appear. As well as the various changes introduced (i.e. addition of the flight controls in the weapon officer's position and widening of the cockpit), Rostvertol is especially proud of the fact that the helicopter employed electronic design for the first time in the factory's history. The electronic model of the front section of the new fuselage was created using Siemens NX (Unigraphics) software.

Plans for 2016 provide for the production of 20 Mi-28 helicopters, including eight for the Russian Air Force and 12 for export. Interestingly, all helicopters from 2016 production are to be fitted with N025 radars (or N025E for export); those helicopters for the Russian Air Force will be the first radar-equipped Mi-28Ns for that operator.

These are the first two Mi-28NE helicopters with dual controls manufactured by Rostvertol in March 2016. Deliveries of this version to Algeria and Iraq started in May 2016. (Erik Romanenko, Rostvertol)

Current-production helicopters are also being fitted with Vitebsk (L370V28) or, for export, President-S28 (L370V28E) self-protection systems.

To date, over 90 Mi-28Ns have been delivered to the Russian Air Force. Rostvertol is also implementing two export contracts. The export Mi-28NE has two designations: izdeliye 2941 is the export equivalent of the Russian Mi-28N (izdeliye 294) version, and izdeliye 299 is the export equivalent of the Russian Mi-28UB (izdeliye 298) version. The first contract for 15 Mi-28NE helicopters (11 izdeliye 2941 and four izdeliye 299 versions) for Iraq was completed between August 2014 and June 2016. The helicopters for Iraq are the first operational Mi-28s with the mast-mounted N025E radars. Algeria ordered 42 izdeliye 299 helicopters; deliveries began in May 2016. Mi-28s have taken part in combat operations in Iraq (Iraqi Mi-28NEs) and in Syria (Russian Mi-28Ns).

Thanks to the embargo on military supplies from Ukraine, current-production Mi-28N helicopters have introduced certain production changes. In particular, the I-256 radio-command missile guidance datalink fitted in the nose tip, produced in Ukraine, has been replaced by the Russian 9S477K-1 system, also used in current-production Mi-35M helicopters.

Chapter 2: Future Army Aviation helicopters, pp161–166

The Ka-62 made its first hovering flight on 28 April 2016 at Arsenyev, with Vitaliy Lebedev and Nail Azin at the controls. The delay was caused by the Austrian Zoerkler Gears GmbH company that produces gearboxes and transmissions for the helicopter, and which failed to meet the deadline. It is likely that there are still problems afflicting the programme; as of September 2016 there was no information concerning additional flights by the Ka-62.

On 29 December 2015 the izdeliye 3701 helicopter, or LL PSV, completed its maiden flight. This is a modified Mi-24 attack helicopter, used for testing solutions developed for the new-generation high-speed PSV (Perspektivnyi Skorostnoy Vertolet, Future High-speed Helicopter); LL stands for Letayushchaya Laboratoriya, flying test-bed.

Left: The Ka-62 completed its first hovering flight on 28 April 2016.
(Russian Helicopters)

Right: First flown on 29 December 2015, the izdeliye 3701 helicopter, or LL PSV, utilises a modified Mi-24 airframe.
(Mil)

The LL PSV has a longer wing, a narrow forward fuselage with a single-seat cockpit and, most importantly, a new main rotor. The powerplant comprises two VK-2500-01 engines rated at 1,790kW (2,400hp) for take-off and 2,013kW (2,700hp) emergency power. The new main rotor blades tested on the LL PSV will be employed in the future Mi-37 as well as current military helicopters. In case of the Mi-28NM and Mi-35M, the use of the new rotor blades will increase maximum speed by 10 per cent and by 13 per cent, respectively; cruising speed will be increased by 13 per cent and 30 per cent, respectively.

In May 2016 the deputy CEO of Russian Helicopters Andrei Shibitov announced that in the coming weeks the LL PSV experimental helicopter would attain a speed of 400–450km/h (249–280mph). In the event, it attained a speed of 360km/h (224mph), which is close to maximum for this design.

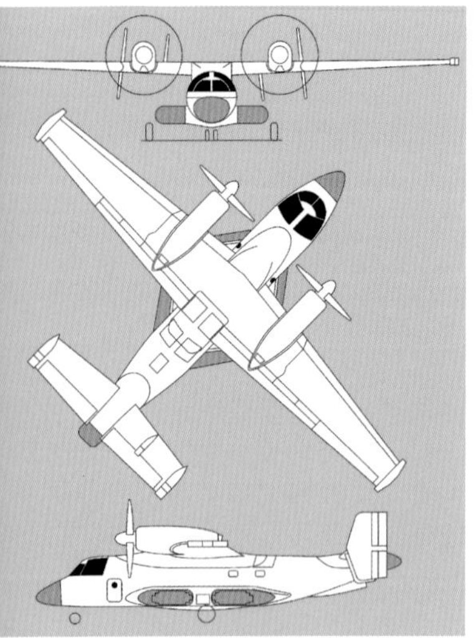

The latest design of Beriev's AEW&C aircraft, as patented in 2015.
(Piotr Butowski)

Chapter 3: Future airborne early warning and control aircraft, pp202–203

The Beriev Company has patented its design for a carrier- and land-based airborne early warning aircraft. Although the designation remains unknown, it represents an alternative design to the A-110, as described in Volume 1. The patented aircraft is a high-wing aircraft with an H-tail, powered by two turboprop engines. The most important novelty is the positioning of fixed, all-round observation antennas in large fairings within the lower fuselage, under the wing. Additional antennas are mounted in the forward and aft fuselage.

Chapter 3: New generation of large unmanned aircraft, pp207–209

In the last year much has happened in the field of Russian unmanned aerial vehicles (UAVs), but little of it has been officially confirmed.

In mid-July 2016 the large, five-tonne Altair UAV, built by OKB Simonov of Kazan under the Altius-M research and development programme, completed its maiden flight. The UAV can be seen in a satellite photo of Kazan airfield dated 25 September 2014, near a Tu-22M3 bomber. Later (reportedly in February 2015), the Altair/Altius-M attempted to take off, but these efforts ended with a broken undercarriage strut.

In July 2016 the UAV made several circuits over the Kazan airfield and successfully landed. Bearing in mind a year and a half passed between the take-off attempt and the successful take-off, it is likely that significant changes were introduced in the UAV, probably relating to its flight control system.

The smaller, one-tonne Orion UAV, built by the Kronshtadt Company under the Inokhodets programme, completed a first series of 'hops' at Zhukovsky in July 2016, lifting off the runway for a moment.

According to further, similarly unofficial information, in August 2016 the demonstrator of the small Vega Korsar UAV crashed.

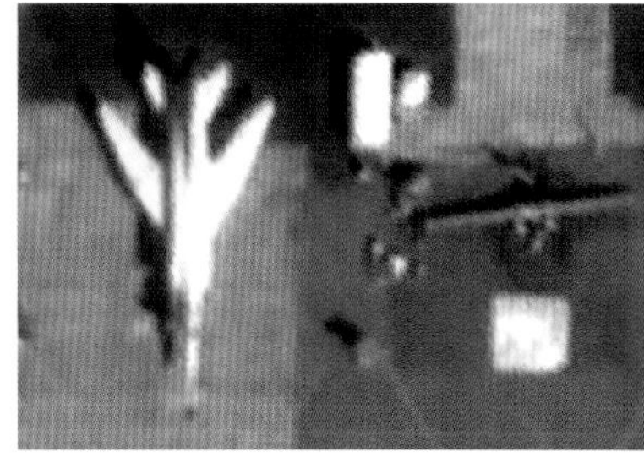

The satellite image of the Altius-M next to a Tu-22M3 bomber at Kazan on 25 September 2014. (Google Earth)

Chapter 4: Ilyushin Il-80, pp227–229

RF-93645 appears to be the second Il-80 aircraft upgraded as part of the Zveno-2S strategic command system. Official reports suggest that the second Il-80M upgrade will be completed in 2018. However, this date may refer to the aircraft's return to service. (Dmitry Müller)

The United Instrument Corporation of Russia announced in December 2015 that the upgraded Il-80M airborne command post had completed state evaluation; in early 2016 the aircraft was returned to service. No information about the scope of the Il-80M modernisation effort is available; however, new antennas have appeared on the fuselage, including a dozen very small blade-shaped antennas on the aircraft's spine, and a new 'hockey stick' antenna just behind them. The official press release says that the new system 'features increased survivability, functionality and reliability, lower weight and size, as well as lower energy consumption'. The Il-80M is part of the automatic command system of the Russian nuclear forces, codenamed Zveno-2S (leading squad), and includes an advanced communications suite developed by the Polyot Company of Nizhny Novgorod; prior to upgrade, the Il-80 was equipped with the Zveno-S system. A second Il-80 will be upgraded to the Il-80M standard in 2018.

Chapter 4: Mil Mi-8 electronic warfare variants, pp233–236

Russia's Concern Radio-Electronic Technologies (KRET) has announced the handover for evaluation of a test example of the modernised Rychag-AVM electronic countermeasures (ECM) system for Mi-8 helicopters. The baseline Rychag-AV (lever; AV stands for Aviatsionnyi Vertoletnyi, airborne for helicopter) system has been in series production since 2015 at the Kazan Optical Mechanical Plant (KOMZ), a subsidiary of KRET. The KOMZ deputy CEO Aleksey Panin said that series production of the modernised Rychag-AVM will begin in 2017. The modernised system emits higher power than the Rychag-AV and can complete more functions. The KRET deputy CEO Igor

Nasenkov added that the new Rychag-AVM systems are to be fitted to Mi-8AMTSh transport helicopters made by the Ulan-Ude plant, while the current Rychag-AV systems are being mounted on Kazan-made Mi-8MTV5-1 versions (eight delivered in 2015 and 10 in 2016); essentially, there is no difference between these two helicopters.

Chapter 4: Military balloons, pp237–244

Between 13–28 August 2016 the upgraded variant of the Tigr tethered aerostat, made by Augur, underwent tests at Kirzhach airfield, 80km (50 miles) northeast of Moscow. In comparison with the first version of the Tigr, which was developed and tested in 2010–11, the new aerostat employs new fabric. The ground station is entirely new, as is the control system and data transfer system.

According to data released by Augur, the upgraded Tigr has an envelope with a volume of 3,000m^3 (3,924 cu yd) and length of 39m (127ft 11in). It can carry a load (mission systems) weighing 100kg (220lb) to an altitude of 3,000m (9,843ft) or a load of up to 600kg (1,323lb) to a lower altitude; the mission systems are provided with an 8kW power supply. The aerostat can be airborne for up to 15 to 25 days; the maximum permitted wind speed at altitude is 30m/s (5,906ft/min). The Tigr is a mobile system, which can be quickly moved from one location to another. The Tigr has been developed under the Multiplikatsiya (animation) research and development programme that was ordered by the Russian Ministry of Defence in 2007 and which is aimed at the development of the PAK-RT (Perspektivnyi Aerostatnyi Kompleks Re-Translatsyi, Future Aerostat Complex of Relay) communication and command signal relay system; a surveillance version may be fitted with a radar and an electro-optical sensor package.

Augur also announced that its Jaguar aerostat, twice as large as the Tigr, would ascend for the first time at Kirzhach in September 2016. The Leninets Company is currently producing the Mars ground surveillance radar for the Jaguar.

An Augur Tigr military balloon photographed in August 2016. (Augur)

Russian military aviation in Syria

Since the appearance of the first volume in this series, the most important event for the Russian Air Force (more properly, the Vozdushno-Kosmicheskiye Sily, VKS, or Russian Aerospace Forces) has been its involvement in the military intervention in Syria, which commenced in autumn 2015. The use of Russian air power in Syria has several objectives. The political objective is to support Moscow's ally, Bashar al-Assad, and return to a position of influence in the Middle East, a status that Russia almost entirely lost in recent years. Russia is concerned about retaining its naval base at Tartus in Syria, the only such facility it has in the region. The military objective is to test new weapon systems in real battlefield conditions; Russia has employed virtually all types of combat aircraft operated by the Air Force, from fighters to strategic bombers, as well as helicopters, reconnaissance aircraft and unmanned aerial vehicles (UAVs); the Syrian conflict has also seen the use of aircraft that have only recently entered service. Several types of air-to-ground guided munitions have also been used for the first time. The propaganda aspect, i.e. demonstrating that Russia is still a superpower, is not to be discounted, as well as the use of the conflict as a 'shop window' from which to sell arms to prospective customers.

For some missions, including the use of strategic aircraft, the propaganda value was the most important aspect. The final rehearsal before the deployment to Syria was the large-scale Tsentr-2015 exercise, held between 18 and 20 August 2015, in which a total of 150 aircraft took part. Some footage from this exercise, including bombing by Tu-22M3 aircraft, very closely resembles later imagery from Syria.

Tactical aviation at Hmeimim

During summer and autumn 2015, Russia re-established Hmeimim air base, on the edge of Bassel al-Assad International Airport, 20km (12 miles) southeast of the city of Latakia in Syria. Hmeimim has been home to most of the Russian air assets during

In Syria, Mi-24P combat helicopters were typically armed with four tube-launched anti-tank missiles and two rocket pods. This photo was taken at Hmeimim on 6 October 2015. (TASS)

the operation in Syria. Previously, the airfield served as a base for Ka-28 helicopters of the Syrian Navy. New infrastructure was erected including an air traffic control tower, staff accommodation, taxiways, and fuel and storage facilities. The base is protected by surface-to-air missiles, including Buk-M2 and Pantsyr-S systems, and the latest S-400 long-range system, delivered to Hmeimim by An-124 transport aircraft on 26 November 2015, two days after downing of a Su-24M by the Turkish Air Force.

In September 2015, Russia ferried to Hmeimim a so-called Special-Purpose Air Brigade commanded by Major General Alexander Maksimtsev. Fixed-wing combat aircraft arrived by air via Iran and Iraq, while helicopters were brought by An-124 airlifters. On 30 September the air group commenced combat operations in support of Syrian government forces. In the first weeks, the Russian air contingent at Hmeimim comprised 32 combat aircraft including 12 Su-24M tactical bombers from the 2nd Composite Aviation Regiment at Chelyabinsk (Su-24M SVP-24 versions) and the 277th Bomber Aviation Regiment at Khurba (Su-24M2 versions), 12 Su-25SM and UB attack aircraft from the 960th Attack Aviation Regiment at Primorsko-Akhtarsk, four Su-34 tactical bombers from the 47th Composite Aviation Regiment at Voronezh (now temporarily deployed to Buturlinovka) and four Su-30SM multirole fighters from the 120th Composite Aviation Regiment at Domna near the Chinese border. The rotary-wing assets included 12 Mi-24P combat helicopters and four Mi-8 transports. In the early days some aircraft had their Russian stars and registrations painted over; later the insignia was reinstated. In the initial period the intensity of operations was fairly low and between 30 September and 8 October a daily average of 25 sorties was performed.

In the following months until March 2016, the aircraft and helicopters at Hmeimim were flying 30 to 80 sorties per day, for a daily average of around 50. The air brigade was also growing in size. In November 2015 four Su-27SM fighters were deployed to Hmeimim, and in January 2016 four Su-35S fighters joined them; additional Su-24M and Su-34 bombers also arrived. At its peak, 68 combat aircraft were based in Syria, including 32 Su-24Ms, 12 Su-34s, 12 Su-25SMs, four each of the Su-27SM, Su-30SM and Su-35S fighters, as well as 37 helicopters. Apart from the aircraft at Hmeimim, Russian tactical aircraft sporadically joined the action from Russian territory, in addition to the strategic bombers (see below). For example, on 20 November 2015 eight Su-34s flew 16 sorties over Syria from Krymsk air base in Russia.

Su-34 '03 Red' from the Voronezh regiment deployed at Hmeimim, 20 January 2016. (AP)

'Dumb' bombs rule

Although widely publicised by Russia, precision-guided airborne weapons only played a small part in these operations. The most widely used weapons were free-fall bombs; the two most widespread bomb types were the 250kg (551lb) OFAB-250-270 high-explosive fragmentation bomb and 500kg (1,102lb) FAB-500M-62 high-explosive bomb, both designed to defeat manpower, lightly armoured materiel, industrial facilities and field fortifications. Some footage also showed RBK-500 cluster bombs filled with fragmentation, incendiary or anti-armour bomblets being used in Syria. Weapon loads carried by the aircraft were surprising small. Su-25s usually flew with four 250kg bombs, although they are capable of carrying up to four tonnes. Su-24Ms flew with a maximum of four 500kg or six 250kg bombs, although the full load is 7.5 tonnes.

With the exception of the 10km (6.2-mile) range Kh-25ML laser-guided missile dating back to the Soviet era, and seen once under a Su-24M, tactical guided air-to-ground weaponry has only been carried by Su-34s. As such, Su-34s usually carried two satellite-guided 500kg KAB-500S bombs; this weapon entered service in 2006. Other types of guided weapon were employed for testing purposes. For example, on 11 February 2016, the Russian Ministry of Defence (MoD) released video of a Su-34 taking off for a mission over Syria with new Kh-35U missiles suspended under its wing. The Kh-35U is a 550kg (1,200lb) subsonic anti-shipping missile with a maximum range of 260km (162 miles); it remains unclear what Syrian targets it could be used against. Series production of the Kh-35U was launched two to three years earlier and this was its first combat use. A photograph shows another Su-34 with a 1,500kg (3,307lb) KAB-1500LG laser-guided bomb, which also entered production only recently.

Su-30SM and Su-35S fighters arrived in Syria with their standard medium-range R-27 and close-combat R-73 air-to-air missiles (AAMs). The Su-35S was seen also with new R-77-1 medium-range AAMs that entered service recently. Sometimes, R-27 and R-73 missiles were also carried by Su-34s.

The full range of Russian air-launched weaponry will be described in detail in the forthcoming title *Russia's Air-launched Weapons.*

For the Russian Air Force contingent in Syria – like this Su-25 on the apron at Hmeimim – 'dumb' bombs have provided the primary armament. However, weapons loads on individual aircraft have been noticeably small. (Russian MoD)

Unexpected withdrawal

On 14 March 2016, President Vladimir Putin announced the start of a withdrawal of 'the main part of the Russian military contingent' from Syria, noting that 'the task set for the Ministry of Defence and Armed Forces in general is fulfilled'. By that time, according to a statement from the MoD, the Russian aviation had executed 8,922 sorties in Syria. Within the next two days the first groups of Russian strike aircraft left Syria and returned to their home bases at Buturlinovka near Voronezh (Su-34s), Chelyabinsk (Su-24Ms) and Primorsko-Akhtarsk (Su-25s); within several days two thirds of the Russian contingent had returned to Russia, including all the Su-25s. The Su-30SM and Su-35S fighters remained in Syria.

After Putin's declaration of withdrawal of the main forces from Syria, Russia has released much less information concerning its operations. Reports on the activity of Russian aircraft are no longer being published. The few available photographs (and satellite imagery) of Hmeimim reveals the presence of about 20 combat aircraft, including six to 10 Su-24Ms, four Su-34s, four Su-30SMs and four Su-35s; however, the inventory has been subject to change.

Along with the return of some combat aircraft to Russia, more helicopters have been deployed to Syria, including the latest types that entered service only recently. Still the most numerous helicopters are a dozen or so each of the Mi-8AMTSh and Mi-24P. However, there are also several (reportedly, four of each) of the new Mi-35M (since December 2015) as well as Ka-52 and Mi-28N attack helicopters (both since March 2016). The Mi-8AMTSh serves in Syria for combat search and rescue and auxiliary transport duties; when armed, it carries a typical load of four 20-round 80mm (3.1in) B-8V-20 rocket pods. Mi-24Ps typically fly armed with two Shturm tube-launched anti-tank guided missiles (ATGMs) and four B-8V-20 pods, or four Shturms and two B-8V-20s. The Mi-35Ms are seen with a pack of eight Ataka ATGMs and two B-8V-20 rocket pods; the armament of the Mi-28N is similar.

Initially, the deployed Mi-8AMTSh and Mi-24P helicopters were not equipped with advanced self-protection systems and had only standard flare dispensers and the old L166V infrared jammers; some Mi-24Ps lacked even this. However, the Mi-8AMTSh helicopters in Syria later appeared with the latest Vitebsk self-protection system. At least one Mi-35M operating in Syria has also been fitted with the Vitebsk system, in a variant not previously seen. Ka-52s are equipped with the Vitebsk as standard.

Left: On occasions, Su-34s in Syria are armed with R-27 beyond-visual-range air-to-air missiles. (Russian MoD)

Right: Except for sporadic use of missiles, the only tactical guided air-to-ground munitions used by Russia in Syria are KAB-500S satellite-guided bombs dropped by Su-34 bombers. (Russian MoD)

Strategic revenge

The first Russian loss in Syria – and the only one suffered by a fixed-wing aircraft – was the Su-24M shot down on 24 November 2015 by a Turkish Air Force F-16C Fighting Falcon. It was a symbolic event – for the first time, a Russian aircraft had been shot down by a NATO aircraft. During the rescue operation a Mi-8AMTSh helicopter was also destroyed. A Mi-28N helicopter from the Budyonnovsk regiment crashed near Homs on 12 April 2016, reportedly due to pilot error; the crew was killed. The next loss was a Mi-35M, shot down on 8 July 2016 near Palmyra. This helicopter was piloted by the commander of the 55th Helicopter Regiment at Korenovsk; the crew was also killed. Another Mi-8AMTSh from the Novosibirsk air base was shot down by ground fire on 1 August 2016; five crew were killed. Moreover, on 14 May 2016 four Mi-24Ps were burnt out on the ground at Tiyas (T4) air base; this was claimed to be an accident and not a result of combat action.

Russia has used strategic aviation in Syria as a retaliatory weapon. The largest operation by strategic bombers over Syria lasted four days and began on 17 November 2015, the day after official acknowledgement by Russian that a Metrojet Airbus A321 airliner downed over the Sinai was brought down as the result of a terrorist act. The operation saw the first combat use of Tu-160 and Tu-95MS strategic bombers as well as their Kh-555 and Kh-101 cruise missiles.

Between 17 and 20 November 2015, Russian long-range bombers flew 112 sorties, including 96 sorties performed by Tu-22M3s, 10 by Tu-160s and six by Tu-95MS bombers. The Tu-95MS and Tu-160 operated from their permanent base at Engels near Saratov. They flew to their target via the Caspian Sea and launched their missiles over Iranian territory, near the Iraqi border. The exception was the mission conducted on 20 November. That day, two Tu-160s took off from Olenyegorsk base on the Kola Peninsula in northern Russia, flew around Norway and the British Isles, entered the Mediterranean Sea via Gibraltar and flew over the entire Mediterranean to launch eight Kh-555 missiles against targets in Syria. Then, flying over the territories of Syria, Iraq, Iran and the Caspian Sea they returned to their home base at Engels; the route was more than 13,000km (8,100 miles) long. Over Syria, the Tu-160s were assisted by Su-30SM fighters from Hmeimim. The use of strategic bombers and long-range cruise missiles in Syria, especially the flight around Europe on 20 November, was a demonstrative action; Russian tactical aircraft could have accomplished the same task much more simply and cheaply from their base within Syria.

Tu-160s launched 48 Kh-101 and 16 Kh-555 cruise missiles, while Tu-95MS bombers launched 19 Kh-555 missiles. The Kh-101 was the most interesting airborne weapon

Left: Su-24M '26 White' takes off from Hmeimim. Both upgraded Su-24M SVP-24 and Su-24M2 versions of the aircraft have been employed in the Syrian campaign. (Russian MoD)

Right: Dating back to the Soviet era, the 10km (6.2-mile) range Kh-25ML laser-guided missile is seen under a Su-24M's wing. (Russian MoD)

During the mission around Europe on 20 November 2015, a pair of Tu-160 strategic bombers was assisted by Su-30SM fighters from Hmeimim while over Syria. (Russian MoD)

used during the Syrian operation; it is a 4,000km (2,500-mile) range subsonic cruise missile, series production of which began in 2010–11, first in nuclear-armed Kh-102 form and then in the conventionally armed Kh-101 version. Only a few operational Tu-160 and Tu-95MS bombers have been adapted to carry these missiles to date. It may be supposed that Russia expended a significant portion of its Kh-101 stocks over Syria. The Kh-555 is a conversion of older Kh-55 nuclear missiles into non-nuclear weapons; it has been part of the inventory since around 2003. Not all missiles reached their targets; photographs in social media show that some missiles were downed or crashed prior to reaching their targets. At least one Kh-101 crashed in Iran just after launch, with its wings still folded.

For their missions over Syria, Tu-22M3s (some of them SVP-24-22 versions) were temporarily deployed to Mozdok airfield in North Ossetia, from where they had to fly some 2,200km (1,400 miles) to their targets, based on the route over the Caspian Sea, Iran and Iraq. After 17–20 November 2015, Tu-22M3s performed several more operations including 60 sorties in early December 2015, and the next series of strikes in July and August 2016. On 12 July 2016, a few days after the downing of the Mi-35M, six Tu-22M3s took off from a base in Russia and conducted a retaliatory bombing of targets near Palmyra, as well as in Homs province. In all cases, the Tu-22M3s dropped free-fall bombs only, usually salvoes of 12 250kg (551lb) bombs, reduced in summer 2016 to 10 250kg or six 500 kg (1,102lb) bombs; one of the released videos shows a single 3,000kg (6,614lb) bomb being dropped.

Reconnaissance component

The Russian contingent in Syria is supported by reconnaissance assets including satellites, one or two Il-20M reconnaissance aircraft based at Hmeimim as well as various UAVs. Most of the 70 or so UAVs used by Russia in Syria are small, launched by hand or using a small catapult, like the Orlan-10, Eleron-3SV and Granat-4. A larger UAV in Syria is the 140kg (309lb) Yakovlev Pchela-1 developed in the early 1980s. Another Russian UAV spotted over Syria is the 454kg (1,000lb) Forpost, which is an Israel Aerospace Industries (IAI) Searcher Mk II assembled in Russia. This is the largest and most advanced reconnaissance UAV at the disposal of the Russian armed forces. Another surveillance system used by Russia in Syria is the Augur Au-17 Bars aerostat with elec-

Largest of the Russian UAVs that have been deployed in Syria is the Forpost. (Russian MoD)

Left: Bomb-armed Su-25s roll for take-off at Hmeimim. As part of the Russian 'withdrawal' from Syria, the Su-25 fleet returned to Russia in spring 2016.
(Russian MoD)

Right: The Syrian campaign has seen combat debut for new Russian Air Force types including the Su-30SM. '29 Red' is seen recovering an air-to-air armament of R-27 and R-73 missiles.
(Russian MoD)

tro-optical payload, probably used for observation of the area around Hmeimim air base; two such aerostats have been seen near Palmyra and one near Hmeimim.

Other Russian aircraft have appeared occasionally in Syria for brief periods. When the S-400 air defence system was being transported to Syria in November 2015, an A-50U airborne early warning aircraft was used to cover the transport operation. On 15 February 2016 a Tu-214R multi-sensor reconnaissance aircraft arrived at Hmeimim and remained there for two weeks. Earlier, in June 2015, a Tu-214R had been spotted patrolling along the Russian-Ukrainian border and in December 2012 an example was intercepted near Japan. The second Tu-214R, RF-64514, was deployed again to Hmeimim on 28 July 2016. On 5 June 2016, a day after the US Navy's *Harry S. Truman* Carrier Strike Group launched its first strikes over Syria and Iraq from the Mediterranean Sea, Russia sent a large Tu-142MK anti-submarine aircraft from Kipelovo base to the Eastern Mediterranean; it was seen over Aleppo.

Aircraft carrier plans

In July 2016, Russia's TASS news agency reported that Moscow was to send its only aircraft carrier, *Admiral Kuznetsov*, to the Syrian coast in October 2016; the carrier is to remain on station until January/February 2017. The air group on board the ship will comprise around 15 MiG-29KR/KUBR and Su-33 fighters, as well as around a dozen helicopters: Ka-52K for attack, Ka-31R for radar surveillance and Ka-27 for anti-submarine warfare/rescue. The deployment will be the operational debut for the MiG-29KR/KUBR, Ka-52K and Ka-31R.

MiG-29KR prototype '941' undergoes trials on board the *Admiral Kuznetsov* ahead of the planned Eastern Mediterranean cruise, slated to begin in October 2016. Note the TV-guided KAB-500KR precision-guided munitions underwing.
(RAC MiG)

The Russian press reported on the *Admiral Kuznetsov*'s planned Mediterranean cruise as early as autumn 2015, soon after the Russian operation in Syria had begun. According to these reports, the ship had recently undergone a three-month overhaul in a dock of the 35th Ship Repair Plant at Murmansk, after which she set off for the Barents Sea where Su-33 pilots commenced flight training. However, in January 2016 it was reported that the carrier could not be used in Syria 'because she is currently undergoing repair'. It may be surmised that the test cruise revealed technical problems that forced a return to dock. Furthermore, the ship was supposed to be adapted for the use of new MiG-29KR/KUBR fighters. Participation of the *Admiral Kuznetsov* in the Syrian operation only makes sense if MiG-29KR/KUBR multirole fighters are on hand to deliver guided air-to-ground munitions. The current Su-33s are pure air-defence fighters without a ground-attack capability.

A modernisation package for the *Admiral Kuznetsov* had been drafted by the end of 2015, with assistance from Nevskoye PKB, the ship's design bureau. The first stage of repairs began in early January 2016 and was completed by mid-June, when the ship left dock. The Murmansk repair plant carried out repair of the boilers and steam turbines, electric generators, and other items. Storage for aerial ordnance was converted to fit new weapons; additional systems necessary to operate the new aircraft types were also installed.

On 2 July 2016, a Su-33 and a Su-25UTG landed on board the carrier for the first time after repairs, while the first MiG-29KR arrived on 8 August; helicopters, including a Ka-52K, were also tested on board. After several weeks spent training the air group, the *Admiral Kuznetsov* returned to dock in Murmansk for completion of repairs; she was due to leave Murmansk for the Mediterranean Sea at the end of October.

The *Admiral Kuznetsov*'s deployment will have no practical significance for the operation in Syria; with a permanent base at Hmeimim, Russia can conduct strike missions more effectively using the land-based aircraft already deployed in Syria. Because of the small number of multirole fighters, the lack of combat-experienced pilots and certain features of the ship (including the lack of a steam catapult), strike missions launched from the *Admiral Kuznetsov* will necessarily be limited. The main objective of the deployment to Syria – apart from propaganda value – is developing basic skills in conducting strike operations from a carrier.

The Russian Navy's carrier aircraft and their operations will be discussed in detail in a future Harpia title, *Carrier Aviation Today*, while the continued developments within the Russian aviation arms in general, including orders of battle and structure, will also be the subject of a forthcoming book.

LONG-RANGE BOMBERS

Tupolev Tu-22M

NATO reporting name: Backfire

Tu-22M3 '46 Red' RF-94223 carries a pair of Kh-22 heavy anti-shipping missiles – which remain the aircraft's primary armament. Note also the external MBD3-U9M multiple bomb racks under the engine air intake trunks.
(Avtor)

Manufacturer

The Tu-22M was developed by the Tupolev Design Bureau in Moscow and series manufacture was undertaken by the Kazan Aircraft Plant named after S. P. Gorbunov. Currently, both entities belong to the Tupolev Company.

Role

The Tu-22M is a nuclear and conventional intermediate-range bomber and missile carrier; a reconnaissance version was built in a small series only. During the Cold War, the primary targets for Tu-22Ms would have been the US Navy's aircraft carriers and cruisers armed with Tomahawk cruise missiles operating in the Mediterranean and in the Atlantic Ocean. With the express purpose of defending US Navy aircraft carriers against Tu-22Ms, the Grumman F-14A Tomcat interceptor was developed and intro-

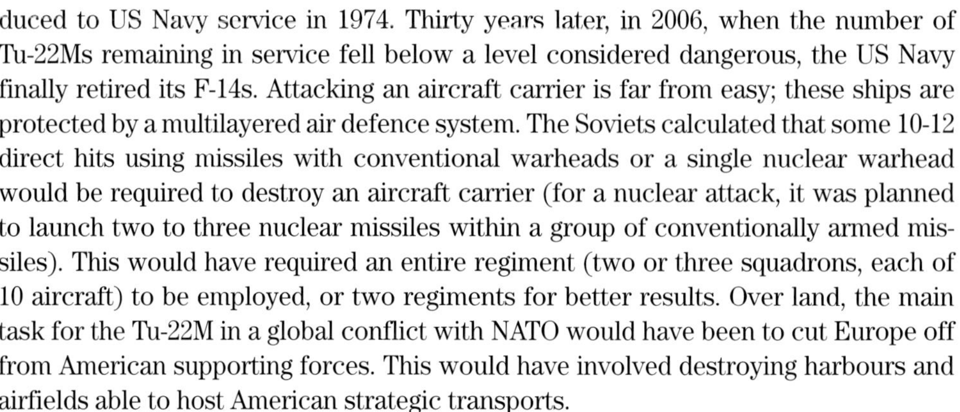

duced to US Navy service in 1974. Thirty years later, in 2006, when the number of Tu-22Ms remaining in service fell below a level considered dangerous, the US Navy finally retired its F-14s. Attacking an aircraft carrier is far from easy; these ships are protected by a multilayered air defence system. The Soviets calculated that some 10-12 direct hits using missiles with conventional warheads or a single nuclear warhead would be required to destroy an aircraft carrier (for a nuclear attack, it was planned to launch two to three nuclear missiles within a group of conventionally armed missiles). This would have required an entire regiment (two or three squadrons, each of 10 aircraft) to be employed, or two regiments for better results. Over land, the main task for the Tu-22M in a global conflict with NATO would have been to cut Europe off from American supporting forces. This would have involved destroying harbours and airfields able to host American strategic transports.

Crew

The crew of four consists of two pilots seated side-by-side in front, and the navigator and weapons system officer seated to their rear. All crewmembers have KT-1M (kreslo Tupoleva, 'Tupolev's seat') ejection seats, connected within the ASS automatic rescue system. A minimum speed of 130km/h (81mph) is required for safe ejection at altitudes below 60m (200ft); at higher altitudes there is no speed restriction. The crew are provided with LAS-5M lifesaving dinghies. The cockpit features conventional instrumentation and control yokes.

Airframe and systems

The variable-geometry wing has large, fixed gloves at the centre section and hydraulically driven wing panels (the motion of which is synchronised). Fowler-type trailing-edge flaps (62° deflection) are fitted on the fixed glove sections. There are three sections of double-slotted flaps (deflected 23° for take-off and 40° for landing), and three-section full-span leading-edge slats on each outer wing panel. There are no ailerons; instead, control is performed by three sections of spoilers/lift dumpers on the outer panels and by differential deflection of the elevators. The slab-type tailplanes can be deflected +9° or -20° symmetrically or differentially. The large tailfin has a conventional rudder. The ABSU-145M flight control system is of the hydraulic/electric type. The landing gear features main legs attached to the fixed wing gloves, which retract into the wings, while the wheels retract partly into the fuselage. Each main bogie comprises three pairs of 1,030 x 350mm (40.6 x 13.8in) wheels in tandem. The nose leg has twin 1,000 x 280mm (39.4 x 11.0in) wheels, which retract rearwards into the fuselage.

A Tu-22M3 undergoes refuelling. The aircraft carries 67,700 litres (17,881 gallons) of fuel in the fuselage and wing and in the fence ahead of the tailfin. (Stanislav Bazhenov)

Powerplant

The Tu-22M3 is powered by two Kuznetsov NK-25 (izdeliye Ye) afterburning turbofans rated at 140.2kN (31,526lbf) dry and 245.18kN (55,115lbf) with afterburning; the time from low to full thrust is nine seconds, or 18 seconds to full thrust with afterburning. A TA-6A auxiliary power unit (APU), installed in front of the tailfin root, supplies power for engine start and for on-board systems. Two or four 736AT rocket-assisted take-off (RATO) boosters can be used. The fuel system contains 67,700 litres (17,881 gallons) of internal fuel, equivalent to 53,550kg (118,057lb). Fuel is located in the fuselage and wing (including the movable outer wing panels) and in the fence in front of the tailfin; standard fuels are T-1, TS-1 or RT. There is no provision for auxiliary fuel tanks. In line with 1980 treaty restrictions, a fairing above the nose replaced the previous in-flight refuelling probe; theoretically, the probe can be reinstated, but this is not an easy operation. Furthermore, there are currently no Tu-22M pilots trained for this operation.

Dimensions

Wingspan 23.3m (76ft 5in) fully swept or 34.28m (112ft 6in) fully spread; maximum length 42.46m (139ft 4in); maximum height 11.05m (36ft 3in); wing area 175.78m^2 (1,892 sq ft) fully swept increasing to 183.58m^2 (1,976 sq ft) fully spread; sweepback of wing fixed glove 56°; sweepback of wing movable panels 20° to 65°; tailplane span 11.26m (36ft 11in); tailplane area 61.7m^2 (664.13 sq ft); tailfin area 32.98m^2 (355 sq ft); tailfin sweepback 57°15' at leading edge; wheelbase 13.51m (44ft 4in); wheel track 7.3m (23ft 11in).

Weights

Maximum take-off 124,000kg (273,373lb); maximum take-off with RATO boosters 126,400kg (278,664lb); empty 64,750kg (142,749lb); normal landing 78,000kg (171,961lb); maximum landing 88,000kg (194,007lb); the aircraft can land at full weight in an emergency.

Performance

Dash speed 2,300km/h (1,429mph); maximum speed at high altitude 2,000km/h (1,243mph); maximum speed at low altitude 1,000km/h (621mph); cruising speed 900km/h (559mph); ceiling at supersonic speed 14,000m (45,932ft); ceiling at subsonic speed 10,200m (33,465ft); g limit +1.6 wings fully spread or +2.0 wings fully swept; supersonic range 2,000km (1,243 miles); subsonic range 6,800km (4,225 miles) at high altitude or 3,350km (2,082 miles) at low altitude; operational radius with one Kh-22 missile at high altitude, some supersonic flight, 2,200km (1,367 miles); take-off distance 2,000-2,100m (6,562-6,890ft); landing distance 1,200-1,300m (3,937-4,265ft); lift-off speed 370km/h (230mph); approach speed 285km/h (177mph).

Mission systems

The main targeting sensor is the PNA (izdeliye 030A) navigation/attack radar (NATO reporting name Down Beat), which lacks an automatic terrain avoidance capability. The PNA is made by the Almaz Company in Moscow. PNA refers to Planeta Nositel for izdeliye A, in which Planeta (planet) is the designation of the K-22M control system complex (see Armament), Nositel is carrier, and izdeliye A refers to the Tu-22M. It should be noted that the active radar seeker of the Kh-22 missile when allied with this

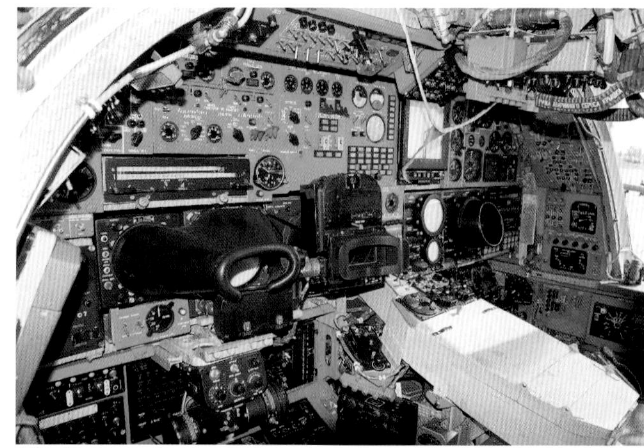

Left: Front cockpit of the Tu-22M3 with the pilot's seat on the left and the co-pilot on the right. The analogue instumentation is typical for Soviet aircraft of the 1980s. (Piotr Butowski)

Right: Rear cockpit of the Tu-22M3 with the weapons system operator's seat on the left and navigator on the right. (Piotr Butowski)

aircraft is designated PG, or Planeta Gruz (load). An izdeliye 015T optical TV bombsight is installed in the fairing under the cockpit. In the early 1990s it was planned to upgrade the PNA radar to the PNA-D standard developed by the Phazotron-NIIR company. However, only a few of these radars were completed and series upgrades were abandoned. In the late 1980s an U001 SURO (Sistema Upravleniya Raketnym Oruzhiyem, missile armament control system) was introduced for use with the Kh-15 missile. Currently, this is being upgraded to the U001M version that is compatible with both Kh-15 and Kh-32 missiles. An AFA-15 photographic camera is installed under the nose.

Avionics

Controlled by an Orbita-10TS-45 computer, the NK-45 Vakhta-2 (watch, or duty) navigation system allows automatic pre-programmed flight at high and low altitudes as well as automatic approach. It includes the MIS-45 inertial navigation system (INS), Rumb-1A (compass point) attitude and heading reference system, A711 long-range radio navigation system, RSBN-PKV short-range radio navigation system, ARK-15M radio direction finder, DISS-7 Doppler radar, Os'-1 instrument landing system (ILS), and RV-5 and RV-18M radio altimeters. Two R-832M UHF radios, one R-847T HF radio and SPU-10 (previously SPU-7) intercom systems are combined within the AS-45 (Apparatura Svyazi, communication system). The identification friend or foe (IFF) system is the Parol-2PV.

Self-protection features

The Ural-M (izdeliye L229) self-protection system combines the SPO-15 (L006) Beryoza radar warning receiver (RWR), Mak-UT (L083) infrared missile launch and approach sensor located on top of the fuselage just behind the rear crew, SPS-171/SPS-172 (L103M /L104M) Geran active response jammers (some of these were later upgraded to L362-1/-3), SPS-5M Fasol or SPS-6 Los' noise jammers, and decoy dispensers. Initially, the aircraft had only two ASO-2B-126 (Avtomat-2) decoy dispensers found on the centreline underneath the rear fuselage, below the engines. Subsequent aircraft added the APP-50A (L-029) decoy system with 16 three-round 50mm (1.9in) launchers installed in the bottom of the tailplane roots (eight launchers on each side; initially, these were KDS-155 launchers) and another 16 launchers under the rear fuselage. The aforementioned describes the full suite of self-defence equipment. However, on many

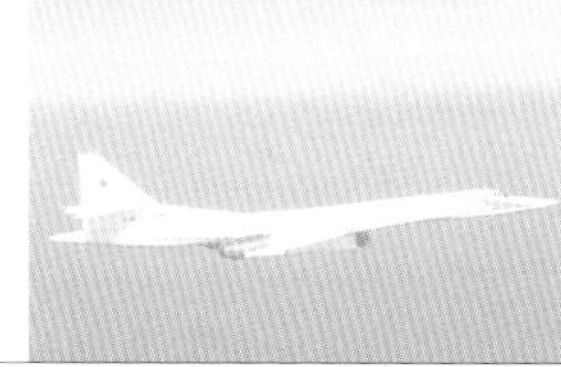

Above: Launchers for infrared decoys can be installed below the tailplane roots and under the rear fuselage. (Avtor)

aircraft this suite is incomplete, with, for example, a reduction in the complement of the Mak sensors and decoy dispensers. Additionally, and not connected to the Ural system, the APP-22MS (Avtomat-3) dispenser with large decoys (chaff bundles) can be fitted in the rear of the internal weapons bay for escort jamming missions (the dispenser must be removed when the under-fuselage missile is carried). Externally, the APP-22MS fairing is visible when fitted.

Defensive armament includes a 23mm GSh-23M twin-barrel cannon (one barrel above the other) with a firing rate equivalent to 4,000rpm, and provided with 750 rounds of ammunition. The gun is installed in a 9A-502M tail turret that is remotely controlled by means of a PRS-4KM (izdeliye 4DK) Krypton radar sight (NATO reporting name Fan Tail) and a TP-1KM TV sight. Heat-resistant steel shrouds protect the gun barrels, which enter the wake of the exhaust gases when deflected downwards. As in other Russian heavy aircraft, the primary purpose of this cannon is to jam enemy anti-aircraft missiles and the radars of enemy fighters. For this purpose, the cannon fires rounds carrying thermal or radar decoys.

Tu-22M3 tail turret. (Piotr Butowski)

Armament

The primary armament of the aircraft is the Raduga Kh-22 supersonic heavy missile. The Tu-22M aircraft, Kh-22 missile and Planeta control system (comprising the aircraft's radar and missile guidance system) are together known as the K-22M aircraft-missile complex. Two basic versions of the Kh-22 are used, comprising an active-radar seeker version for use against ships and an inertial-guidance version for use against large ground targets. The active-radar Raduga Kh-32 missile, which is a direct succes-

This Tu-22M3 was armed with a single Kh-32 anti-shipping missile semi-recessed under the fuselage when spotted by a Norwegian fighter on 29 October 2014. (Royal Norwegian Air Force)

sor to the Kh-22 and has the same shape and size, has been in limited service since the early 2000s; a new Kh-32M version was under test at the time of writing.

The nominal weapon load is 6,000kg (13,228lb), equivalent to a single Kh-22/Kh-32 missile; any greater load compromises the fuel load carried. The maximum weapon load is 24,000kg (52,911lb). The bomber can carry a maximum of three Kh-22/Kh-32 missiles, one semi-recessed on the under-fuselage BD-45F pylon and two under the fixed wing glove on BD-45K pylons. In the late 1980s, the Tu-22M3s of the final production series were armed with six Kh-15 inertial-guidance short-range attack missiles carried on an MKU6-1 (Mnogozaryadnaya Katapultnaya Ustanovka, multiple launching device; izdeliye 9A827) rotary launcher inside the weapons bay; four more Kh-15s could be suspended under the wings on single AKU-1 ejection launchers.

Free-fall bombs can be carried on KD3-22R multiple racks (for bombs up to 500kg, 1,102lb) or KD4-105A multiple racks (for bombs of 1,500-3,000kg, 3,307-6,614lb) inside the bomb bay as well as on four external MBD3-U9M multiple racks (two under the engine air intake trunks and two under the wings, in place of the BD-45Ks, each rack carrying six 500kg bombs). Bomb load options include 69 250kg (551lb), or 42 500kg (1,102lb), or eight 1,500kg (3,307lb), or two 3,000kg (6,614lb) weapons. Mine-laying loads for maritime missions include eight RM-1, UDM, UDM-5, Serey, Lira, APM, AMD-2M or AGDM mines, or 12 AMD-500M mines, or 18 IGDM-500 or UDM-500 mines.

History

On 28 November 1967 the Soviet government charged Andrey Tupolev's design team with the creation of the Tu-22M (izdeliye A, or izdeliye 145). The bomber was required to attain a maximum speed of 2,300-2,500km/h (1,429-1,553mph) and to achieve a subsonic range of 7,000km (4,350 miles) with a single Kh-22 missile. An initial batch of eight Tu-22M0 (izdeliye 45.00) (NATO reporting name Backfire-A) versions was com-

pleted by the Kazan factory; the first of these performed a maiden flight on 30 August 1969, with Vasili Borisov at the controls.

The Tu-22M0 was much too slow (1,530km/h, 951mph) and its range was far too short (4,140km, 2,572 miles). On 28 July 1971 the Tu-22M1 (izdeliye 45.01) was flown for the first time, this variant introducing new movable outer wing panels. The range was improved slightly to 5,000km (3,107 miles) and speed was increased to 1,660km/h (1,031mph). The Tu-22M1 was produced in a small series of nine aircraft.

The subsequent Tu-22M2 (izdeliye 45.02) (NATO reporting name Backfire-B) with slightly modified airframe first flew on 7 May 1973 and became the first large-scale production version. Its performance was not much improved (range 5,100km, 3,169 miles; speed 1,700km/h, 1,056mph) but the decision was taken to commence production because of its much improved mission systems. The factory in Kazan completed 211 Tu-22M2s until 1983.

The Tu-22M2 was still far from meeting the original requirements of 1967. The bomber's problems were solved by introducing modern NK-25 engines offering 245.18kN (55,115lbf) of thrust, a 25 per cent increase over the previous powerplant, while specific fuel consumption was reduced by 11 per cent. Since the fuselage had to be changed to incorporate the new engines, the opportunity was taken to redesign the entire airframe. The new Tu-22M3 (izdeliye 45.03) (NATO reporting name Backfire-C) received larger, wedge-type air intakes; the wings can be folded back to 65° (compared to the previous 60°). The aircraft's speed was increased to 2,000km/h (1,243mph) while the dash speed was increased to 2,300km/h (1,429mph). Action radiuses were increased by 14-45 per cent, depending on mission profile. The first Tu-22M3 flew on 20 June 1977 and the factory in Kazan built 268 examples up to 1993. Initially, the Soviet Air Force reserved the Tu-32 designation for the bomber but finally opted for Tu-22M3. The aircraft was officially commissioned in March 1989.

One further production version was the Tu-22MR (izdeliye 45.09) reconnaissance aircraft. The prototype made its maiden flight on 6 December 1985 and a dozen examples were built between 1989–93. In the mid-1980s, a prototype of the Tu-22MP (Pomekhovyi, jamming) escort jammer version was developed but the programme was discontinued due to the disappointing performance of this system. Design of the Tu-22M4 (izdeliye 45.10) was launched in 1983; the aircraft was to carry Kh-32 and Kh-57 (a reduced-range derivative of the Kh-55) missiles as well as UPAB-1500 glide bombs. The targeting suite was to be built around the Obzor radar of the Tu-160. The new bomber was to be powered by two NK-32 turbofans, also inherited from the Tu-160. In 1990, Tupolev adapted Tu-22M3 '4504' to serve as a flying test-bed for the NK-32 engines, but it was never fitted with these. Aircraft '4504' features 12 (instead of the standard nine) auxiliary air inlets on each engine air duct. The aircraft was seen on many occasions during airshows at Zhukovsky in the 1990s. Today, it is preserved at a small museum in Ryazan, home of the Long-Range Aviation evaluation centre. The Tu-22M4 programme was cancelled in November 1991. The next variant, the Tu-22M5, attained the very early design phase in the mid-1990s, but progressed no further.

Production and operators

After the disintegration of the Soviet Union, Tu-22Ms remained in Russia and Ukraine only (the aircraft previously based in Belarus and Estonia were transferred to Russia). The Ukrainian aircraft were scrapped in 2002–06. The Tu-22M has never been exported.

The Tu-22M3's variable-geometry wing has large, fixed gloves located at the centre section, each of which can carry a single Kh-22/Kh-32 missile on a BD-45K pylon.
(Avtor)

During a visit to India in October 1999, the then Russian Air Force commander-in-chief Anatoly Kornukov submitted to New Delhi an offer for the lease of four Tu-22M3s, but this never materialised.

Between 1969 and 1993 a total of 514 Tu-22M aircraft of all versions were built, including fatigue and static-test examples. Today, Russia's long-range bomber force includes 80 Tu-22M bombers at three operational bases — Belaya, Olenyegorsk and Shaykovka — and at the Ryazan crew conversion centre. More than 60 additional Tu-22Ms are in storage at aircraft depots or lie abandoned at various airfields; some of them may be returned to service after appropriate restoration. A number of Tu-22M bombers were previously under Russian Navy command, but in 2011 all were put under Russian Air Force command.

Variants

Tu-22M0 (izdeliye 45.00) (NATO reporting name Backfire-A). An initial batch of eight aircraft built at the Kazan factory.

Tu-22M1 (izdeliye 45.01) new movable outer wing panels for improved performance. Nine aircraft completed.

Tu-22M2 (izdeliye 45.02) (NATO reporting name Backfire-B). Incorporating a slightly revised airframe, this became the first large-scale production version. The factory in Kazan completed 211 Tu-22M2s until 1983.

Tu-22M3 (izdeliye 45.03), (NATO reporting name Backfire-C). As described above, this is currently the only operational bomber version of the Tu-22M.

Tu-22M3 '9804' operated by the Tupolev Company prepares to land with two test Kh-32M missiles.
(Piotr Butowski)

Tu-22MR (izdeliye 45.09) is a theatre-level reconnaissance aircraft equipped with a BKR-2 (M200) suite including the M202 Shompol side-looking radar, SRS-13 Tangazh electronic intelligence (ELINT) system, Osen infrared (IR) scanner, and A-81, A-84 and AP-402 photo cameras. The PNA radar was replaced by the Leninets U006 Obzor-MR, while the 015T TV sight was replaced by the OPB-18 from the Tu-160. One aircraft remains operational at Belaya air base. In the early 1990s design work began on the **Tu-22MR1**, which was to feature a new BKR-4 reconnaissance suite; the project was later abandoned.

Tu-22M4 (izdeliye 45.10). This aircraft was intended to carry Kh-32 and Kh-57 missiles as well as UPAB-1500 glide bombs. The Tu-22M4 program was cancelled in November 1991.

Tu-22M5. This aircraft reached only a very early design stage in the mid-1990s.

In 2000, Tupolev presented a concept for the **Tu-344**, a supersonic business/VIP jet converted from a Tu-22M3. This would have been able to carry 12-18 persons over a distance of 7,700km (4,785 miles) at a cruising speed of Mach 1.7.

Tu-22M3 mid-life upgrade programmes

For a period of around 10 years, Tu-22M3s have been slowly upgraded to carry the Kh-32 missile, a direct successor to the Kh-22. The subsequent Kh-32M missile is currently being evaluated on Tu-22M3 '9804' (serial number 98-04, c/n 4898649), an aircraft that belongs to the Tupolev design bureau. The research and development programme for the adaptation of the Tu-22M3 to carry the Kh-32M missile is codenamed **Poten-**

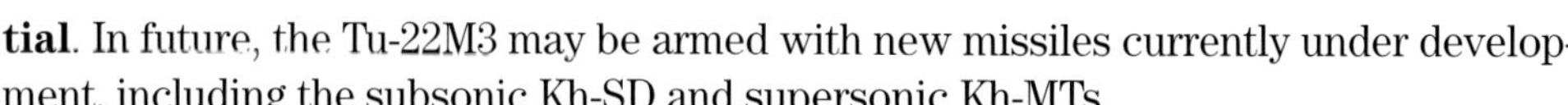

tial. In future, the Tu-22M3 may be armed with new missiles currently under development, including the subsonic Kh-SD and supersonic Kh-MTs.

Tu-22M3 SVP-24-22 is an upgrade programme by the Gefest & T company that repeats solutions implemented by the company in its upgrade of the Sukhoi Su-24M tactical bomber (see Volume 1). In October 2008, Gefest & T signed a contract with the Russian Ministry of Defence for the adaptation of the SVP-24 suite for the Tu-22M3 bomber; the adapted avionics suite was designated SVP-24-22. The suite comprises the SV-24 computer, SRNS-24 navigation system, and two new displays added to the navigator's instrument panel. The PNA radar remains unchanged, but its image is now digitally processed. The only way to distinguish an upgraded aircraft (apart from the inscription 'Gefest & T' that is sometimes worn on the port side) is a small white flat antenna on the spine, aft of the Mak radome. This new antenna is part of the satellite navigation system.

The first Tu-22M3 upgraded by Gefest & T, '37', underwent trials in 2009, and even took part in the Russian-Belarusian Zapad-2009 exercise that took place in Belarus. According to Alexander Panin, the head of Gefest & T, the accuracy of the aircraft's navigation is increased by a magnitude of eight to 10, while the precision of free-fall bomb delivery is increased by a magnitude of seven to nine; the reliability of the systems is also considerably increased. In 2012 the Russian Air Force ordered serial upgrades of the Tu-22M3 according to the pattern developed by Gefest & T; these aircraft have not received a separate designation and are usually referred to simply as 'Tu-22M3 with SVP-24-22'. In 2012 the Myasishchev Company of Zhukovsky modified three Tu-22M3s in line with an order from Gefest & T calling for retrofit of the bombers with the new equipment; the upgrades continue. A statement from the Russian Ministry of Defence issued on 31 January 2012, to mark the beginning of the training year at the Ryazan centre, announced that 'by 2020, upgrade of about 30 bombers to Tu-22M3M [sic; the statement in fact referred to the SVP-24-22 upgrade – author's note] version is planned'.

Tu-22M3M (izdeliye 45.03M). This upgrade programme formally began as early as June 1990, when the Soviet Ministry of Defence ordered Tupolev to begin work on the **Adaptatsiya-45.03M** (adaptation). The programme has retained the same codename, but has made little progress in the years since. The exact form of the upgrade has, until recently, been subject to change. The upgraded Tu-22M3M will receive the NV-45 (Novella-45) radar complex with the 1NV-1 radar produced by the Zaslon (formerly Leninets) Company of St Petersburg. As early as 2008, Tu-22M3 '9804' was retrofitted with a prototype of the Novella-45 radar. In 2011 the plans suddenly changed and it was decided that the Tu-22M3M (and Tu-160M) would utilise a different radar developed by the NIIP Company on the basis of the Irbis electronically scanned unit. However, a contract for the new radar was not signed and in autumn 2013 the previous plans were reinstated. Leninets announced that it delivered the first NV-45 radar system for tests in 2014; reportedly, it has been upgraded when compared to the radar of the 2008 version. Other changes in the upgraded Tu-22M3M include an advanced NO-45.03M navigation system with INS-2000-04 inertial navigation, S-505-45 communication suite, 623-3D-23 IFF, as well as a digitally controlled ABSU-145MTs flight control system. Self-defence systems are also being improved. There will be no changes in terms of the Tu-22M3's airframe and engines.

In 2016 the Russian Ministry of Defence placed a contract for the upgrade of a first four operational Tu-22M3M bombers. A subcontract provides for the delivery of four NV-45

radar systems beginning in the fourth quarter of 2016 (one radar each quarter). It may therefore be supposed that the first aircraft will be returned to service in mid-2017. Tu-22M3 bombers are now being overhauled by two repair facilities: ARZ-150 near Kaliningrad and ARZ-360 at Ryazan, as well as by the manufacturer, KAPO of Kazan. Upgrade of the Tu-22M3 is to be conducted only at Kazan.

Tu-22M3 '9804' belongs to Tupolev and is based at Zhukovsky. Among other test duties, it is used as a platform for live tests of Russian **hypersonic flying vehicles**. The hypersonic vehicle to be tested is launched by the Tu-22M3 attached to the forward section of a Kh-22 missile. The test vehicle then separates from the Kh-22 and can accelerate to Mach 8. Originally, this test-bed suite was facilitated in order to support the French LEA programme, but Russia's participation in this project has since been suspended. Instead, Russia is using the Tu-22M3/Kh-22 to test its own similar hypersonic vehicle. Reportedly, this was launched for the first time in summer 2012; the tests continue.

In the conventional bombing role, as employed over Syria, the Tu-22M3 has been typically armed with 12 250kg (551lb) free-fall bombs in the internal weapons bay.
(Stanislav Bhazenov)

Combat service

Tu-22Ms have seen action in several local wars; however, they have only employed free-fall bombs, and not the heavy supersonic missiles that comprise their main weapons. In 1984 targets in Afghanistan were bombed for the first time by Soviet Tu-22M2s. On a second occasion, from October 1988 to January 1989, Tu-22M3s blocked the approaches to roads being used for the evacuation of Soviet troops. In Chechnya, between November 1994 and January 1996, Tu-22M3s performed in excess of 100 sorties, mainly conducting free-fall bombing as well as illuminating the battlefield with illumination bombs.

During its third conflict, Russia's war with Georgia in August 2008, the Tu-22M suffered its first combat loss. On 9 August 2008 a group of bombers from the 52nd Heavy Bomber Aviation Regiment (TBAP) from Shaykovka was bombing targets near Gori in central Georgia. On the return to base one of the bombers was shot down by a Georgian surface-to-air missile, probably a Buk-M. Only one of four crewmembers (the co-pilot) survived. Immediately after the loss, Russia announced that the destroyed Tu-22M 'was performing reconnaissance tasks'; the objective was not to admit it had been flying a bombing sortie while the fate of the crew remained unknown. The statement led to much speculation about the use of the Tu-22MR reconnaissance aircraft in the war with Georgia, although this variant was not involved.

More recently, Tu-22M3s performed 96 sorties during Russia's first strategic-aviation attack on Syria between 17 and 20 November 2015. Over Syria, the Tu-22M3 has been used to drop salvoes of 12 250kg (551lb) free-fall bombs or single 3,000kg (6,614lb) bombs. For this operation, the Tu-22M3s have been temporarily deployed to Mozdok airfield in Northern Ossetia, from where they are required to fly some 2,200km (1,367 miles) to reach targets in Syria, presumably utilising a route over the Caspian Sea, Iran and Iraq. The aircraft fly in pairs; the leader in each pair is an upgraded Tu-22M3 SVP-24-22, equipped with a much more precise navigation system. During the following months, Tu-22M3s have performed further sorties over Syria, including an intensive series of strikes in July and August 2016. For a brief period in August 2016 the aircraft made use of Hamedan air base in Iran for refuelling.

Tupolev Tu-95MS

NATO reporting name: Bear-H

A Tu-95MS from Engels air base takes on fuel from an Il-78 tanker.
(Sergey Krivchikov)

Manufacturer

The Tu-95MS was designed by the Tupolev Company in Moscow and series manufacture was undertaken by the Aviacor Aircraft Plant in Samara.

Role

Intercontinental-range cruise missile carrier.

Crew

The Tu-95MS is operated by a crew of seven including two pilots, a navigator (with access to the astrodome), a navigator/defence system operator, a communications operator, and a flight engineer in a pressurised compartment within the forward fuselage, and a tail gunner in a separate rear compartment. All crew (except the tail gunner) enter the cockpit via the front undercarriage bay. No ejection seats are provided.

Airframe and systems

The aircraft is an all-metal monoplane. The swept, mid-mounted wing has 2.5° anhedral and +1° incidence. The wings have four-spar 35° (at quarter-chord) inner panels and three-spar 33.5° outer panels. The main wing is provided with two-section double-slotted trailing-edge flaps (20° for take-off and 30° for landing) and three-section ailerons (16° up and down) with tabs on each wing; spoilers are fitted on the upper surface of the wing. Three boundary layer fences are fitted on each wing. The conventional tail control surfaces include a variable-incidence tailplane, adjustable in flight according to the fuel used (1° down, 3° up); elevators (26° up and 13° down) and rudder (25° each side), all with tabs. The SAU-3-021 flight control system is mechanical and is hydraulically actuated. The retractable undercarriage has steerable twin nosewheels (1,140 x 350mm, 44.9 x 13.8in) and four-wheel (1,450 x 450mm, 57.1 x 17.7in) bogies on each main unit. The main undercarriage units retract into the large fairings on the wing trailing edges, in line with the inner engines.

Powerplant

The Tu-95MS is powered by four Kuznetsov/Samara NK-12MP turboprops, each developing 11,185ekW (15,000ehp) maximum power or 7,360ekW (9,870ehp) for cruise. Each eight-blade AV-60K propeller unit comprises two four-blade coaxial contra-rotating reversible-pitch propellers, 5.6m (18ft 4in) in diameter. A maximum of 84,000kg (185,188lb) of internal fuel is carried in eight wing tanks plus three fuselage tanks; there is no provision for auxiliary tanks. An in-flight refuelling probe is installed on the nose, ahead of the cockpit. The Sprut sub-variant incorporates a TA-12A auxiliary power unit. Thanks to its four powerful engines and swept wing, the Tu-95 is the world's fastest turboprop production aircraft.

Dimensions

Maximum length 49.13m (161ft 2in); wingspan 50.04m (164ft 2 in); wing area 289.9m^2 (3,120 sq ft); maximum height 13.30m (43ft 8in); maximum fuselage diameter 2.9m (9ft 6in); wheelbase 14.83m (48ft 8in); wheel track 12.55m (41ft 2in).

Weights

Maximum take-off 185,000kg (407,885lb); maximum after in-flight refuelling 187,000kg (412,264lb); maximum landing 135,000kg (297,624lb); empty 94,400kg (208,116lb).

Performance

Maximum speed 830km/h (516mph); maximum speed at sea level 550km/h (342mph); cruising speed 735km/h (457mph); take-off speed at maximum take-off weight (MTOW) 300km/h (186mph); approach speed 275km/h (171mph); take-off distance at MTOW 2,540m (8,334ft); g limit +2; ceiling 10,500m (34,450ft); range with six internal cruise missiles 10,500km (6,524 miles) without in-flight refuelling; range with six internal and 10 external cruise missiles 6,500km (4,039 miles) without in-flight refuelling; range with single in-flight refuelling 14,100km (8,761 miles); flight duration without in-flight refuelling 14 hours.

Mission systems

The Leninets Obzor-MS (coverage; izdeliye U009; NATO reporting name Clam Pipe) navigation/attack radar is fitted in the nose, with a weather radar above. The Sprut (octopus; izdeliye K-016) missile initialisation and launch system is designed to align the coordination axes of the navigation systems of the aircraft and the Kh-55SM mis-

sile, and to transmit a digital map of the terrain along the planned missile path from the aircraft to the missile before launch; early aircraft have the Osina (aspen; izdeliye K-012) system that supports only the earlier Kh-55 missile. In the second half of the 2000s, Russian strategic aviation introduced the SVVI-021-16 pre-flight data management system coupled with the Sigma mission-planning system.

Crew positions in the Tu-95MS comprise (clockwise, from top left): the pilots' positions, with the crew commander on the left, in the front cockpit; the rear-facing navigator's position at the rear end of the pressurised crew compartment; the navigator/self-defence system operator's position; the communications operator's position; and the flight engineer's position. (Piotr Butowski)

Avionics

The NPK-VP-021 flight-navigation complex is controlled by an Orbita-10 computer and consists of an AP-15PS autopilot, Bort-42 path control system, Rumb-1B attitude and heading reference system, and L14MA astro-inertial navigation system. The system receives data from ARK-15M and ARK-U2 radio direction finders, DISS-7 Doppler radar, RV-5M and RV-18G radio altimeters, A711, A713 and A722 long-range navigation

systems, and an RSBN-PKV short-range radio navigation system. The Os'-1 instrument landing system enables the aircraft to take off in 400m (1,312ft) visibility and 30m (98ft) cloud base, and land under 1,000m (3,280ft) and 100m (328ft) conditions, respectively. The Strela-AM communication suite includes two R-832M VHF and two R-857G HF radios as well as an R-866G HF receiver. The IFF suite is the Type 6202.

Self-protection features

The Meteor-NM (Meteor-N on early aircraft) self-defence system allies SPO-15 (L006) Beryoza (SPO-10 Sirena-3M on early aircraft) radar warning receivers at the nose and tail, L083 Mak-UT IR missile launch and approach sensors under the nose and on the rear fuselage, SPS-171/SPS-172 (L103Zh/L104Zh; Geran-1DU/-2DU) active radar jammers on the nose and rear fuselage and in pods under the tail turret, and 50mm (1.9in) APP-50 chaff/flare dispensers in the undercarriage fairings. (The number of APP-50 dispensers varies; most aircraft have eight three-round launchers in each of two fairings, while some aircraft have around 30 launchers in each fairing).

Defensive armament includes two twin-barrel 23mm GSh-23 cannon installed in a 9A-503M tail turret that is remotely controlled using a Krypton radar sight (NATO reporting name Box Tail); two AM-23 single-barrel guns were fitted in early aircraft.

Armament

A normal weapon load weighs 7,800kg (17,196lb), while a maximum load weighs 21,000kg (46,297lb). The normal load consists of six Kh-55 (on Osina aircraft) or Kh-55SM (Sprut aircraft) long-range nuclear cruise missiles carried on the MKU-6-5 (9A829) rotary launcher fitted inside the fuselage; the weapons bay is 7.5m (24ft 7in) long, 1.78m (5ft 10in) wide and 2.9m (9ft 6in) deep. Each missile is dropped by pneu-

Left: Eight three-tube 50mm (1.9in) chaff/flare dispensers are built into the undercarriage fairing of a Tu-95MS. Some aircraft have additional dispensers on the upper surface of the fairing. (Piotr Butowski)

Right: The two twin-barrel 23mm GSh-23 cannon and Krypton radar sight in the Tu-95MS's tail turret. (Piotr Butowski)

Tu-95MS '21 Red' reveals the distinctive undercarriage of the 'Bear', with twin nosewheels and four-wheel main bogies that retract into large fairings on the wing trailing edges, in line with the inner engines. (Avtor)

matic catapult from the lowest point of the revolving drum and then fired. Afterwards the drum is rotated 60° ready for the next launch. Additionally, approximately half the fleet comprises Tu-95MS16 aircraft able to carry 10 more missiles suspended under the wings in four clusters (two missiles on each inner pylon and three missiles on each pylon between the engines). Note that when used on the Tu-95MS, the Kh-55SM missiles are not fitted with their additional fuel tanks. During upgrades, the aircraft were adapted to carry up to six Kh-555s (internally) and the fleet is currently being adapted for the carriage of up to eight Kh-101/Kh-102 cruise missiles; see below for more details.

History

On 11 July 1951, Andrey Tupolev was assigned the task of building the Tu-95 (izdeliye V) intercontinental bomber; on 12 November 1952 a crew led by Aleksei Perelet took off for the maiden flight of the first prototype. Series production began in autumn 1955 and by 1969 the Samara (then Kuibyshev) plant had built 173 aircraft in several versions including Tu-95M bombers, Tu-95K missile carriers and Tu-95RTs maritime reconnaissance aircraft. After production of the Tu-95 ceased in Samara, production of the Tu-142 maritime patrol aircraft – based on a thoroughly upgraded Tu-95 airframe – continued in Taganrog.

At the end of the 1970s, and several years after production of the Tu-95 had ceased, a new generation of long-range cruise missiles appeared, first in the United States (AGM-86 Air-Launched Cruise Missile), and then in the Soviet Union (Kh-55). A test-bed for trials of the Kh-55 missile was converted from a Tu-95M aircraft, and the resulting Tu-95M-55 or izdeliye VM-021 took off for the first time on 31 July 1978 with Nikolay Kulchitsky at the controls. (It seems likely that the 021 number originates from a reverse reading of the index for the Kh-55 missile: izdeliye 120.) Between 1978 and 1982, the aircraft completed 107 experimental flights and launched 10 Kh-55 missiles. On 28 January 1982 the Tu-95M-55 crashed during take-off from Zhukovsky, killing all 10 members of the crew.

Looking for an operational platform for the missiles, the Soviets selected (along with new Tu-160, see separately) the Tu-142 airframe. In July 1977, Tupolev was ordered to redesign the Tu-142M to create a Kh-55 missile carrier designated Tu-142MS. The

Tu-142MS prototype was built by the Taganrog factory on the basis of Tu-142MK airframe c/n 42105 and first flew at Taganrog on 14 September 1979, with a crew led by Slava Gordiyenko. Externally, when compared with the Tu-142MK, the aircraft has a shorter forward part of the fuselage with a new, wider cockpit. Along with the start of series production, the aircraft was redesignated as the Tu-95MS. In 1981 the factory in Taganrog completed a few aircraft intended for testing. On 3 September 1981 the first Tu-95MS performed a first successful launch of a Kh-55 missile. On 17 December 1982 the first two aircraft were delivered to the 1023rd TBAP at Semipalatinsk, Kazakh SSR. On 31 December 1983, upon introduction of adjustments resulting from the state acceptance tests, the Tu-95MS aircraft with Kh-55 missiles was officially commissioned into service. The size of the planned production series exceeded the capability of the factory in Taganrog, especially as the plant was simultaneously manufacturing Tu-142s and converting Il-76MD transport aircraft into A-50 early warning aircraft (see Volume 1). Therefore, at the beginning of 1983 production of the Tu-95MS was moved to Samara, where the last Tu-95s had been completed 14 years earlier.

Production and operators

During the first production period (1955 to 1969) the Samara plant built 173 aircraft. Subsequently, 88 Tu-95MS bombers were produced during 1982–92 including the first 12 in Taganrog and the remainder in Samara. After the collapse of the USSR, 40 of these aircraft remained in Kazakhstan with the 79th Heavy Bomber Aviation Division (TBAD) based at Semipalatynsk and were handed over to Russia in 1994 in exchange for fighter aircraft. Another 25 remained in Ukraine with the 182nd TBAP at Uzin-Shepelovka; the three newest of these had been manufactured in 1991, and were the only Sprut versions in Ukraine. These were sold to Russia in November–December 1999 (Russia was not interested in obtaining the older Osina versions).

At present, Russia has 60 Tu-95MS bombers, with an equal division between Osina and newer Sprut sub-variants. These are found at two operational air bases at Engels and at Ukrainka in the Far East, and in the Russian Air Force's crew conversion centre at Ryazan (five or six aircraft). Additionally, four or five Tu-95MS aircraft are used for tests at Zhukovsky near Moscow. Since 1999, Russian Tu-95s have received the names of towns and cities, as follows: *Irkutsk* (01, the first aircraft to be named), *Mozdok* (02), *Kurgan* (04), *Saratov* (10/1), *Vorkuta* (11), *Moskva* (12), *Voronezh* (14), *Kaluga* (15), *Veliky Novgorod* (16), *Krasnoyarsk* (19), *Ryazan* (20), *Dubna* (20/1), *Samara* (21/1), *Kozelsk* (22), *Chelyabinsk* (22), *Tambov* (23), *Sevastopol* (28/1), *Smolensk* (29/2, formerly 08) and *Blagoveshchensk* (59).

Variants

Tu-95MS (izdeliye VP-021) is the initial service version that exists in two sub-variants; older aircraft have the Osina missile system that only operates with Kh-55 missiles, while later aircraft have the more modern Sprut system, as used in the Tu-160, also capable of controlling the Kh-55SM missile. The aircraft self-defence and communication systems have been improved, and an APU added. The Sprut sub-variant entered service in 1986.

Another difference between the Tu-95MS sub-variants is related to the number of missiles that can be carried: the aircraft designated conventionally as **Tu-95MS6** carry six missiles within the fuselage weapon bay, whereas the **Tu-95MS16** bombers carry

Tu-95MS RF-94259 is escorted by a Eurofighter Typhoon of No. 6 Squadron, Royal Air Force, off the coast of the United Kingdom in 2011. (RAF)

an additional 10 missiles under the wings; these are not official designations and were used during START (Strategic Arms Reduction Treaty) 1 negotiations, together with the corresponding Bear-H6 and Bear-H16 NATO reporting names.

Introduction of new missiles

The first modernisations implemented on operational aircraft consist of the introduction of new weapons; the aircraft type designation has not been changed during these upgrades. Since around 2003, the aircraft have been armed with Kh-555 missiles (six carried inside the fuselage on the MKU-6-5 launcher), these being non-nuclear conversions of Kh-55 missiles.

Subsequently, the aircraft were adapted to carry eight new nuclear Kh-102 and then non-nuclear Kh-101 very-long range cruise missiles. As the aircraft's internal weapons bay was tailored for the 6m (19ft 8in) long Kh-55 missile, the 7.5m (24ft 7in) long Kh-101/-102s have to be carried externally on four underwing pylons, each with two missiles on AKU-5M launchers. The external carriage of Kh-101/-102 missiles causes a significant reduction in the aircraft's range; it may be estimated that with eight missiles, the range of the Tu-95MS is around 7,000km (4,350 miles). Only the later Tu-95MS aircraft with the Sprut system are being upgraded to carry the Kh-101/-102 missiles.

The first tests of the Tu-95MS with Kh-101/Kh-102 missiles were carried out at Zhukovsky and involved two test aircraft belonging to Tupolev, '01' and '317'. Aircraft '01' (c/n 15101) is used for tests of the missile itself including launches, and has only one weapon pylon; the first launch of the Kh-101/-102 missile by this aircraft was conducted around 2004. Tu-95MS '317' (c/n 19317) is used for tests of the aircraft's flight handling and performance and usually flies with a full load of eight missiles; the aircraft has no mission systems and carries only mock-ups of the missiles.

Production of the pylons required to carry the new missiles is undertaken at the Beriev plant in Taganrog. The same plant conducted the first serial upgrades and adaptations of the bombers, consisting of reinforcing the wing structure in the area of the new pylons. The first Russian Air Force aircraft adapted for carrying Kh-101/-102 missiles, Tu-95MS '10/1', named *Saratov* and registered RF-94128, was rolled out of the Beriev plant in early 2015. Formally, the upgraded aircraft is designated **Tu-95MS updated according to bulletin No 021-1170BU**.

In 2015 the Aviakor Plant at Samara commenced overhauls of Tu-95MS aircraft and installation of pylons for the new missiles. On 18 November 2015 the plant delivered the first aircraft ('20' *Dubna*, c/n 34666, registered RF-94122) to the Russian Air Force; the overhaul and adaptation to carry the Kh-101/-102 missiles took three months. The upgrades continue in Samara at a rate of three aircraft per year. Overhauls of the Tu-95MS aircraft are also conducted by the ARZ-360 repair facility in Ryazan.

Tu-95MSM upgrade programme

Simultaneous with the implementation of the new armament, an independent upgrade of the bomber's systems is being conducted. The **Tu-95MSM** (**izdeliye VP-021MSM**) upgrade was ordered by the Russian Ministry of Defence on 23 December 2009, within a research and development programme codenamed **Litograf** (lithographer); the main contractor is Tupolev. As with other Russian aircraft upgrades, the programme is being conducted in stages. The first stage, sometimes referred to as **M1**, concerns the replacement of the navigation equipment, usually the secondary equipment. In the course of the upgrade the A737I satellite navigation receiver, VIM-95 VHF omnidirectional range/instrument landing system (VOR/ILS), RSBN-85V short-range radio navigation system, ARK-40 automatic direction finder, A-053 and A-075 radar altimeters and other devices are installed. The aircraft are first overhauled and upgraded by the Beriev plant at Taganrog and then the new equipment is adjusted and probably supplemented with additional devices by a Tupolev subsidiary at Zhukovsky airfield.

The first aircraft in which this minor upgrade was implemented, Tu-95MS '50' (c/n 00822), was overhauled by Beriev during 2009–10 and then handed over to Tupolev. At the time of writing the aircraft was still at Zhukovsky; it will probably be used as the prototype for subsequent stages of the upgrade. Serial upgrades began in 2014. On 18 December 2014, Tupolev handed over to the Russian Air Force at Zhukovsky the first Tu-95MS ('62') upgraded in accordance with this pattern; the second aircraft was handed over on 29 December 2014 and the third on 27 January 2015. On 29 December 2014, Tupolev announced that that 20 bombers would be upgraded by the end of 2016.

The complete Tu-95MSM upgrade provides for further systems improvements, including replacement of the Obzor-MS radar with the new NV1.021 radar from the Novella family, made by the Zaslon (until October 2014 Leninets) Company. A test example of the radar is currently being built and should soon be fitted to an Tu-95MSM test aircraft. The Moscow MIEA Institute is developing for the upgraded Tu-95MSM the new KSU-021 flight control system and S-021 navigation complex that combines BINS-SP-1 inertial navigation, ANS-2009 astro-navigation and NVS-021M (S-021-22) navigation computer. The Vega Concern is producing the new DISS-021-70 Doppler navigation radar. The UKBP Design Bureau of Ulyanovsk is responsible for the SOI-021 data display system with five liquid-crystal displays (LCDs) for the 'glass' cockpit of the Tu-95MSM. The TsNIRTI Institute is upgrading the current Meteor-NM self-defence suite to NM2 standard with broader function bands and digital signal processing. The Kuznetsov NK-12MP turboprop engines will be upgraded to the NK-12MPM version. The AV-60K airscrews will be replaced by AV-60T (Tyazholyi, heavy) propeller units

Tu-95MS test aircraft '317' is owned by the Tupolev Company and is seen carrying a full load of eight Kh-101/-102 missiles. Note also the new AV-60T propellers with wide blades. (Piotr Butowski)

to reduce vibration. The new propeller's cruise efficiency is increased from 0.89 to 0.90; the strength and lifetime are improved, but the weight is increased from 1,190kg (2,624lb) to 1,350kg (2,976lb). The trials of the AV-60T propellers began in 2015 at Zhukovsky using test aircraft '317'. New weapons may be expected for the Tu-95MSM, including medium-range Kh-SD and Kh-MTs missiles.

Combat service

The Tu-95MS was used for the first time in combat operations on 17 November 2015, when three bombers struck targets in Syria using eight Kh-555 cruise missiles; Tu-22M3 and Tu-160 bombers also took part in the strike. The Tu-95MS bombers continued the strikes on subsequent days. The bombers operated from their permanent base at Engels, flying over the Caspian Sea and launching their missiles over Iranian territory, near the Iraqi border.

Tupolev Tu-160

NATO reporting name: Blackjack

The Tu-160 features a retractable probe for the in-flight refuelling system, mounted in the upper part of the aircraft's nose. (Sergey Krivchikov)

Manufacturer

The Tu-160 was designed by the Tupolev Company in Moscow and series manufacture is undertaken by the Gorbunov KAZ factory in Kazan.

Role

A supersonic intercontinental-range missile carrier and bomber, the Tu-160 is a multimode aircraft. In its primary intercontinental mission as a strategic missile carrier it flies at a speed of Mach 0.77 and altitude of 11,000-12,000m (36,089-39,370ft) to attain maximum range. For these kinds of sorties, the aircraft is armed with subsonic cruise missiles. When operated at the theatre level, the aircraft can penetrate enemy air defences in two ways: flying at a speed of 2,000km/h (1,243mph) at high altitude or flying at 1,030km/h (640mph) close to the ground with the use of automatic terrain following/avoidance. For the defence suppression mission the Tu-160 can be armed with supersonic Kh-15 short-range attack missiles. However, it is very likely that the Kh-15 has now been withdrawn from operational service.

Crew

The crew of four is seated in the aircraft's nose within a common pressurised cockpit. The commander-pilot occupies the front port-side seat, with the co-pilot to his right. Fighter-type control sticks are used rather than the traditional wheels or yokes. The rear seats are occupied by the navigator/offensive weapons operator and the navigator/electronic warfare/communications operator. Each crewmember has a Zvezda K-36L.70 'zero-zero' ejection seat, ejecting upwards. The cockpit is accessed via the nose undercarriage bay. A small galley and toilet are provided.

Airframe and systems

Tu-160 is a four-engine all-metal low-wing monoplane with variable-geometry wings. The fuselage and central section of the wing form a common shape with appended empennage and movable wing panels. The long and narrow fuselage/wing centre section (leading-edge root extension – LERX – type) is blended for stealth, and is subdivided into four compartments: nose (radar unit, crew cockpit and nose landing gear unit), front (fuel tanks and front weapons bay), centre (main undercarriage units, engine nacelles and rear weapons bay) and rear (fuel tanks and equipment).

The variable-geometry wing has slight anhedral. In terms of strength, the main structural element of the aircraft is the central wing stringer, which measures 12.4m (40ft 8in) long and 2.1m (6ft 10in) wide, and which interconnects with both wing-pivoting nodes. The stringer is comprised of two halves, upper and lower, which are milled from titanium alloy and welded together in a vacuum chamber according to a unique engineering process. The outer, movable panels can be set at one of three manually selected positions: 20° for take-off and landing, 35° for Mach 0.77 cruising speed, and 65° for supersonic flight. Each movable wing panel has four-section leading-edge slats, a three-section double-slotted trailing-edge flap, and an aileron; five-section spoilers are installed ahead of the flaps. With the wings fully swept, the inner section of each three-section trailing-edge flap is raised to become a large aerodynamic fence between the wing and the fixed glove, which serves to improve directional stability. The mid-mounted slab (taileron) tailplane can be deflected symmetrically or differentially. The all-moving upper section of the tailfin, above the tailplane, forms the rudder. The flight control system is of the quadruple analogue fly-by-wire type, supplemented by a standby mechanical system. The use of the mechanical control system is severely limited since the aircraft is statically unstable.

The hydraulically retractable undercarriage has twin nosewheels (1,080 x 400mm, 42.5 x 15.7in) retracting backwards and two six-wheel (1,260 x 425mm, 49.6 x 16.7in) main bogies (three tandem pairs) retracting into the wing centre section between the weapons bay and the engine nacelles. Three braking parachutes of 105m^2 (1,130 sq ft) gross area are located in the aircraft's tail.

Powerplant

The propulsion system consists of four Kuznetsov NK-32 (izdeliye R) turbofans in widely separated pairs (to make room in the fuselage for the weapons bay) under the wing centre section, with the nacelles protruding far beyond the wing trailing edge. Each engine is rated at 137.3kN (30,865lbf) dry and 245.18kN (55,115lbf) with afterburning. The NK-32 is a three-spool turbofan with a bypass ratio of 1.36:1; it has 3+5+7 compressor stages and 1+1+2 turbine stages. The engine weight amounts to 3,650kg

(8,047lb), inlet diameter is 1,455mm (57.3in), and overall length is 7,453mm (293in). The engine nozzles are automatically adjustable; the air intakes are also adjustable, with a vertical wedge for each pair of engines. The aircraft has a TA-12 auxiliary power unit.

The Tu-160 can carry 148,000kg (326,284lb) of T-8 azoted fuel in 13 tanks installed inside the fuselage/wing centre section and in the movable wing panels. The fuel transfer system is used to balance the aircraft when accelerating to supersonic speed. A retractable probe for the in-flight refuelling system is mounted in the upper part of the aircraft's nose.

Dimensions

Wingspan 35.6m (116ft 9.5in) at 65° sweep, 50.7m (166ft 4in) at 35° sweep and 55.7m (182ft 9in) at 20° sweep; maximum length 54.1m (177ft 6in); height 13.1m (44ft); length of engine nacelle 13.28m (43ft 7in); wing area 232m^2 (2,497 sq ft) fully swept, increasing to 293m^2 (3,154 sq ft) fully spread; tailplane span 13.25m (43ft 6in); wheelbase 17.88m (58ft 8in); wheel track 5.4m (17ft 9in).

Weights

Empty 117,000kg (257,941lb); maximum take-off 275,000kg (606,270lb); maximum landing 155,000kg (341,716lb).

Performance

Maximum speed 2,000km/h (1,243mph); maximum speed at sea level 1,030km/h (640mph); cruising speed Mach 0.77; approach speed at 140,000kg (308,650lb) weight 260km/h (162mph); take-off distance 900-2,200m (2,953-7,218ft) at 150-275 tonnes weight respectively; landing distance 1,200-1,600m (3,937-5,250ft) at 140-155 tonnes weight respectively; maximum climb rate 4,200m (13,800ft) per minute; service ceiling 15,600m (51,181ft); g limit +2; service range without in-flight refuelling, Mach 0.77 and six Kh-55SM missiles dropped mid-range, 12,300km (7,643 miles) with 5 per cent fuel reserve; maximum theoretical range 13,950km (8,668 miles); maximum duration without in-flight refuelling 15 hours; combat radius 2,000km (1,243 miles) at Mach 1.5.

Mission systems

The aircraft has a Buk-K (beech) targeting-navigation complex developed by the Elektroavtomatika Company, controlled by eight Orbita-20 computers. This is responsible for providing semi-automatic flight to the missiles' launch area, preparation and launch of the missiles, and return to the base airfield. The Leninets Obzor-K (izdeliye U008) navigation/attack radar and Sopka (hill) terrain-following radar are fitted in the nose, while the OPB-18 Proyom (aperture) TV-optical bomb sight is located in a fairing under the nose. The Sprut-SM missile initialisation and launch system is designed to control the use of Kh-55SM missiles. The SVVI-70 pre-flight data management system coupled with the Sigma mission planning system developed for Russian strategic aviation was implemented in the second half of the 2000s.

Avionics

The aircraft is equipped with the K-042K astro-inertial long-range navigation system that plots the current position on the map, the Glonass satellite positioning system

Left: The port-side rear position is occupied by the navigator/electronic warfare/ communications operator. (Piotr Butowski)

Right: The two pilots are accommodated in the front of the common pressurised cockpit, with the crew commander on the left and the co-pilot on the right. Note the fighter-type control sticks. (via Georg Mader)

(utilised here for the first time in Russia), ARK-22 radio direction finders, DISS-7 Doppler radar, long-range radio navigation system, Kvitok instrument landing system, SVS-2ts-4 air data system, and other items of equipment. Cockpit instrumentation is the conventional gauge type.

Self-protection features

The L232 Baikal-M self-defence system combines Ogonyok (light) IR and Kiparis (cypress) radar warning sensors, SPS-171/SPS-172 Geran-1DU/-2DU and AG-56 Sevan radar jammers, and APP-50 chaff/flare dispensers (with a total of 24 three-round launchers), all located in the fuselage tailcone.

Armament

Weapons are carried exclusively inside the fuselage, in two tandem weapons bays, each of which is 11.28m (37ft) long, 1.92m (6ft 4in) wide and 2.4m (7ft 10in) deep. Basic armament comprises six (or a maximum of 12) Raduga Kh-55SM cruise missiles installed on one (or two) MKU6-5U (9A829K2) rotary launchers, with one six-round launcher in each of the bays. Alternative armament comprises up to 24 Raduga Kh-15 short-range attack missiles on four 'short' MKU6-1U (9A827K2) revolving drums (fitted in tandem pairs); the Kh-15 has likely now been removed from service.

Beginning in around 2003, the aircraft was adapted to employ non-nuclear Kh-555 missiles (using the same 9A829K2 launchers). Since around 2011 the aircraft has also been able to carry up to 12 Kh-101/-102 missiles. The Kh-101/-102 missile is nearly 1.4m (4.6ft) longer and 1,000kg (2,205lb) heavier than the Kh-55SM or Kh-555; as a result, it was necessary to develop a new, stronger 9A829K3 six-round rotary launcher for carrying these new missiles in the weapons bays of the Tu-160. Initially, there were problems with insufficient rigidity of the rotating mechanism and the launcher's construction had been improved by 2015. As of early 2016, three or four bombers were capable of

Left: The Tu-160 can carry six Kh-55SM cruise missiles installed on an MKU6-5U rotary launcher in each of its two weapon bays. (Archives)

Right: Self-defence equipment, including an Ogonyok infrared warning sensor in the centre and chaff/flare dispensers surrounding it, are located at the end of the fuselage. (Piotr Butowski)

carrying the Kh-101/-102 missiles. Reportedly, the Tu-160 has been adapted for deploying 1,500kg (3,307lb) UPAB-1500 glide bombs. In around 2020, new 1,500km (932-mile) range subsonic Kh-SD and hypersonic GZUR cruise missiles may be expected to be deployed on both the Tu-160M and Tu-160M2.

History

The Soviet government began the programme that led to the Tu-160 on 28 November 1967, opening a competition for a supersonic strategic bomber able to cruise at 3,200-3,500km/h (1,988-2,175mph) and to reach a maximum range of 16,000-18,000km (9,942-11,185 miles). Weapons developed for the new strategic bomber were two 4,500kg supersonic Kh-45 missiles or 24 Kh-2000 short-range attack missiles. In 1972, scaled-down requirements called for a dash speed of 2,500km/h (1,553mph), later reduced yet further to a speed of 2,000km/h (1,243mph) and maximum subsonic range of 14,000-16,000km (8,699-9,942 miles). The armament was changed when the Soviets learned about American work on the AGM-86 strategic cruise missile in 1976–77. Instead of heavy Kh-45s, the Soviet opted for an armament of six to 12 subsonic Kh-55 missiles, while 12-24 Kh-15 missiles (a further development of the Kh-2000 project) were chosen as the alternative weapon. However, the size of the armament bay (11.28m, 37ft in length) remained the same, since it was designed for carriage of Kh-45 missiles (10.8m, 35ft 5in in length). This was much larger than necessary for the Kh-55 missiles (6.04m, 19 ft 10in in length). Within the Tupolev Design Bureau the aircraft received the designations izdeliye 70 and izdeliye K. The first 70-1 prototype flew on 18 December 1981, piloted by Boris Veremey. In February 1982, it performed a first supersonic flight. During early tests a speed of 2,200km/h (1,367mph) was attained; in operation, however, the Tu-160 is limited to 2,000km/h (1,243mph).

Several derivatives of the basic aircraft were under consideration but none was realised. Unbuilt projects included the Tu-160PP (Postanovshchik Perekhvatchik, jam-

In 2006, Tu-160 *Valentin Bliznyuk* was upgraded to become an M1 version and in 2016 was undergoing the second-stage upgrade at the Kazan factory; this picture dates from 2014. (Piotr Butowski)

mer and interceptor) escort electronic warfare aircraft and interceptor armed with long-range air-to-air missiles (AAMs), intended for hunting transport aircraft carrying supplies from the United States to Europe during wartime, and the Tu-160R Rakonda strategic reconnaissance aircraft. The enlarged Tu-160M bomber of the 1980s was to be armed with two Kh-32 supersonic missiles aimed against US aircraft carriers, or future hypersonic Kh-90 missiles. The Tu-160V (Vodorod, hydrogen) was to be powered by liquid hydrogen. The Tu-160SC (space carrier) was a projected commercial version for use as a launching platform for the Burlak space vehicle, similar in concept to the US Pegasus. The Tu-170, a variant of the Tu-160 adapted for carrying exclusively conventional weapons, was also under consideration.

Between 1989 and 1990, the Tu-160 set a series of 44 world records for aircraft. The first records were set by a military crew under the command of Lev Kozlov in aircraft '14', while another two series were established by a crew from the Tupolev Design Bureau under the command of Boris Veremey in prototype 70-03. On 31 October 1989, Kozlov flew at a speed of 1,731.4km/h (1,075.8mph) over a 1,000km closed circuit with a load of 30,000kg, setting a new record in Class C-1r (aircraft weight 240 tonnes). At the same time, records were set with loads of 25, 20, 15, 10, 5, 2, and 1 tonnes and without a load. During the same flight the Tu-160 established an altitude record in level flight of 12,150m (39,862ft), carried a record load of 30,471kg (67,177lb) to an altitude of 2,000m, as well as attaining an altitude of 13,894m (45,583ft) with a 30-tonne load. On 3 November 1989, Veremey, now flying with a take-off weight of 275 tonnes

(Class C-1s), recorded a speed of 1,678km/h (1,042.6mph) over a 2,000km closed circuit with a load of 25 tonnes. On 15 May 1990, Veremey recorded a speed of 1,720km/h (1,068.7mph) over a 1,000km circuit with a load of 30 tonnes (as well as 25, 20, 15, 10, 5, 2, and 1 tonnes and without the load). On this occasion the aircraft weight was 251 tonnes and the performances were achieved in Class C-1s. In June 1995 the Tu-160 had its first international presentation at the Paris Air Show.

Production and operators

After two flying prototypes (70-1 and 70-3) and one static prototype (70-2) built by Tupolev in Moscow, the next 33 aircraft (including one static article) were manufactured at the Kazan KAZ plant. The first Kazan-made Tu-160, serial number 1-01, made its first flight on 10 October 1984; this, and some of the subsequent aircraft were used for tests. At the collapse of the Soviet Union, production of the Tu-160 was at a rate of three aircraft per year, and finally came to the end in 1994, leaving four unfinished aircraft at the Kazan plant. Two of these aircraft were completed after that date, serial number 8-02 in 1999 and serial number 8-03 in 2007; two others, serial number 8-04 and 8-05, still remain at the factory and will probably be used as test aircraft for the forthcoming Tu-160M2 version.

In April 1987 an initial two Tu-160s, serial number 2-03 and serial number 3-01, arrived at the first operational unit, the 184th TBAP at Pryluky in the Ukrainian SSR. In July 1987, Pryluky's bombers performed the first launches of Kh-55SM cruise missiles. At the end of 1991, the regiment had two squadrons of Tu-160s, for a total of 19 aircraft, as well as one squadron of Tu-134UBL aircraft for training (see Chapter 5). In May 1991, Tu-160s flying along the Norwegian coast near Tromsø encountered Western aircraft for the first time met, in the form of General Dynamics F-16A Fighting Falcons of the Royal Norwegian Air Force's 331 Skvadron. After the disintegration of the USSR, these aircraft remained in Ukraine.

Six subsequent Tu-160s were assigned between February 1992 and June 1994 to the 1096th (in 1994 renumbered 121st) TBAP in Engels, these being the only Tu-160 units in Russia. These six aircraft remained the only operational Tu-160s in Russia until 6 October 1999, when in Russia bought eight Tu-160s from Ukraine. These aircraft were selected on the basis of being in the best technical condition among those at Pryluky (of the remaining 11 Ukrainian aircraft, 10 were scrapped and one, '26', was put on display at an aviation museum in Poltava). The ex-Ukrainian bombers came to Engels between 5 November 1999 and 21 February 2000. The next bomber, serial number 8-02 ('07', *Alexandr Molodchiy*) arrived at Engels on 5 May 2000, and one more, serial number 8-03 ('08', *Vitaliy Kopylov*) arrived on 29 April 2008. In 2000, Russia decided to repair and introduce into service aircraft serial number 2-02, which had been completed in 1986 and was then used by the Tupolev Design Bureau for testing. The repair work lasted six years and in July 2006 the bomber was transferred to the regiment at Engels and named *Valentin Bliznyuk* (after the chief designer of the Tu-160). Russian Air Force Tu-160s are named after famed 'strongmen', including mythic folk heroes (Ilya Muromets), wrestling champions (Ivan Yarygin), or famous pilots and air commanders.

On 30 December 2005 the Tu-160 was officially commissioned into service. Prior to this date, and although the bombers had been operated by both the Soviet and Russian Air Forces from 1987, these operations were formally considered as 'trials'.

Tu-160 bombers in current operation

Side number	Serial number	Registration	Name
02	7-02	RF-94102	*Vasiliy Reshetnikov*
03	7-03	RF-94101	*Pavel Taran*
04	7-04	RF-94112	*Ivan Yarygin*
05	7-05	RF-94104	*Aleksandr Golovanov*; previously named *Ilya Muromets*
06	8-01	RF-94105	*Ilya Muromets*
07	8-02	RF-94106	*Aleksandr Molodchiy*
08	8-03	RF-94115	*Vitaliy Kopylov*
10	6-01	RF-94100	*Nikolay Kuznetsov*
11	6-02	RF-94114	*Vasiliy Senko*
12	6-03	RF-94109	*Aleksandr Novikov*
14	3-04	RF-94103	*Igor Sikorsky*
15	6-05	RF-94108	*Vladimir Sudets*
16	5-03	RF-94107	*Alexei Plokhov*
17	5-04	RF-94110	*Valery Chkalov*
18	5-05	RF-94111	*Andrey Tupolev*
19 (formerly 87)	2-02	RF-94113	*Valentin Bliznyuk*
– (formerly 63, 342)	4-01	-	*Boris Veremey*

Aircraft '01' (serial number 7-01; *Mikhail Gromov*) crashed in 2003. There are no aircraft with the numbers '09' or '13'.

Two Tu-160s have been lost. In March 1987, serial number 1-02 came down after suffering an engine failure soon after take-off from Zhukovsky airfield; the crew under the command of Valeriy Pavlov initiated ejection and survived. On 18 September 2003 aircraft '01' (*Mikhail Gromov*) crashed near Stepnoye, 40km (25 miles) east of Engels,

Tu-160 *Aleksandr Golovanov* returns to its home base of Engels after a mission over the Atlantic on 20 December 2007. (Piotr Butowski)

killing four crew under the command of Lieutenant Colonel Yuri Deyneko. During the approach to land, at an altitude of 1,200-1,500m (3,940-4,920ft), the aircraft disintegrated. The catastrophe was caused by a failure of the venting system in the fuel tanks: after using up the fuel the resulting negative pressure broke the wing torsion box.

At the time of writing, the Russian Air Force has 16 Tu-160s assigned to the air base at Engels; some of these are undergoing overhaul and upgrade at the Kazan facility. One more aircraft is based at Zhukovsky and belongs to Tupolev. This latter is serial number 4-01 *Boris Veremey* (named after the first pilot to test the Tu-160 in 1981), and without a tactical number. Previously, this aircraft had the side number '63', and then received the side number '342' for its visit to the Paris Air Show at Le Bourget in 1995. It is used as a prototype for future upgrades. A number of additional airframes currently to be found at Zhukovsky are probably beyond repair.

Variants

Tu-160 (**izdeliye 70** or **izdeliye K**) is the initial variant currently in service, as described above.

Tu-160M upgrade programme

The **Tu-160M** (**izdeliye 70M**) represents a mid-life modernisation that provides for the complete replacement of the original bomber's mission system and avionics. According to a statement from the United Aircraft Corporation, the initial technical design of the Tu-160M was completed on 23 October 2014. The Obzor-K radar will be replaced with a new NV1.70 radar from the Novella family, made by the Zaslon Company (until October 2014, Leninets). For some time it was planned to install a radar designed by the Tikhomirov NIIP Company on the basis of the Irbis radar as used in the Su-35 fighter (see Volume 1), but in 2013 this idea was abandoned. The UKBP Design Bureau in Ulyanovsk is developing a new data display system with 'glass' cockpit for Tu-160M. The aircraft is also being fitted with the K-042KM navigation complex with BINS-SP-1 inertial navigation, ANS-2009M astro navigation and a navigation computer. Other new systems include the DISS-021-70 navigation radar, A737DP satellite navigation receiver, ABSU-200MTs autopilot and S-505-70 communication suite. In March 2016 the Tu-160 named *Valentin Bliznyuk* was spotted in the assembly hall at Kazan, where it was probably undergoing upgrade to the Tu-160M version. Earlier in 2006 the same aircraft had served as a prototype for the Tu-160M1 modernisation, described below.

The **Tu-160M1** represents a 'first-stage' upgrade without the most expensive elements such as the new radar and 'glass' cockpit. In addition, certain other new systems are implemented in the Tu-160M1 in their early versions, for example the ABSU-200-1 autopilot and K-042K-1 navigation complex. Simultaneously, some previous devices seem to have been removed. For example, the modernised aircraft have 'blind' windows for the previous OPB-18 optical sights, which suggests that the sights have been disassembled. After the prototype *Valentin Bliznyuk* that appeared in 2006, several aircraft were modernised to Tu-160M1 standard by the KAZ facility at Kazan, starting with *Andrey Tupolev*, first flown after upgrade on 16 November 2014, and then handed over to the Russian Air Force on 19 December, 2014. Two subsequent aircraft, named *Vasiliy Reshetnikov* and *Vasiliy Senko*, were repaired and upgraded to Tu-160M1 standard in Kazan between 2015 and January 2016.

A test rig for the integration of avionics for the Tu-160M and M2 at the GosNIIAS research institute of aviation systems in Moscow. The upgraded cockpit has five large MFDs and a set of conventional standby instruments.
(UAC)

Further operation of Tu-160s – and particularly the new-production Tu-160M2s – requires a supply of new engines. In August 2014 the Kuznetsov Company of Samara was contracted by the Ministry of Defence to restart production of upgraded NK-32 series 02 engines (formally designated 'NK-32 of the second-stage state trials'). After a production pause of nearly 25 years, an initial batch of five new-production engines was to be ready for tests in 2016. The improvements included in the NK-32 series 02 engine are not known, but it is likely that the engine's reliability and lifetime have been improved while the thrust remains unchanged.

Tu-160M2 new-production bomber

The idea of resuming series production of the Tu-160 bomber was disclosed for the first time in public by the Russian Minister of Defence Sergei Shoygu on 29 April 2015, during his visit to the Kazan Aircraft Plant. In August 2016, the commander-in-chief of the Russian Air Force Viktor Bondarev declared that the first new **Tu-160M2** (**izdeliye 70M2**) would fly at the end of 2018, followed in 2021 by series production at a rate of three aircraft per year (some months earlier, Bondarev proclaimed the first flight would take place in 2021; it therefore appears that the programme has been accelerated). The Russian Air Force has declared that it requires at least 50 new Tu-160M2 aircraft, which will be required to serve for at least 40 years. The new-production Tu-160M2 will feature weapons and equipment similar to those of the current Tu-160M mid-life upgrade; the timescale dictates that nothing more ambitious can be realised. The powerplant will comprise newly produced NK-32 series 02 engines.

On 10 March 2016 a large meeting of the United Aircraft Corporation (UAC) management and local authorities was held in Kazan, to discuss the resumption of Tu-160 production. Yuri Slyusar, the UAC president, and Rustam Minnikhanov, the president of Tatarstan, signed an agreement of cooperation in the implementation of this task. Yuri Slyusar commented that the resumption of Tu-160 production is a 'giant project, unprecedented in the post-Soviet history of our aircraft industry' and that it is being implemented in cooperation with 'all leading firms of the Russian aircraft industry.'

Combat service

The Tu-160 was used for the first time in real combat operations on 17 November 2015, when two Tu-160s ('08' and '15') struck targets in Syria with 16 Kh-101 cruise missiles launched from over Iranian territory; Tu-22M3 and Tu-95MS bombers also took part in the same mission. In subsequent days the Tu-160s continued their strikes, using both Kh-101 and Kh-555 missiles. The Tu-160s operated from their permanent base at Engels. Usually they flew towards their targets over the Caspian Sea and launched their missiles over Iranian territory, close to the Iraqi border. In a mission conducted on 20 November 2015, two Tu-160s took off from Olenyegorsk air base on the Kola Peninsula in northern Russia, flew round Norway and the British Isles, entered the Mediterranean Sea via Gibraltar and flew the entire length of the Mediterranean Sea to launch eight Kh-555 missiles against targets in Syria. Then, flying over Syria, Iraq, Iran and the Caspian Sea, the bombers returned to their home base at Engels; the entire route was more than 13,000km (8,078 miles) long. While over Syria, the Tu-160s were escorted by Su-30SM fighters (see Volume 1) operating from the air base in the province of Latakia.

FUTURE LONG-RANGE BOMBERS

MARK

The **MARK** represents a relatively unknown strategic system, which was mentioned by Alexander Zelin, the former commander-in-chief of the Russian Air Force during a lecture delivered in April 2013 concerning the service's acquisitions plans up to 2025. In a chart presented by Zelin, the MARK was located within programmes for the 2021 to 2025.

The MARK abbreviation has not been explained by Zelin. However, another slide from his aforementioned presentation showed a picture of a Tu-160 bomber with an intercontinental ballistic missile (ICBM) carried under the fuselage. There was once such a project, involving a Tu-160 carrying a 32-tonne Burlak space rocket, and this was even displayed in model form at the Paris Air Show in 1991. Known as Burlak, and developed by the Raduga Company, this was intended to be a system equivalent to the American Pegasus.

However, alternative launching platforms will likely be considered. The Tu-160 is currently unsuitable for this role because there are simply too few examples in service (the Zelin lecture was delivered long before Russia decided to resume production of the Tu-160) and the type already has other, no less important tasks. Another probable option is the use of a heavy transport aircraft. Such projects existed during the 1970s and 1980s and even bore the designation MARK (Mezhkontinentalnyi Aviatsionnyi Raketnyi Kompleks, intercontinental airborne missile complex). At that time, there were plans to use the An-22 as a launch platform, and then an An-124 or purposely-built Il-76MF with stretched fuselage (all three types are described in detail in Chapter 3). It may be supposed that the new MARK will involve a launch system for an ICBM from the new Il-76MD-90A transport aircraft. In comparison with the An-124, also well-suited for this role, the Il-76MD-90A has the advantage of being manufactured entirely in Russia.

Tupolev PAK DA Poslannik

In August 2009 the Tupolev Company was awarded a three-year contract by the Russian Ministry of Defence for the **Poslannik** (envoy) research and development work. This resulted in a preliminary design for the next-generation strategic bomber within the **PAK DA** (Perspektivnyi Aviatsionnyi Kompleks Dalney Aviatsii, Future Air Complex of Long-Range Aviation) programme. The concept for the aircraft, which received the designation **izdeliye 80** within the Tupolev Design Bureau (the Tu-160 is izdeliye 70), was approved in spring 2013.

On 23 December 2013, the United Aircraft Corporation was awarded a follow-on contract for the detailed design of the PAK DA; it was followed by subcontracts for development of the aircraft's systems. The detailed design and construction of the prototype was to be finished within five years of the work beginning. Commanding officer of Russian Long-Range Aviation Anatoly Zhikharev stated in a press interview on the centenary of the service in December 2014 that the PAK DA prototype would fly in 2019, and that the aircraft would gradually replace all three current types of long-range bombers in Russian Air Force service beginning in 2023–25. He also said that the PAK DA will be 'a subsonic all-wing aircraft able to reach 15,000km (9,321 miles) without refuelling'. A little earlier, the commander-in-chief of the Russian Air Force Viktor Bondarev said that the bomber would be able to carry more weapons than the current Tu-160, and that these will comprise 'more serious weapons' including hypersonic missiles. The engines for the PAK DA will be based on the core of the NK-32 series 02 turbofan, according to Vladislav Masalov, head of the United Engine Corporation. The Kuznetsov Company was charged with development of an engine for the PAK DA in December 2014.

In 2015, however, the idea of resuming series production of the Tu-160M2 was put forward and, together with this, plans for the PAK DA programme were moved back. In July 2015, during a visit to the Kuznetsov plant in Samara, the Deputy Minister of Defence Yuri Borisov announced that due to the launch of the Tu-160M2 programme, the PAK DA project would be 'a bit postponed'. If the Tu-160M2 enters production, it will consume the production capacity of the Kazan plant and Ministry of Defence funding for many years and will also reduce the demand for the PAK DA.

As early as the 1980s, Tupolev was undertaking design work on the Tu-202 heavy subsonic all-wing combat aircraft. Later, in 1993, the company showed a model of the huge 850-seat Tu-404 airliner that utilised a similar all-wing configuration with a span of 95m (312ft).

MARITIME AIRCRAFT

Beriev Be-12

NATO reporting name: Mail
Nickname: Chaika

Russian Navy Be-12 '28 Yellow' is seen at Kacha airfield in 2012. This Crimean air base is the last bastion of the Be-12 in Russian military service. (Alexander Golz)

Manufacturer

The Be-12 was designed by the Beriev Company in Taganrog and serially manufactured by production plant in the same town, today belonging to Beriev.

Role

Short-range anti-submarine warfare (ASW) and search and rescue (SAR) amphibian.

Crew

The Be-12 is manned by a crew of four, including two pilots seated side-by-side in the upper cockpit, a navigator in the glazed fuselage nose, and a radio officer in the cabin.

Airframe and systems

The Be-12 is an all-metal, high-wing amphibian aircraft. The single-step boat hull has two anti-spray strakes each side of the forward section. High-mounted, cranked wings

are employed to keep the propellers clear of the water. Two-section trailing-edge flaps and an aileron (with tabs) are found on each wing. The H-type tail unit incorporates a sharply dihedral tailplane. Two oval endplates are located in line with the propellers for improved efficiency at low speed on water. The elevators and rudders are fitted with tabs. Mechanical control is provided for the ailerons, elevators and rudders, with hydraulic boost. The flaps have hydraulic control while the tabs utilise electric control. The fully retractable landing gear incorporates single mainwheels of 1,450 x 520mm (57 x 24in) size and a tailwheel of 950 x 350mm (37 x 14in) size; the wingtip floats are non retractable.

Powerplant
Two Progress AI-20D series 4 (series 3 in earlier aircraft) turboprops, each rated at 3,863ekW (5,180ehp), are fitted over the highest points of the wing, with four-blade AV-68D variable-pitch propellers, each with a diameter of 5.0m (16ft 5in). An AI-8 auxiliary power unit is provided. A total of 11,300 litres (2,984 gallons) of internal fuel is carried, equivalent to 9,000kg (19,842lb); there is provision for an additional 1,800 litres (475 gallons) of fuel within a tank fitted inside the cabin. Fuel is of the T-1 or TS-1 type.

Dimensions
Wingspan 29.842m (97ft 11in); maximum length 30.11m (98ft 9in); maximum height when parked 9.1m (29ft 10in); height in flight line 7.94m (26ft 1in); wing area 99m^2 (1,066 sq ft); tailplane span 8.90m (29ft 2in); wheelbase 14.436m (47ft 4in); wheel track 5.00m (16ft 5in); float track 26.50m (87ft).

Weights
Empty, operating 24,500kg (54,013lb); maximum take-off 36,000kg (79,366lb) from concrete runway or 35,000kg (77,162lb) from water; maximum landing 30,500kg (67,241lb).

Performance
Never-exceed speed (VNE) 580km/h (360mph); maximum level speed 530km/h (329mph); cruising speed 440-450km/h (273-280mph); approach speed 195km/h (121mph); ceiling 12,100m (39,698ft) limited to 8,000m (26,247ft) during service because of lack of oxygen equipment; minimum level flight altitude over sea 20m (66ft); range with 3,000kg (6,614lb) of weapons 1,500km (932 miles); range with 1,500kg (3,307lb) of weapons 2,720km (1,690 miles); maximum range 3,600km (2,237 miles); patrol duration at 500km (311 miles) from base 3 hours with normal weapons load; required sea run length 1,800m (5,906ft); take-off distance to 15m (50ft) 2,000m (6,562ft) from concrete runway or 2,300m (7,546ft) from water; landing from 15m (50ft) at 30,500kg (67,241lb) weight 1,800m (5,906ft) on shore or 2,100m (6,890ft) on water; required minimum depth of water 3m (9.8ft); allowable wave height 0.8m (2.6ft).

Mission systems
The basic submarine-detection system used by the Be-12 is the Baku (named after the capital city of Azerbaijan) radio sonobuoy system including the Baku-S (SPARU-55, Samolyotnoye Priyomnoye Avtomaticheskoye Radio-Ustroystvo, airborne automatic receiving radio device) airborne receiver that can receive and process signals from 18 expandable RGB-NM/NM-1 and RGB-1 buoys (18 is the number of available com-

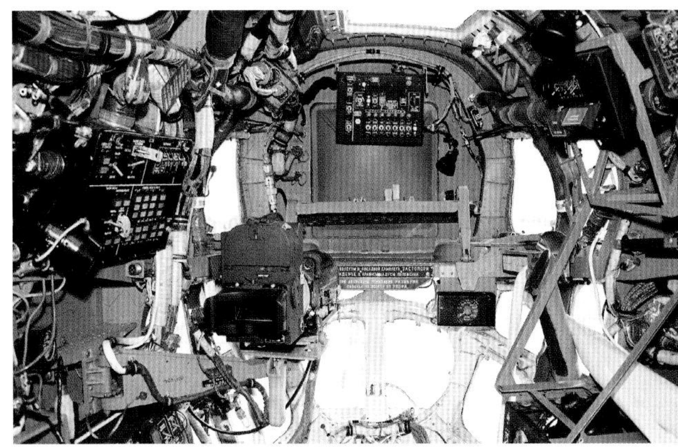

Left: The Be-12's pilots are seated side-by-side in the upper cockpit.
(Piotr Butowski)

Right: The Be-12's navigator has a position in the glazed fuselage nose. Note the radar sight with its rubber hood.
(Piotr Butowski)

munication channels). Other elements of the Baku system comprise the ANP-1V-1 navigational device, PVU-S-1 Siren-2M computing device and AP-6Ye autopilot. The APM-60Ye Orsha (named after a town in Belarus; APM is Aviatsionnyi Poiskovyi Magnitometr, airborne search magnetometer) magnetic anomaly detector (MAD) includes an antenna extending rearwards from the tail and can detect a submarine range from a range of 250m (820ft). The Initsiativa-2B search/attack radar is fitted in the fuselage nose; the radar is able to detect the periscope of a submerged submarine from a distance of 10-12km (6-7 miles). The upgraded Be-12N has a Nartsiss-12 (narcissus) targeting computer, Nara (named after a river in Russia) sonobuoy receiver that communicates with new RPG-2 directional buoys (taken from the Berkut system of the Il-38, described later), APM-73S Bor-1S MAD (providing submarine detection at a range of 400m, 1,312ft) and Initsiativa-2BN radar.

Avionics

A DISS-1 Doppler navigation radar is carried; cockpit instrumentation is of the analogue gauge-type.

Self-protection features

None.

Armament

A nominal load of up to 1,500kg (3,307lb) of weapons and stores can be carried in an internal bay in the bottom of the fuselage, aft of the step, and on four pylons under the outer wing panels; the maximum load is 3,000kg (6,614lb) at the expense of reduced fuel. The aircraft's armament consists of RYu-2 nuclear depth charges, AT-1 (AT-1M) torpedoes, PLAB-250-120 and PLAB-50-65 depth charges, AMD-2-500 mines, and signal bombs. The most typical mixed load consists of 36 RGM-NM1 and 10 RGB-2 sonobuoys, plus one AT-1M ASW torpedo. In a pure attack configuration, the Be-12 carries three torpedoes. For nuclear attack, the aircraft carries a single RYu-2 charge plus 29 sonobuoys.

History

Nicknamed Chaika (seagull), the Be-12 (izdeliye Ye) was created in line with a governmental order of 28 March 1956 and took off for its maiden flight from a shore airstrip

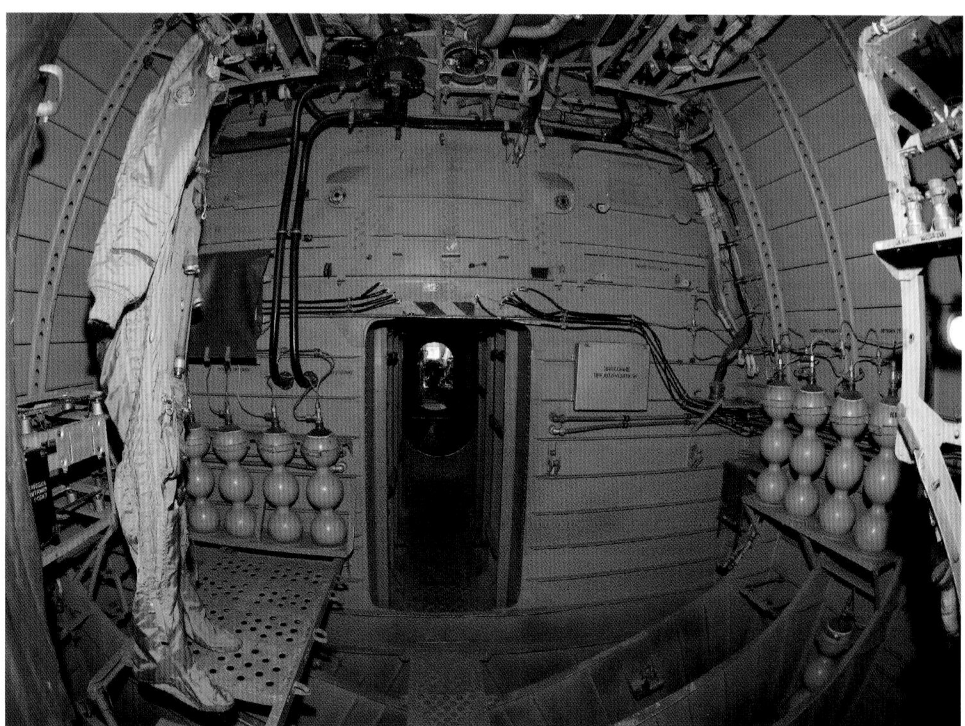

An interior view looking towards the forward bulkhead reveals details of the main cabin of a Russian Navy Be-12. (Fydor Borisov)

at Taganrog on 18 October 1960, piloted by Pyotr Bobro. The M-12 prototype differed from later series aircraft in that the radar was installed in a retractable housing under the fuselage (in series-production aircraft the radar is installed in the nose) and that the engines were installed under the wings (later the engines were moved to the upper surface of the wing). The Be-12 was presented to the public for the first time in July 1961, over Tushino, Moscow. The Be-12 amphibian was officially commissioned into service with the Soviet Navy on 29 November 1968. A search and rescue variant, the Be-14 (izdeliye 2Ye) incorporating significantly revised construction came into being in 1965 but remained as a one-off prototype, while the Navy instead ordered the more modest Be-12PS (izdeliye 3Ye) for the same role.

In the early 1990s the Beriev Company completed several conversions of Be-12s into civil versions. Four Be-12s were redesigned as firefighting Be-12P (Pozharnyi, izdeliye YeP) versions. The first of these was c/n 9601404, coded '40', which was first tested in flight after conversion on 27 April 1992, on the Sea of Azov. Another three aircraft were converted into Be-12NKh (Narodno-Khoziaystvennyi, economic) transport versions. None of the civilian Be-12s remains in use. One more aircraft was the experimental Be-12P-200 (c/n 8601301) that tested the new water-filling system for the Be-200 firefighting amphibian (see below), and which was first flown in August 1996.

Production and operators

After three prototypes (including one Be-14), the Taganrog factory produced 140 series aircraft between December 1963 and June 1973, most of which (130) were of the ASW version. The remaining 10 aircraft were of the Be-12PS SAR version (four Be-12s were later converted into PS versions). A peak output rate of 20 aircraft a year was reached in 1969–70, subsequently reduced to 15. During the 1970s, in the course of major

Ukrainian Navy Be-12 '04 Yellow' drops a rescue payload from its internal stores bay over its Saki base in 2012. At the time of writing, two Ukrainian aircraft were still active at Mykolayiv. (Alexander Golz)

repairs, 27 aircraft were upgraded into Be-12N versions at the Yevpatoriya plant; this variant was commissioned into service in April 1976.

The first Be-12s were assigned to the Naval Aviation evaluation centre at Mykolayiv, Ukrainian SSR, in 1964, and then to operational ASW regiments at Kacha within the Black Sea Fleet, Yelizovo and Nikolayevka within the Pacific Fleet, Severomorsk-1 within the Northern Fleet, and Kosa within the Baltic Fleet. Between August 1969 and June 1971 three Be-12s from the Kacha regiment were deployed in Marsa Matruh, Egypt. These received Egyptian markings, but were manned by Soviet crews (for more on this deployment, see *Arab MiGs Volume 4: The Attrition War 1967–1973*, Tom Cooper et al, Harpia Publishing, 2013). In 1981, four aircraft were sold to Vietnam in the ASW configuration. After the disintegration of the USSR, 55 aircraft remained in Russia and 14 in Ukraine. Within the Russian Navy, the Be-12 was officially decommissioned in 1992, but the type actually remained in service. At the time of writing the Russian Navy operated several Be-12s at Kacha air base in Crimea; meanwhile, the Ukrainian Navy operated two aircraft at Mykolayiv.

In 2012, Russia decided to conduct major overhauls of its surviving Be-12s, including engine overhauls and replacement of propellers. For this purpose four aircraft flew from Kacha to Taganrog during 2012 and 2013. In November 2014 the first of these aircraft, '12' (RF-12007) was returned to service after overhaul; the fourth and final overhauled aircraft, '01', arrived at Kacha in June 2015. After this overhaul the aircraft are once again capable of waterborne operations (previously, Russian Be-12s had ceased landing on water in 2006). In June 2015 overhauls of further Be-12s commenced at the plant at Yevpatoria, Crimea, which had previously overhauled these aircraft in Soviet times.

Unexpectedly, in February 2015 the commander of the Russian Naval Aviation Major General Igor Kozhin declared that the Be-12 would be modernised, with particular focus on its anti-submarine systems. The scope of the upgrade remains unknown and had probably not yet been specified at the time of writing. For the time being, Russia will conduct restorative maintenance of non-flying aircraft, a number of which are to be found at various airfields. Currently, about a dozen aircraft are suitable for return to service. According to available satellite imagery, the largest collections of Be-12 aircraft are to be found at Yelizovo (six aircraft), Taganrog (six) and Kacha (five).

Military variants

Be-12 (**izdeliye Ye**) is the standard ASW version, as described.

Be-12N (**izdeliye YeN**) is a mid-life upgrade with the Nartsiss system, as described. The modernisation was very significant; indeed, the capabilities of the new mission system were close to those of the Berkut system installed in the larger Il-38 aircraft.

Be-12PS (Poiskovo-Spasatelnyi, search and rescue, **izdeliye 3Ye**) has weapons and ASW equipment deleted while adding a number of items of medical and rescue equipment, a motor dinghy and a small hatch in the starboard fuselage. The aircraft is able to carry 13 survivors.

Beriev Be-200

Be-200ChS RF-21512 demonstrates the type's firefighting capability. A full load of 12,000kg (26,455lb) of water can be dropped in a single salvo within one second, through doors in the hull. (Fydor Borisov)

Manufacturer

The Be-200 was designed by the Beriev Company in Taganrog. An initial 11 aircraft were built by the Irkutsk Aircraft Plant; production was then moved to the Beriev facility in Taganrog. On 30 May 2016 the Taganrog plant rolled out the first Be-200 completed at the facility, and this aircraft completed its maiden flight at Taganrog on 16 September 2016.

Role

Multi-purpose amphibian, initially for search and rescue (SAR) and then maritime patrol, while other military versions are also possible. The basic civilian version is used for firefighting.

Details for Be-200ChS

Crew

The flight crew consists of two pilots. Optional crewmembers include an observer and on-board technician.

Airframe and systems

The fuselage is subdivided into an upper pressurised compartment, 18.765m (61ft 8in) long, 2.50m (8ft 2in) wide and 1.895m (6ft 3in) high, and an unpressurised lower section containing firefighting equipment. The slightly swept, shoulder-mounted wing has no dihedral/anhedral. The T-tail incorporates a variable-incidence swept tailplane with elevators. The retractable landing gear has twin 950 x 300mm (37.4 x 11.8in) mainwheels and twin 620 x 180mm (24.4 x 7.1in) nosewheels; the wingtip floats are fixed. The EDSU-200 fly-by-wire (FBW) control system was developed by Moscow's Avionika Company.

Powerplant

Two Ivchenko Progress D-436TP turbofans, each producing 73.55kN (16,535lbf) of take-off thrust, are carried above the fuselage, aft of the wings. Two wing-box fuel tanks each contain 8,050 litres (2,126 gallons) of fuel, equivalent to 12,500kg (27,558lb) at 0.775kg/litre. A TA12-60 auxiliary power unit is fitted, with the TA18-100 APU planned for future production aircraft.

Dimensions

Wingspan 32.78m (107ft 7in); length 32.049m (105ft 2in); height 8.90m (29ft 3in); tailplane span 10.114m (33ft 2in); wing area 117.44 m^2 (1,264 sq ft); cabin volume 80.8m^3 (2,853cu ft); wheelbase 11.143m (36ft 7in); wheel track 4.9m (16ft 1in) to outer wheels.

Weights

Maximum take-off 41,000kg (90,390lb) from shore or 37,900kg (83,555lb) from water, or 43,000kg (94,799lb) after water scooping; empty operating 27,900kg (61,5089lb); maximum landing 35,000kg (77,162lb) to shore or 37,900kg (83,555lb) to water.

Performance

Maximum Mach number 0.64; maximum cruising speed 650km/h (404mph); stall speed with flaps 155km/h (96mph); maximum climb rate 15.5m/s (3,051ft/min); service ceiling 8,100m (26,575ft); range with full payload 1,000km (621 miles); maximum range 3,150km (1,957 miles); maximum endurance 7.5 hours; take-off distance at MTOW 1,400m (4,593ft) from both concrete runway and water; landing distance at maximum landing weight 750m (2,461ft) on concrete or 1,400m (4,593ft) on water; allowable wave height 1.2m (4ft); required water depth 2.6m (8ft 6in).

The Israeli IAI Tamam Airborne Observation System (AOS) thermal/TV turret installed under the wing of the Be-200ChS for SAR operations. (Alexei Petrov)

Transport capabilities

The aircraft can carry a payload of 5,000kg (11,023lb) in the cabin. For SAR operations, it is capable of carrying up to 57 survivors/passengers in seats or up to 30 stretcher cases. As a water bomber, it can carry 12,000kg (26,455lb) of water in eight tanks under the cabin floor. The water can be dropped in a single salvo within one second, through doors in the hull.

Mission systems

The KSO-200 (Kompleks Spetsialnogo Oborudovaniya, special equipment complex) search system consists of the Ukrainian Buran-A200 weather radar (or Russian-made Kontur 200-A813Ts radar for the Russian Ministry of Defence version) fitted in the air-

The two-person cockpit of the Be-200 is dominated by six 6 x 8in (152 x 203mm) multifunction displays. (Fyodor Borisov)

craft's nose, an NPO Karat Lanner-M (early aircraft have the Israeli AOS system) gyro-stabilised electro-optical turret mounted under the port wing, a multifunction indicator and video display at the observer's position in the aircraft cabin, as well as a data recording system. The aircraft also has an SX-5 Starburst searchlight.

Four droppable KAS-150 or UKAS-200 rescue capsules can be carried under the wing, each weighing 150kg (331lb) or 200kg (441lb) respectively. A dinghy or life-raft, as well as medical, radio and other equipment necessary for the survivors can be stored inside these containers.

Avionics

The Be-200ChS utilises Allied Signal avionics integrated by the Russian NIIAO Institute within the ARIA-200M system (American-Russian Integrated Avionics). It includes NSI-2000MT inertial navigation combined with a Glonass/GPS receiver, ARK-32 radio direction finder, A-053 radio altimeter and other devices. The 'glass' cockpit is fitted with six 6 x 8in (152 x 203mm) multifunction displays. Communication devices include two Orlan-85ST UHF and one Prima-400 HF radios, as well as Prima-DMV-1B UHF/VHF radio for communication with ships.

History

In the 1980s, Beriev developed a heavy, 86-tonne military amphibian known as the A-40 (NATO reporting name Mermaid). During Mikhail Gorbachev's policy of 'perestroyka', Russia offered the A-40 as a civilian aircraft (it was shown at the Paris Air Show in 1991), but it was obvious that there was no civilian customer for such a large amphibian. The company then decided to repeat the A-40's configuration in the form of a civilian aircraft that would be two times lighter. This was the A-200 project, later designated as the Be-200. The Be-200 performed its maiden flight on 24 September 1998, in Irkutsk, piloted by Konstantin Babich.

For medical evacuation missions the cabin of the Be-200ChS can be outfitted to accommodate up to 30 stretcher patients. (Alexei Petrov)

Production and operators

The Irkutsk Aircraft Plant completed four Be-200 test aircraft (three of these still fly, and are operated by Beriev) and seven production Be-200ChS versions (six of these were delivered between 2003 and 2011 to Russia's Ministerstvo Cherezvychainykh Situatsiy, MChS, Ministry of Emergency Situations and one was delivered in 2008 to the similar service of Azerbaijan). On 25 May 2011 the Russian MChS ordered another six Be-200ChS aircraft from the Taganrog production line, to be delivered between 2013 and 2014; in summer 2015 the delivery dates were revised to 2015–18. In the event, the aircraft completed its first flight at Taganrog on 16 September 2016.

On 23 May 2013 the Russian Ministry of Defence signed a contract with Beriev for the delivery of six Be-200 amphibians between 2014 and 2016. Two aircraft were to be completed in the form of the Be-200ChS standard production version, and the other four as the new, simpler Be-200PS search and rescue version without the firefighting function of the ChS variant. The value of the order was 8.408 billion roubles (USD275 million at the then exchange rate), equivalent to around USD46 million for one aircraft. The aircraft are to be equally divided between the Naval Aviation evaluation centre at Yeysk and the Navy's air base of Artyom-Knevichi near Vladivostok in the Far East. The first Be-200ChS was to be delivered to Yeysk in November 2014, and another example was to go to Artyom in November 2015. Also in November 2015, Yeysk was to receive two Be-200PS amphibians, and in November 2016, the last two Be-200PS aircraft were to arrive at Artyom. In fact, none of these aircraft had been delivered by autumn 2016. In February 2016, a source within the Russian Ministry of Defence claimed that the contract had been delayed by two years and the first aircraft would be ready at the end of 2016. Another problem facing the programme is the D-436TP engine, which is being manufactured by the Salyut factory in Moscow in cooperation with Ukraine. In future, Russia intends to replace the D-436 with its own PD-7 turbofan developed from the PD-14's core. However, this is not likely to happen before 2020–22.

Following the Russian Ministry of Defence's initial order, the same customer is expected to order two Be-200s completed in a special command post version with modified cabin configuration and equipment.

On several occasions the Russian Navy has declared its intention to purchase Be-200 aircraft in the anti-submarine warfare Be-200P version, which in future would replace the Be-12. However, this intent has not progressed beyond general declarations. Among Russia's approved future maritime patrol aircraft programmes (see below) there is currently no place for the Be-200.

Variants

Be-200ChS (Chrezvychainykh Situatsiy, emergency situations; izdeliye **A201**) version is a combination firefighting and SAR aircraft. For SAR operations, the aircraft is equipped with an Airborne Observation System (AOS) provided by Israel Aircraft Industries' Tamam Division (or the Russian Lanner-M turret in current production aircraft) with a thermal/TV turret installed under the wing; it is also capable of carrying up to 57 survivors/passengers in seats or up to 30 stretcher cases.

Be-200ChS-E is a sub-variant with European EASA certificate issued in 2010.

Be-200PS (Poiskovo-Spasatelnyi, search and rescue) is to be as the Be-200ChS but without the firefighting capability.

Future projects

Be-210 is a project for a passenger amphibian capable of carrying 72 passengers over a distance of 1,850km (1,150 miles).

Be-220 (**Be-200MP**, Morskoy Patrulnyi, maritime patrol) is to be an ASW and surveillance aircraft with an advanced mission system including radio sonobuoy, magnetometric, electro-optical and electronic intelligence subsystems. Two available Russian ELINT options are the Kasatka-S (cowfish) suite produced by the Radar MMS Company, or the Novella suite from Leninets, both based in St Petersburg. Weapons options include depth charges and ASW torpedoes carried in an internal armament bay, as well as on six underwing pylons. The Be-200MP version is to be based on a

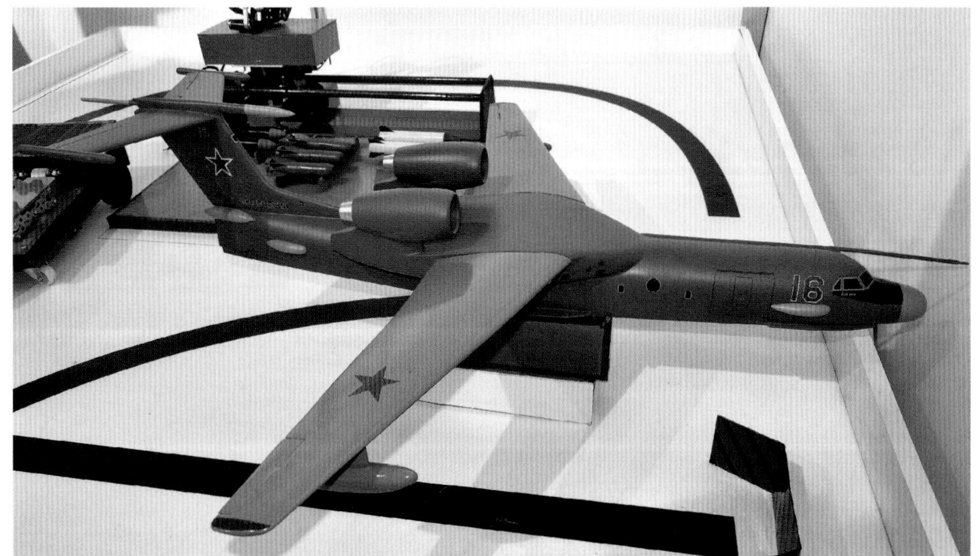

A model of the Be-200MP maritime patrol and anti-submarine aircraft with Kasatka-S mission suite, as presented at the Army-2016 exhibition at Kubinka in September 2016. (Piotr Butowski)

strengthened airframe and powered by uprated 80.4kN (18,078lbf) engines providing for an increased take-off weight of 45,000kg (99,208lb) from shore bases and 39,790kg (87,722lb) from water. According to the specifications of the project, the aircraft will be able to patrol for four hours at a distance of 850km (528 miles) from its base; ferry range is 3,900km (2,423 miles).

At the Farnborough Airshow in 2012, the Russian arms trade company Rosoboronexport and Finmeccanica (now Leonardo-Finmeccanica) of Italy signed an agreement concerning cooperation in the development of the Be-220 with the Selex ES Airborne Tactical Observation and Surveillance (ATOS) mission system, backed up with mechanical Gabbiano or electronically scanned Seaspray E surveillance radars, intended for export to third countries. The first proposed customer was India.

Be-250 is a Beriev proposal for an airborne early warning and target indication aircraft based on the Be-200 platform; see Volume 1.

Be-300 is being designed as a shore-based derivative of the Be-200 amphibian with a completely new fuselage without the boat-shaped hull; the wing, tailplane and engines will remain unchanged while the undercarriage will undergo modest modifications.

Be-300MP is similar to the Be-200MP but with the fuselage of the Be-300. It is being offered to the Indian Coast Guard.

Be-310 is a proposed regional airliner intended to carry 102 passengers over a distance of 2,100km (1,305 miles) at a cruising speed of 750km/h (466mph).

Ilyushin Il-38

NATO reporting name: May

'Yellow 19' was the first Il-38 upgraded to Il-38N standard. From 2001 it served as a prototype for an early version of the upgrade. By 2014 it had been upgraded to the final Il-38N version and was ceremonially handed over to the Naval Aviation on 15 July 2014. It bears the name of Radiy Papkovsky, who headed the original Il-38 program. (Piotr Butowski)

Manufacturer

Designed by the Ilyushin Company in Moscow, series manufacture of the Il-38 was undertaken by Moscow's Znamya Truda Plant (which currently belongs to Russian Aircraft Corporation MiG, within which it is incorporated as the Production Centre No. 2).

Role

The Il-38 is a shore-based medium-range ASW aircraft; expanded maritime patrol and surveillance roles, as well as detecting and combatting surface targets (Indian version) are possible after the Novella/Sea Dragon upgrade.

Crew

The flight crew of five comprises two pilots, a navigator, flight engineer and communications operator. The tactical crew comprises a commander and two operators. All are located in the aircraft's pressurised nose compartment (entry is via a forward hinged/rear-opening ventral hatch, just behind the radar bulge). The crew are provided with a PSN-6A rescue dinghy and life jackets.

Airframe and systems

The Il-38 retained the wing, empennage, engines, landing gear, most systems and the cockpit of the Il-18 passenger aircraft, as described in detail in Chapter 4. The fuselage retained the outer contour, while inside, two stores/weapons bays and a mission systems operators' cabin were incorporated. The wing was moved forward considerably to compensate for the moving of the aircraft centre of gravity due to installation of the weapons bays. A bulbous antenna for the Berkut radar appeared under the nose, and

a magnetic anomaly detector was fitted in the tail. Most of the windows found on the Il-18 airliner were deleted.

Powerplant

The four Ivchenko Progress AI-20M (AI-20K on early-series aircraft) turboprops are each rated at 3,169ekW (4,250ehp) for take-off, and drive AV-68I four-blade propellers. A TG-16M auxiliary power unit is fitted. A total of 35,153 litres (9,284 gallons) of fuel is carried, equivalent to 26,650kg (58,753lb).

Dimensions

Wingspan 37.42m (122ft 9in); length 40.135m (131ft 8in); height 10.17m (33ft 4in); wing area 140m^2 (1,507 sq ft); tailplane span 11.8m (38ft 8in); wheelbase 12.78m (41ft 11in); wheel track 9m (29ft 6in).

Weights

Empty operating 34,630kg (76,346lb); maximum take-off 66,000kg (145,505lb); maximum landing 52,200kg (115,081lb).

Performance

Maximum speed 650km/h (404mph) at 6,000m (19,685ft) altitude; cruising speed 530km/h (329mph); mission speed 320-400km/h (199-249mph); mission altitude between 100-1,000m (328-3,280ft); ferry range 9,500km (5,903 miles); range with 5,430kg (11,971lb) weapons and stores 6,500km (4,039 miles); patrol duration 4 hours at 2,000km (1,243 miles) from base; maximum endurance 16 hours; take-off distance 1,700m (5,577ft); landing distance 1,070m (3,510ft).

Mission systems

Il-38: The Leninets Berkut (golden eagle) anti-submarine warfare system is controlled by a TsVM-264 Plamya (flame) digital computer (8,192 bytes ROM, 256 bytes RAM) that combines a radio sonobuoy subsystem (i.e. a suite of expendable sonobuoys and an airborne receiver of information from the buoys), 2BS1 Berkut search/attack radar (NATO reporting name Wet Eye; wavelength 2cm, 0.8in; weight 334kg, 736lb), as well as indication and data input subsystems. The Berkut automatically receives the data from the navigation system and autopilot. The system performs semi-automatic and automatic cruise flight and patrol flight in the operational area, radar search for surface targets (including searching for submarine periscopes), automatic laying of a barrier of sonobuoys and tracking of the buoys' signals, and finally, processing of data for the attack. The Il-38 uses two types of buoys, the RGB-1A and RGB-2. (RGB-3 and RGB-4 buoys were also developed for the Il-38, but are large and expensive. RGB-3s were used very seldom while the even larger RGB-4 never entered the production stage.) The passive omnidirectional RGB-1A buoy (weight 15kg, 33lb) can detect a submarine from a distance of up to 2,000m (6,562ft) and relays the detected sound via radio to the aircraft (over a distance of up to 40km, 25 miles). The passive directional RGB-2 buoy (47kg, 104lb) specifies the direction from which the sound of the submarine is coming from and is used immediately before attack, to gain exact positioning of the target. Another sensor aboard the Il-38 is the APM-60 Orsha (a town in Belarus) magnetic anomaly detector (MAD) housed in a long 'sting' aft of the empennage and

The conventional cockpit of the Il-38 is little changed from that of the original Il-18 airliner. (Rob Schleiffert)

not connected to the Berkut system; the signals acquired by the MAD are classified by the operator.

The Il-38's equipment has been subject to minor modifications throughout the years. During 1974–75 the aircraft's navigation system was supplemented with the ANP-3V device that improves accuracy when laying a sonobuoy field. The APM-60 magnetometer was replaced by the newer APM-73S Bor-1S (forest). Later, in the 1990s, some aircraft were retrofitted with the MMS-114 Ladoga (a lake near St Petersburg) MAD. During the 1990s, around 10 aircraft were retrofitted with the Izumrud-8 (emerald; Id-8) radio sonobuoy system that includes a Volkhov (a town in Russia) airborne receiver and new passive omnidirectional RGB-16-1 buoys; RTB-91 Nerchinsk (a town in Russia) auxiliary telemetric buoys were also added.

Il-38N/Il-38SD: The core of the Leninets Novella-P-38 (novel; izdeliye 1NV) and Sea Dragon (2SD) systems is the 1NV4 (2SD4) computerised operational centre that includes two operators' stations. Each position is fitted with two colour 15in (381mm) liquid-crystal displays (LCDs) and the control panel. The third station, for the system's commander, features only one large display and a control panel. The system comprises the following sensors, all of which are integrated:

- 1NV1 (2SD1) radar used for detecting aerial and surface targets (the stated detection range for a submerged submarine's periscope is 30–35km, 19–22 miles); the Russian 1NV1 radar operates in two bands: C (wavelength 30–60cm) and I (3–3.75cm), while the export variant 2SD1 has only the I-band;
- 1NV2 (2SD2) radio sonobuoy system using new buoys;
- NV3 (SD3) MAD with a range up to 900m (2,953ft);
- NV5 (SD5) electro-optical turret with TV, IR imaging, laser rangefinder and automatic target tracking; the target for observation can be preliminary 'pointed' using the radar;
- NV9 (SD9) electronic support measures (ESM) with sensors situated in a circular pattern in a box fairing located over the forward section of the fuselage.

Above: Indian Navy Il-38SD IN305 test launched a Kh-35E anti-shipping missile in 2005. (Tactical Missile Corporation)

Right: RGB-1A buoys are loaded into the internal bay in cassettes, each with 18 buoys. Typically, the Il-38 carries eight cassettes, together with other weapons and stores. (Piotr Butowski)

Leninets also developed and launched production of new radio sonobuoys for the Novella/Sea Dragon system: the passive omnidirectional RGB-41 and passive directional RGB-48; it is likely that the RGB-41 buoys are not used in the Russian Novella version. The sonobuoys are used in conjunction with GB-58 noise generators and RTB-93 auxiliary telemetric buoys (which measure and relay the speed of sound in the location of operation). A new feature is the RMB-81 magnetometer buoy.

Avionics

Il-38N/Il-38SD: This aircraft received a new navigation system including the I-21-5 inertial navigation system, A-737 satellite navigation receiver, SVS-2TsU air-data system, RV-21 radio altimeter, as well as new communication equipment including R-862 UHF and R-865NZh HF radios.

Self-protection features

Indian aircraft can carry four large, 192-round packs of chaff/flare dispensers, one on each side of the nose and one on each side of the MAD antenna. The Russian aircraft do not carry self-protection equipment.

Armament

Il-38: A maximum 8,400kg (18,519lb) or nominal 5,430kg (11,971lb) load of buoys and weapons is carried in two bays in the fuselage, one forward and one aft of the wing's spar; there is no provision for external stores. The most popular combined 'search and strike' load variant comprises 144 RGB-1A (RGB-16-1) buoys and 10 RGB-2 buoys, plus two APR-2 Yastreb-M rocket-propelled torpedoes, or two AT-2 torpedoes, or two UMGT-1 (AT-3) Orlan torpedoes, or 10 PLAB-250-120/RBK-100 depth charges, or one RYu-2 nuclear depth charge. In the mine-laying role, the Il-38 carries eight AMD-2-500M mines or four UDM mines.

Il-38SD: The upgraded aircraft received new weapons including Zagon/Zagon-2 guided depth charges (up to 20) and new APR-3 Oryol-M rocket-propelled torpedoes. India ordered its Il-38SDs with the capability to carry Kh-35E anti-ship missiles (not intro-

Il-38SD IN305 is one of five aircraft operated by India, all of which have now been upgraded to the Il-38SD version. The operator is Indian Naval Air Squadron (INAS) 315 at Dabolim, Goa. (Angad Singh)

duced in the Russian aircraft) on two APU-38 launchers fitted at the wing roots. A successful test launch of the Kh-35E (or izdeliye 5-78) was conducted on 14 November 2005; finally, India ordered a batch of Kh-35E missiles for its Il-38SD aircraft in early 2013.

History

The Tunyets (tuna fish) programme was launched on 18 June 1960 with the task of creating the Il-38 ASW aircraft. This was required to be able to patrol for three hours at a distance of 2,200km (1,367 miles) from its base and detect and fight submarines. A prototype (at this stage without the Berkut system) made its maiden flight on 28 September 1961, piloted by Vladimir Kokkinakki. In the 1970s, several improved versions were completed, but did not enter series production. These comprised the Il-38M of 1972 with the new Korshun-M search/attack system and provision for in-flight refuelling; meanwhile, the Il-38MZ was to be used as a tanker.

Production and operators

On 23 December 1967, Moscow's Znamya Truda Plant (now belonging to the MiG Corporation) built the first production Il-38; the 65th and final aircraft left the factory on 22 February 1972. The first aircraft were deployed to Soviet Naval Aviation's evaluation centre at Mykolayiv, Ukrainian SSR. Beginning in March 1968 they were delivered to the first operational regiments in Severomorsk-1 (Northern Fleet) and Nikolayevka (Pacific Fleet). In 1973, a Baltic Fleet squadron was established at Skulte, Latvian SSR.

During Soviet times, Il-38s were often deployed to overseas bases. In 1970–72, Il-38s were used to patrol the Mediterranean from Marsa Matruh air base in Egypt (the aircraft wore Egyptian markings but were piloted by Soviet crews). From 29 March 1976, Il-38s operated from Hargeisa airfield, and then from Daafeed in Somalia. Between 1978 and 1979 and later from 1985, the aircraft operated from Aden air base in Yemen, and from 1980 they operated from Asmara air base in Ethiopia (where in May 1984, Eritrean separatists destroyed two Il-38s on the ground). From 1982 onwards, Il-38s patrolled the Mediterranean from air bases in Libya, Mozambique and Syria. The Pacific Fleet's aircraft were often based in Vietnam.

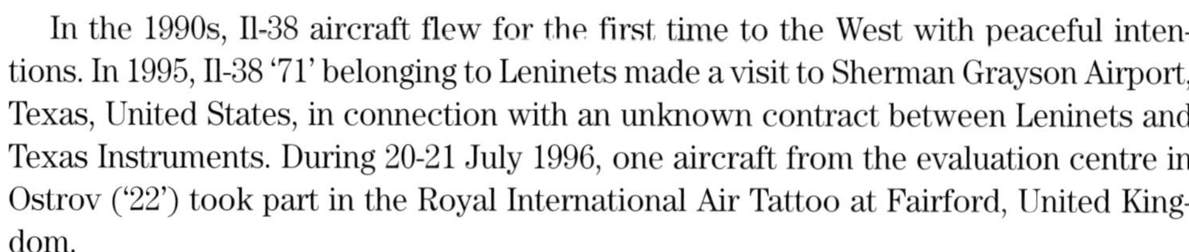

In the 1990s, Il-38 aircraft flew for the first time to the West with peaceful intentions. In 1995, Il-38 '71' belonging to Leninets made a visit to Sherman Grayson Airport, Texas, United States, in connection with an unknown contract between Leninets and Texas Instruments. During 20-21 July 1996, one aircraft from the evaluation centre in Ostrov ('22') took part in the Royal International Air Tattoo at Fairford, United Kingdom.

The Soviet and Russian Navies have lost only two aircraft (plus the two destroyed on the ground in Ethiopia). One crashed on 9 December 1987, when taking off from Nikolayevka airfield (the crew survived); another example crashed while landing at Severomorsk on 3 February 1994, killing the crew. Two aircraft crashed in India (see below).

Currently the Russian Navy has a fleet of 22 Il-38s assigned to three air bases: Severomorsk-1 within the Northern Fleet, and Yelizovo and Nikolayevka within the Pacific Fleet. Some aircraft are also to be found at the Naval Aviation's new evaluation centre at Yeysk on the coast of the Sea of Azov. There are also approximately 20 more non-airworthy specimens stored at different airfields; some of these are suitable for overhaul and return to service.

On 25 May 2012 the Russian Ministry of Defence signed a first contract with Ilyushin for the series upgrade of five aircraft to the Il-38N standard over a period of three years (earlier, a prototype aircraft, '15', had been completed and returned to service). The value of the contract amounted to 3.45 billion roubles, which was equivalent to around USD20 million per aircraft (at the then exchange rate). The contract fulfilment is divided between two companies: Ilyushin modernised the first, third and fifth aircraft while Myasishchev was responsible for the second and fourth. The first aircraft for the series upgrade was '19' (serial number 107-06), which had previously served to test the Il-38N upgrade as early as 2001. After the overhaul and upgrade, '19' flew again in April 2014. In July 2014, the aircraft was painted in dark grey colours, received the registration RF-75355 as well as the previous tactical number '19'. It also received the name *Radiy Papkovsky*, who headed the Il-38 project for many years and died in 2014. On 15 July 2014, aircraft '19' was ceremonially handed over to the Naval Aviation and was transferred to the evaluation centre at Yeysk; the subsequent upgraded aircraft comprised '27', '24' and '23'. The fifth aircraft from the first contract ('78', serial number 106-08, RF-75138) was handed over to the military after its modernisation on 30 June 2015; it received the name *Fedor Zolotukhin*, after the chief designer of the Novella system. Another contract of 26 May 2015 covers the upgrade of five more aircraft (two by Ilyushin and three by Myasishchev) by September 2017. By 2020 it is planned that a total of 28 aircraft will have been upgraded to the Il-38N standard.

The only foreign operator of the Il-38 is India, which acquired five aircraft in 1977. These feature a downgraded Berkut-E system. India also did not receive some items of equipment and armament; in particular, the Indian aircraft were armed only with AT-1E torpedoes rather than AT-2s. Two Indian Il-38s collided in mid-air on 1 October 2002 and were replaced by another two examples supplied from Russian Navy stocks. All five Indian Il-38s were upgraded to the Il-38SD version; they are operated by Indian Naval Air Squadron (INAS) 315 at Dabolim, Goa.

Il-38 '01 Red' takes off from its airfield in Russia's Far East. Plans call for additional Russian Navy aircraft to be upgraded to Il-38N standard, including returning to service aircraft that are currently no longer airworthy.
(Armen Gasparyan)

Variants

Il-38 (izdeliye 8) is the standard operational version, as described.

Il-38SD (izdeliye 8SD) is an upgraded export version with the Sea Dragon mission system. In September 2001, Rosoboronexport signed a contract worth USD205 million for the upgrade of the Indian aircraft to Il-38SD standard. The aircraft were supposed to have been upgraded by the end of 2004, but the system was still unproven and the deadline was significantly exceeded. The first Indian aircraft, IN305, flew in Moscow after its upgrade on 3 July 2003 and returned to India in January 2006. The fifth and final Il-38SD, IN307, flew to India in February 2010. The Sea Dragon is an export version of the Novella system with simplified radar and software.

Il-38N (izdeliye 8N) is the mid-life upgrade with Novella mission system that is currently being implemented for the Russian Navy's aircraft. Work on the Novella began in 1992; it is an all-new system with nothing of the previous Berkut remaining. The prototype Il-38N (tail number '19', serial number 107-06, or the sixth aircraft from the 107th production batch) flew for the first time from Pushkin airfield near St Petersburg on 4 April 2001, with Vladimir Irinarkhov at the controls. Trials with the mission systems began in November 2002, but the Novella did not initially meet the requirements and work on it was halted. In the meantime, the Sea Dragon export system took the lead. The definitive Novella-P-38 mission system was completed years later on the basis of the Sea Dragon by adding functions that were unavailable in the export version. In the latter half of 2008 aircraft '15', serial number 104-07, was equipped with the Novella-P-38 and underwent state evaluation with the system during 2009–10. Since March 2012 the aircraft has been assigned to Russia's Northern Fleet, operating from the base at Severomorsk-1. At the time of writing, the next batch of Russian Navy aircraft are being upgraded to the Il-38N standard.

Kamov Ka-27

NATO reporting name: Helix

A Ka-27PS search and rescue helicopter of the Ukrainian Navy taking part in the multinational maritime exercise 'Sea Breeze' in 2016.
(Stefan Fax via Alexander Golz)

Manufacturer

The Ka-27 was designed by the Kamov Company in Lyubertsy and manufactured by the Kumertau Aircraft Production Enterprise.

Role

Ship- or shore-based anti-submarine and search and rescue helicopter.

Crew

The basic Ka-27 anti-submarine helicopter is manned by a crew of three including a pilot and navigator seated side-by-side, with a dipping sonar operator in the cabin. (When operated in an attack configuration, the sonar operator is not required.) Cabin access is via rearward sliding doors on both sides of the fuselage, these being fitted with bulged windows, or through the cabin.

Airframe, rotor system and transmission

The fuselage is made of aluminium alloy with extensive use of titanium and composite materials. The crew cabin is located at the front, with mission system 'boxes' and a weapons/stores bay in the centre part. The engines, transmission gear and rotors are mounted on the top of the cabin. The rear part of the helicopter consists of a tail beam

The Ka-27 has manually folding rotor blades to save space on board ship. This is the Ka-27PS search and rescue version featuring an LPG-300 winch above the cabin door and additional fuel tanks fitted on the cabin sides (the upper, white box, while the lower box contains flotation gear. (Piotr Butowski)

carrying a tailplane with elevator and inward-toed endplates, each with a rudder and fixed leading-edge slat. The two coaxial, contra-rotating, three-blade fully articulated main rotors feature asymmetric blade aerofoils, with ground adjustable tabs. The bottom rotor has vibration dampers. The D2-4 composite blades incorporate manual folding. The rotor head is manufactured from titanium/steel. A rotor brake is fitted and the rotor blades have electrical de-icing. The main gearbox is of the VR-252 type. The fixed four-leg undercarriage has a single wheel on each unit; the mainwheels measure 620 x 180mm (24.4 x 7.1in), while the nosewheels measure 480 x 200mm (18.9 x 7.9in). Safety features include large flotation gear on each side of the lower fuselage and ahead of the main undercarriage legs. The fuselage is watertight in case of emergency ditching.

Powerplant

The two Klimov TV3-117KM (Kamov Morskoy, Kamov sea-borne) turboshafts are each rated at 1,618kW (2,200shp) for take-off, 1,250kW (1,700shp) nominal and 1,765kW (2,400shp) emergency for a period of 2.5 minutes when one engine is shut down. High-altitude TV3-117VK (Vysotnyi Kamov, high-altitude for Kamov) turboshafts are provided for later-production Ka-27 aircraft; TV3-117VKR or TV3-117VMAR engines with a nominal rating of 1,397kW (1,900shp) (other ratings unchanged) are found on export Ka-28 aircraft. All aircraft feature an AI-9 auxiliary power unit.

Eight fuel tanks under the cabin floor (on both sides of weapons bay) plus two inside the cabin provide for a total of 2,940 litres (776 gallons). The Ka-27PS version has no cabin tanks, but has two additional tanks in place of the Ka-27's weapons bay plus two more tanks fitted externally on the cabin sides, for a total of 3,450 litres (911 gallons). The long-range Ka-27PSD carries 4,830 litres (1,276 gallons) of fuel. The Ka-28 has larger internal tanks, as well as the external cabin tanks, for a total fuel volume of 4,760 litres (1,257 gallons).

The anti-submarine Ka-27 can carry the towed APM-73V Bor magnetometer suspended under the tailboom as an option; this requires the sonar to be removed. The orange bulge at the rear tip of the fuselage is a floating emergency data recorder. (Piotr Butowski)

Dimensions

Maximum length, blades folded 12.25m (40ft 2in); fuselage length 11.3m (37ft 1in); width, blades folded 3.8m (12ft 6in); height 5.4m (17ft 8in); rotor diameter 15.9m (52ft 2in) each; wheelbase 3.02m (9ft 11in); main wheel track 3.5m (11ft 6in); front wheel track 1.4m (4ft 7in).

Weights

Nominal take-off 10,700kg (23,589lb); maximum take-off 11,000kg (24,251lb).

Performance

Maximum operating speed at nominal take-off weight (TOW) 290km/h (180mph); maximum operating speed at maximum TOW 270km/h (168mph); cruising speed at MTOW 230km/h (143mph); service ceiling 3,500m (11,480ft); hovering ceiling out of ground effect (OGE) 2,200m (7,220ft) with TV3-117KM engines or 2,900m (9,515ft) with TV3-117VK engines; normal range 700km (435 miles); patrol duration at 200km (124 miles) 2 hours 15 minutes in search configuration or 1 hour 25 minutes in search/attack configuration; maximum duration 3 hours 30 minutes.

Mission systems

The Osminog (octopus) automated search/attack system was designed by the Kvant Company in Kiev, Ukraine, and is manufactured by the Radar plant in Kiev. It comprises the Initsiativa-2KM (initiative) radar, VGS-3 Ros'-V (a river in Ukraine; VGS is Vertolyotnaya Gidroakusticheskaya Stantsiya, helicopter hydroacoustic station) dipping sonar housed in the bottom of the fuselage aft of the cabin, a tactical indicator and a digital computer. The radar can detect a large ship at a range of 180km (112 miles); a surfaced submarine (with a radar cross section of 250m^2, 2,691 sq ft) can be detected

from a range of 30km (19 miles). The Ros'-V sonar has a 96kg (212lb) antenna dipping to a depth of 150m (492ft) and capable of detecting a submarine from up to 20km (12 miles) with a distance accuracy of 4 per cent and azimuth accuracy of 2°. The towed APM-73V Bor (pine forest) magnetic anomaly detector (detection range 400m, 1,312ft) can be optionally suspended under the tailboom when the sonar is removed. Additionally, the helicopter has a radio sonobuoy system that includes the A-100 Pakhra (a river near Moscow) airborne receiver and RGB-NM-1 sonobuoys, not integrated with the Osminog. The radio sonobuoy system detects submarines travelling at a depth of up to 500m (1,640ft) and at speeds of up to 40kt (75km/h, 47mph).

Avionics

The NKV-252 (Navigatsionnyi Kompleks Vertolotnyi, helicopter navigation complex) enables a pre-programmed flight path and autonomous flight back to the ship. This suite includes the DISS-015 Doppler radar mounted under the tailboom, Privod (drive) ILS that is combined with ship systems, a radio direction finder, Greben-1 (comb) heading system, MGV-1V gyroscopic system and A-031 radio-altimeter. The PKV-252 (Pilotazhnyi Kompleks Vertolotnyi, helicopter piloting complex) includes the VUAP-1 four-channel autopilot and provides for automatic hovering at altitudes greater than 25m (82ft). The R-832M and Zhuravl (crane) communication radios, SPU-8 intercom, and a data transmission system enable operations by the 'mother' ship and a group of helicopters within a common data network.

Self-protection features

None.

Cockpit of the anti-submarine Ka-27 with the pilot's seat on the left and the navigator's seat on the right; note the radar screen ahead of the navigator's position. When use of dipping sonar is planned, a third crew member, the sonar operator, takes up a position in the rear cabin.
(Piotr Butowski)

'Yellow 19' is a prototype of the export Ka-28 version, displayed here with its armament and stores including an APR-3E anti-submarine missile, a pack of 16 RGB-16 sonobuoys and a container with the Izumrud device for receiving and processing data from the buoys. (Piotr Butowski)

Armament

Nominal 600kg (1,323lb) and maximum 1,000kg (2,205lb) loads of weapons and stores are carried within the heated weapons bay under the cabin floor. Weapons loads include a single AT-1MV or UMGT-1 torpedo, or a single APR-2 rocket-powered torpedo, or six to eight PLAB-250-120 depth charges, or six to eight Zagon/Zagon-2 guided depth charges, or a single nuclear depth charge. Up to 36 RGB-NM-1 sonobuoys can be carried.

History

Design of the Ka-27 began in 1968 and on 3 April 1972 the design was officially ordered by the Soviet Navy as a replacement for the Ka-25, the requirement calling for a helicopter capable of operating for two hours at a distance of 200km (124 miles) from the 'mother' ship. It is possible that this requirement, which effectively doubled the patrolling time of the new helicopter, is the origin of its original designation: Ka-252 (Ka-25-2) or izdeliye D2 (Ka-25 was izdeliye D). The Soviet Navy also required that the external dimensions not exceed those of the Ka-25, so that it could use the same facilities on board the ship. On 8 August 1973, Ka-252 prototype '01' made the first hovering with Yevgeniy Laryushin at the controls. On 24 December 1973 the same pilot completed the first circuit flight. Series production of the Ka-27 began in July 1979 in the factory at Kumertau (Bashkortostan). During 1977 and 1978, five prototype and pre-series helicopters were subject to state acceptance tests on board the Project 1143 aircraft-carrying cruiser *Minsk*. The state acceptance tests were completed in December 1978 and then, on 14 April 1981, the helicopter was officially accepted into service with the Soviet Navy as the Ka-27. In the West, the Ka-27 was identified for the first time in September 1981, when two helicopters were photographed on board the destroyer *Udaloy*

A Ka-27 deploys its Ros'-V dipping sonar. The antenna weighs 96kg (212lb) and can be submerged to a depth of 150m (492ft).
(Piotr Butowski)

(Project 1155) during exercises in the Baltic Sea. The Ka-27PS search and rescue version first flew on 8 August 1974 and passed state acceptance tests between August 1978 and February 1979.

In addition to the standard Ka-27 ASW and Ka-27PS SAR production versions, a sequence of prototype or short-series helicopters was completed in the 1980s. These included the Ka-27K (izdeliye 09D2) ASW version with the new Kamerton-1M search/attack system, the Ka-27TL telemetric version used as a data-collecting platform to trace the flight path of intercontinental ballistic missiles, the Ka-27RTs (izdeliye 12D2) reconnaissance and target acquisition helicopter, the Ka-27PV (izdeliye 19D2) border-guard version and the Ka-27PK anti-ship version armed with Kh-35 missiles.

Production and operators

Beginning in 1979, the Kumertau Aircraft Production Enterprise completed around 280 Ka-27 helicopters including export Ka-28 versions. After 1991, low-rate production continued for export only; the last nine Ka-28s were completed for China in 2009–10. Around 80 examples are in service with the Russian Navy, comprising over 60 ASW versions and almost 20 SAR versions. A small number (around 16) are operated by Ukraine. Ka-28s were exported to China (17), India (14), Vietnam (10) and Yugoslavia (1). The Russian Navy now operates only one large ship capable of carrying groups of helicopters, the aircraft carrier *Admiral Kuznetsov* (up to 28 helicopters). Smaller missile cruisers, destroyers and frigates can each carry one or two helicopters. The helicopters are not assigned to the ships permanently and are deployed only for the duration of the cruise. The Russian Navy's Northern Fleet operates Ka-27s based at Severomorsk-1, the Pacific Fleet has Ka-27 bases at Yelizovo and Nikolayevka, the Baltic Fleet has a Ka-27 base at Donskoye, and the Black Sea Fleet has a base for the type at Kacha in Crimea. The Russian Border Guard, or FPS (Federalnaya Pogranichnaya Sluzhba), uses numerous Ka-27 helicopters to patrol Russia's sea borders.

The Indian Navy was recipient of 14 examples of the Ka-28, and 10 aircraft are to be upgraded to Ka-28M standard, equivalent to the Russian Navy's Ka-27M. (US DoD)

Now under Vietnamese Navy control, Hanoi's Ka-28 fleet is operated by the 954th Naval Aviation Air Brigade based at Cam Ranh.
(via Albert Grandolini)

At the beginning of 2015, the Kumertau factory began repairs (in order to extend the service life) and upgrades of the first eight helicopters to Ka-27M standard. Russia's National Armament Programme provides for the upgrade of 46 helicopters to Ka-27M standard by 2018. However, only two upgrade contracts had been signed as of September 2016, for a total of 22 helicopters (eight plus 14).

On 29 July 2016, India placed contracts with Russia for the repair and upgrade of 10 Ka-28s at a reported price of almost USD30 million per helicopter. The contract is to be completed by the end of 2019.

Variants in service

Ka-27 (**izdelye D2** or **izdeliye 500**, NATO reporting name Helix-A) is the basic anti-submarine version, as detailed. Some sources apply the incorrect name Ka-27PL.

Russian Navy Ka-27PS '27 Red' represents the search and rescue version of the 'Helix'. As well as the winch above the cabin door, this view reveals the radio signal buoys below the tailboom. (Stanislav Bazhenov)

Ka-27PS (Poiskovo-Spasatelnyi, search-rescue; **izdelye 501**, NATO reporting name Helix-D) is the SAR version, with ASW equipment removed (but retaining the Osminog-PS radar). Two radio signal buoys are suspended below the tailboom, and an LPG-300 winch is added at the cabin door. The helicopter carries life-rafts, and containers for clothes, food, medicines, etc. In daily use, Ka-27PS helicopters are mainly used as a transport between the ship and shore.

Ka-27PSD (Dalnyi, long-range) is a derivative of the Ka-27PS with increased fuel (total of 4,830 litres, 1,276 gallons) carried in two additional tanks on the fuselage sides. Maximum take-off weight is increased to 12,000kg (26,455lb), and strengthened undercarriage is provided. The helicopter has a range of 1,050km (652 miles) compared to 750km (466 miles) for the basic Ka-27PS.

Ka-27PST is the designation of a single helicopter with the GOES-337 electro-optical turret added.

Ka-27Ye is a special reconnaissance version with sensors used for detecting nuclear charges on board potentially hostile or enemy ships. Single helicopters are in use within each of the Russian Navy's fleets.

Ka-28 (**izdeliye 330**) is the export version of the Ka-27 ASW helicopter. It was first flown in 1982 and was originally completed to fulfil an order from India. The radio sonobuoy system was replaced by the Leninets Izumrud (emerald) system using new RGB-16 sonobuoys. Maximum permitted take-off weight was increased to 12,000kg (26,455lb) since there was no requirement for dipping the sonar (long-duration hovering) immediately after take-off from the ship's deck (i.e. with maximum take-off weight) using the rated power of the engines only – this was required by the Soviet Navy for its Ka-27s. Maximum fuel load was increased to 4,760 litres (1,257 gallons), equivalent to 3,680kg (8,113lb), normal combat load is 800kg (1,764lb), and maximum range is 1,240km (770.5 miles). The helicopter is powered by TV3-117VKR or VMAR

engines with the nominal (long-duration) rating increased to 1,397kW (1,900shp); the take-off rating remains unchanged at 1,618kW (2,200shp).

Ka-27M (izdeliye 27D2; izdeliye 520) is a mid-life upgrade programme that was launched in the early 2000s. The helicopter's rotor system, powerplant and airframe are unchanged while the mission system is completely new. Two configurations were considered for the new mission systems: the Lira (lyre) proposed by Leninets of St Petersburg, and the Bumerang (boomerang) by Phazotron-NIIR of Moscow. The Lira system was originally designed for the unrealised Ka-40 (izdeliye 17D2) helicopter in the late 1980s, and was a derivative of the Novella system that was later implemented in the Il-38N. In around 2002 the Lira was tested on Ka-27 '0909'. Tests of the Bumerang system began in early 2004 on the same helicopter, and ultimately, the Bumerang was selected. However, the design phase and subsequent tests of the Ka-27M's mission suite proved to be very protracted. The prototype Ka-27M, '0909', completed preliminary tests in 2011. In 2012 the second Ka-27M, '48', joined the test campaign. In summer 2013 the Ka-27M completed the first stage of state trials, and in 2015 these trials were completed. Series upgrades were launched at the beginning of 2015.

The upgraded Ka-27M includes the RKTS (Radiolokatsyonnaya Komandno-Takticheskaya Sistema, radar command-tactical system) Bumerang integrated by Phazotron-NIIR around the FHA (or Alba, or Kopyo-A) radar and also including the all-new Kema (a river in Russia) radio sonobuoy system with RGB-16MK buoys, the Ros'-VM dipping sonar, MMS-27 fixed magnetic anomaly detector, electronic support measures suite and navigator's tactical display. The X-band (3cm wavelength) radar can detect an aerial target (with a radar cross section (RCS) of 5m^2, 54 sq ft) from a distance of 70km (44 miles), a small sea object (RCS of 1m^2, 11 sq ft) from 30km (19 miles), a motorboat (RCS of 150m^2, 1,615 sq ft) from 130km (81 miles), and a large surface ship within the horizon. The Ka-27M can be armed with all available Russian weapons in the

The GOES-337VKA electro-optical turret contains thermal imaging and television cameras as well as a laser rangefinder. (Piotr Butowski)

'Red 57' is the only Ka-27PST search and rescue helicopter fitted with the GOES-337VKA installed on the port-side undercarriage leg. It was tested in 2003 on board the cruiser *Petr Velikiy*. (Piotr Butowski)

The Chinese People's Liberation Army Naval Air Force received 17 examples of the Ka-28. This example, serial number 9184, is equipped with a towed APM-73V Bor MAD 'bird'. (Top 81.cn)

appropriate class, including APR-3 anti-submarine missiles. The weapon's use is managed by the SUO-27D2P stores management system. Navigation and communication devices are also replaced by new equipment including the SSP-V-27M satellite system for approach and landing on the ship, as well as the S-403-1 communication suite.

The FHA radar alone, without the other elements of the mission system, has been proposed for an upgrade of Ka-27PS search and rescue helicopters.

Ka-28M is the export version, offered to India in particular as a mid-life upgrade for its Ka-28 fleet, and contracted in July 2016.

Ka-29 (**izdeliye 02D2**, or **D2B**, or **502**) is a naval assault helicopter; see separate entry in Volume 1.

Ka-31 (**izdeliye 03D2**) is a naval radar picket helicopter; see separate entry in Volume 1.

Ka-32 (**izdeliye 320**) is a civilian derivative of the Ka-27 that is beyond the scope of this book. However, it should be noted that the Ka-32 is in service with South Korea, where seven examples are operated by the Republic of Korea Air Force under the local designation **HH-32A**. Another eight examples are operated by the South Korean Coast Guard.

Ka-35 (**izdeliye 23D2**) is a battlefield surveillance helicopter; see separate entry in Volume 1.

Mil Mi-14

NATO reporting name: Haze

Mi-14PL '37 Yellow' of the Ukrainian Navy. This is the anti-submarine warfare version of the helicopter, with mission equipment based around the Kalmar search/attack suite. (Alexander Golz)

Manufacturer

Developed by the Mil Design Bureau in Moscow, series manufacture of the Mi-14 was undertaken by Kazan Helicopters.

Role

The Mi-14 is a shore-based anti-submarine amphibious helicopter able to destroy an enemy submarine travelling at a depth of 400m (1,312ft) and at speeds of up to 32kt (60km/h, 37mph). A search and rescue variant also exists.

Details for Mi-14PL

Crew

For standard operations the Mi-14 is crewed by four, including two pilots and a technician seated in the cockpit, and a navigator/weapon systems operator (or rescue equipment operator in the SAR version) seated in the cargo cabin. All crew are equipped with MSK-3M immersion suits; a LAS-5M-3 dinghy is also provided.

Airframe, rotor system and transmission

The watertight boat-type fuselage is subdivided into three compartments comprising the cockpit in the front, a cargo cabin with ASW equipment in the centre portion, and tail beam with tailplane, tail rotor and rear float at the rear. The fuel tanks and weapons bay are located under the cargo cabin. Access to the cabin is via a sliding door in the port side of the fuselage. The helicopter has an LPG-2 or LPG-150 external winch with a lifting capacity of 150kg (331lb), or an LPG-300 (300kg, 661lb) winch in the SAR version fitted at the door. The flight control system is mechanical with hydraulic actuators. The SAU-14 autopilot is equipped with autohover (in the Mi-14PL but not in the Mi-14PS). The four-leg undercarriage is fitted with single 480 x 200mm (18.9 x 7.9in) nosewheels and twin 600 x 180mm (23.6 x 7.1in) mainwheels and retracts into the fuselage (nosewheels) or side sponsons (mainwheels). Two inflatable floats (each with a volume of $4m^3$, 141 cu ft) on the fuselage sides ensure the helicopter remains stable when alighting on water.

The conventional rotor system comprises a VR-14 three-stage planetary main gearbox (weight 842.5kg, 1,857lb; transmission ratio 78.1:1), a five-blade main rotor and a three-blade tail rotor. The Mi-14's dynamics were later implemented in the Mi-8MT (Mi-17) helicopter, described in Volume 1.

Powerplant
The two Klimov TV3-117M turboshafts (M for Morskoi, sea-borne, with special corrosion-resistant coating of certain components) are each rated at 1,454kW (1,950shp) for take-off; the emergency rating is 1,659kW (2,225shp). An AI-9V auxiliary power unit is fitted. A total of 3,795 litres (1,002 gallons) of fuel is carried in six tanks under the cabin floor. An additional 500-litre (132-gallon) tank can be installed inside the cabin for ferry flights.

Dimensions
Main rotor diameter 21.294m (69ft 10in); tail rotor diameter 3.908m (12ft 10in); fuselage length 18.376m (60ft 3in); maximum length with rotors turning 25.315m (83ft 1in); maximum height 6.936m (22ft 9in); wheelbase 4.128m (13ft 6in); mainwheel track 2.82m (9ft 3in); nosewheel track 1.17m (3ft 10in).

Crew
Empty 8,902kg (19,620lb), or 8,821kg (19,447lb) for Mi-14PS; normal take-off 13,000kg (28,660lb); maximum take-off 14,000kg (30,865lb); payload (Mi-14PS) 3,000kg (6,614lb).

Weights
Maximum permitted speed 250km/h (155mph); maximum speed 230km/h (143mph) at sea level or 240km/h (149mph) at 1,000m (3,280ft); maximum speed on water 70km/h (43.5mph); service ceiling 4,000m (13,125ft); normal range 800km (497 miles); maximum range 1,135km (705 miles), with 7 per cent reserves; maximum endurance 5 hours 56 minutes.

Mission systems
The Mi-14PL has a Kalmar (squid) search/attack system that interfaces the Landysh (lily of the valley; izdeliye 7071) analogue mission computer, the Initsiativa-2M (I-2M, M for Mil; I-2ME for export helicopters) radar, the VGS-2 Oka-2 (a river in Russia) dipping sonar and the Snegir' (bullfinch) datalink. Separate devices, not connected to the Kalmar, include the radio sonobuoy system with the A-100 Pakhra receiver (SPARU-55

receiver on early helicopters) and expendable buoys, as well as the APM-60 Orsha magnetic anomaly detector (APM-73 Bor-1 on the final production helicopters). The PK-025 device transmits target-indication data to and from other helicopters or the ship, enabling group operations.

Avionics

The Mi-14 has the DISS-15 Doppler navigation radar (making it the first Russian helicopter with such equipment), ARK-9 and ARK-U2 radio direction finders, RV-3 or RV-5 radio altimeter as well as the Privod-SV-Bort instrument landing system. Communication equipment comprises the R-842M and R-860 radio sets, and SPU-7 or SPU-8 intercom. The IFF system is the SRZO-2.

Self-protection features

None.

Armament

The weapons and expendable stores are carried in the bay under the cabin floor. In the search configuration the helicopter carries 36 RGB-NM-1 or 12 RGB-N sonobuoys. The attack configuration consists of a single AT-1 (AT-1M) torpedo or eight PLAB-250-120 depth charges, or 12 PLAB-50-65 depth charges, or a single SK-1 Skalp nuclear depth charge. In the 1980s some helicopters were upgraded to carry APR-2 rocker-powered torpedoes. Four OMAB-25-12D (day) or OMAB-25-8N (night) marker bombs, plus four Poplavok-B radar beacon buoys are carried in a small bay in the rear part of fuselage.

A Polish Navy Mi-14PL deploys the APM-60 Orsha magnetic anomaly detector. (Piotr Butowski)

History

On 30 April 1965 the Central Committee of the Soviet Communist Party and Soviet government ordered development of the Mi-14 shore-based ASW helicopter from Mikhail Mil's design team. The prototype V-14 or izdeliye 140 (in Aeroflot livery and with CCCP-11051 'registration') first flew on 1 August 1967, piloted by Yuri Shvachko. The first three helicopters were powered by TV2-117 engines, each rated at 1,119kW (1,500shp), which were insufficient for the performance required of the helicopter. New TV3-117 turboshafts rated at 1,491kW (2,000shp) were ordered especially for the Mi-14 (as well as for the Mi-24, see Volume 1). The first Mi-14 with TV3-117 engines made its first flight in September 1969.

Several versions remained 'one-offs', including the Mi-14PLM (V-14M) with the new Osminog system from the Ka-27, flown in December 1975; the V-14R that served as a test-bed for the VGS-3 Ros'-V dipping sonar; and other helicopters for testing of the new APM-73 Bor-M MAD, the Strizh-M wire-guided ASW torpedo, the Kh-23 air-to-surface missile (1983), and the Sura forward-looking infrared (FLIR) sensor (1987).

Production and operators

The first production helicopter flew at Kazan on 24 January 1974. The Mi-14's production run ended in 1986, after 273 examples had been manufactured, including 111 for export. In September 1975 the first helicopters were delivered to an operational unit of the Soviet Navy (the 745th Anti-Submarine Warfare Regiment at Donskoye, near Kaliningrad, Baltic Fleet). On 11 May 1976 the Mi-14PL was officially commissioned. On 25 June 1996 the Mi-14PL was officially withdrawn from the service with the Russian Navy; however, several helicopters remained at Kacha air base in Crimea until 2004, for the training of foreign crews. At the time of writing, dozens of non-airworthy helicopters remain at storage facilities in Russia.

In the 1990s several companies made conversions of former military Mi-14s helicopters into civil versions, including the Mi-14 Helitanker (Eliminator III) firefighter from the German-Russian Aerotec GmbH and the passenger Mi-14P, passenger-cargo Mi-14PG, firefighting Mi-14PZh and geological- and ecological monitoring Mi-14GER from Konvers Avia of Russia. None of these helicopters is currently in use.

Destined for service with Pakistan, this Mi-14PS was noted undergoing overhaul at Sevastopol in 2011. The aircraft had its maritime mission equipment removed to serve as a transport helicopter. (Erwin Poelstra)

Not counting pre-used helicopters, a total of 111 Mi-14s were exported. These were delivered to Bulgaria (12), Cuba (14), East Germany (14; two examples were shipped to the United States in November 1991), Libya (approximately 30), Poland (16), Syria (approximately 20) and Yugoslavia (four). Re-exported helicopters went to Ethiopia, Pakistan and Yemen. At the time of writing, Poland operates eight Mi-14s and Ukraine operates two. The status of the helicopters in the other countries is unknown; however, some may still be in use in Georgia (approximately two examples still in use), Libya (approximately four), Pakistan (perhaps one example), Syria (approximately 10) and Yemen (approximately two).

In 2000, Poland began modernisation of its Mi-14PL helicopters by installing a new Kryl-D (krill) computerised mission system that allies the LS-10 control subsystem and Krab (crab) sonobuoys subsystem. The Kryl-D suite was developed by the Telecommunications Research Institute and Gdańsk Technical University. The original Russian Oka-2 dipping sonar was modernised, while the original MAD was replaced by the Polish Mniszka (moth) device. The sensors were also adapted for Baltic conditions, a sea that is characterised by its limited depth and short wind waves. The helicopter is armed with the Italian A244/S anti-submarine torpedo. On 28 November 2000 the first upgraded helicopter, '1007', re-entered service with the Polish Navy after qualification tests in the Baltic Sea. Polish Mi-14s have also been fitted with Koden 911 GPS and the Radwar RS6106-7 radio, as well as new IFF.

To the surprise of many observers, in June 2015 the Russian Helicopters Corporation announced its intention to return the Mi-14 amphibious helicopter to service. According to Andrey Shibitov, deputy head of Russian Helicopters, the company proposed a two-phase programme to the Russian Ministry of Defence. First, the company will undertake restorative overhaul and partial upgrade of Mi-14s abandoned at various bases. Second, it will start of production of new helicopters. Reportedly, funds for the overhaul of around 10 Mi-14s were secured in the defence budget for 2015.

In September 2015, during ceremonies marking the 75th anniversary of Kazan Helicopters, the Deputy Minister of Defence Yuri Borisov said that the ministry would order new Mi-14s, a move that is connected with Russian plans to secure control of the Arctic. 'Today we have no helicopters with such characteristics, which could be

Georgia has operated a small number of Mi-14s, including '08 White'. A reported two examples of the type may remain in service. (Istvan Topeczer)

used in the Arctic', he said. The primary advantages of the Mi-14 are long range and its ability to land on water, useful especially during rescue operations. Vadim Ligay, the deputy director of the Kazan plant, claimed that tooling required for the production of new Mi-14s could be ready within three to four years. The new-generation Mi-14 will incorporate solutions implemented in members of the Mi-8 family currently in production (see Volume 1), including new rotors, more powerful VK-2500 engines, TA14 APU and new avionics.

Plans to bring the Mi-14 back to service also have a political aspect. The Mi-14 remains in service with the Ukrainian Naval Aviation. Prior to 2014, these aircraft were overhauled by a repair facility at Sevastopol, Crimea. After the annexation of Crimea by Russia, this facility was left in need of work. One solution would be for the Sevastopol facility to restore and modernise Mi-14s for the Russian Navy.

Variants

Mi-14PL (Protivo-Lodochnyi, anti-submarine; **izdeliye 140**, **V-14** or **V-14E** for export; NATO reporting name Haze-A) is the standard ASW version.

Mi-14BT (Buksir-Tralshchik, tug-trawler; NATO reporting name Haze-B) was a mine countermeasures version. It is no longer in use.

Mi-14PS (Poiskovo-Spasatelnyi, search-rescue; NATO reporting name Haze-C) is the SAR version with ASW equipment removed from the cabin, providing room for 20 liferafts, and floating containers carrying clothes, food, medicine, etc. On-board accommodation is provided for 19 survivors. The port-side cabin door is enlarged, and a 300kg (661lb) LPG-300 hoist is installed.

Mi-14PL/R is a specific Polish SAR version (R is for Ratowniczy, rescue) converted from Mi-14PL airframes when Poland retired the Mi-14PS version in 2010. The side door has been enlarged and an SPL-350 hoist installed. The helicopter received a new weather radar in the nose, three searchlights, GPS navigation, new communication radios, and other items of equipment. Two helicopters were converted, '1009' and '1012', and both were in active use at the time of writing.

Tupolev Tu-142

NATO reporting name: Bear-F

Tu-142MK '51' *Yuriy Malinin* returns to its home base of Kipelovo-Fedotovo on 12 August 2016 after a general overhaul completed at the Beriev facility in Taganrog. (Beriev)

Manufacturer

The Tu-142 was developed by the Tupolev Design Bureau and series manufacture was undertaken by the Taganrog factory (now belonging to the Beriev Company); however, the first aircraft were manufactured by the aircraft plant at Kuibyshev (later Samara).

Role

Long-range anti-submarine warfare aircraft derived from the Tu-95 strategic bomber.

Details for Tu-142MK, unless stated

Crew

The Tu-142 is operated by a crew of 10, comprising two pilots, two navigators, a navigator/weapon systems operator, two operators for the radio sonobuoy system, a communications operator, an on-board technician, and a rear gunner. An eleventh crew member, the electronic countermeasures operator, is included in the aircraft with the Sayany-M system (see Self-protection features).

Airframe and systems

The Tu-142 is an all-metal mid-wing monoplane. For a full description of the airframe and systems, see the Tu-95MS in Chapter 1.

Powerplant

The four Kuznetsov NK-12MV turboprops are each rated at 11,185ekW (15,000ehp) for take-off, and drive eight-blade AV-60P propellers with a diameter of 5.8m (19ft); the Tu-142MZ is powered by the more reliable NK-12MP engines with the same rating. The maximum fuel load is 83,900kg (184,968lb) carried in 10 tanks in the wing and one in the fuselage.

The antiquated cockpit of the Tu-142MK. (Viktor Drushlyakov)

Dimensions

Wingspan 50.04m (164ft 2in); length 53.088m (174ft 2in); height 13.623m (44ft 8in); wing area 289.9m² (3,121 sq ft); wheelbase 16.3m (53ft 6in); wheel track 12.55m (41ft).

Weights

Empty 93,900kg (207,014lb); maximum take-off 185,000kg (407,885lb); maximum in flight after in-flight refuelling 187,700kg (413,807lb); maximum landing 135,000kg (297,624lb).

Performance

Maximum speed 855km/h (531mph); cruising speed 735km/h (457mph); take-off distance at MTOW 2,530m (8,300ft); landing distance 1,200m (3,937ft); ceiling 12,000m (39,370ft); maximum range without in-flight refuelling 12,000km (7,456 miles); patrol duration at 4,000km (2,485 miles) from base 4 hours 10 minutes; maximum endurance 16 hours 45 minutes.

Mission systems

Tu-142MK: The 2Korshun-K (kite) search/attack system made by Leninets of St Petersburg is controlled by a 2KNII (II is the Roman numeral 2) computing subsystem with Argon-15 computer. The computing system integrates the 2KNI (I is the Roman numeral 1) radar, the Kayra-P radio sonobuoy subsystem and the 2KNIV (IV is the Roman numeral 4) tactical-data presentation subsystem. The Kayra-P uses new RGB-75 (passive omnidirectional; 9.5kg, 21lb), RGB-15 (passive omnidirectional; 9.5kg, 21lb), RGB-25 (passive directional; 45kg, 99lb) and RGB-55A (passive/active omnidirectional; 55kg, 121lb) sonobuoys, as well as the RGB-1A buoys from the previous Berkut-95 system. The MMS-106 (Magneto-Metricheskaya Sistema, magnetometric system) Ladoga MAD is fitted at the tip of the tailfin and works as a separate device, not connected to the 2Korshun-K system.

Left: Positions for the operators of the Korshun mission system. (Viktor Drushlyakov)

Right: The flight engineer's position. (Viktor Drushlyakov)

Tu-142MZ: In this version the Korshun-N search/attack system features an upgraded KNNII computing subsystem and KNNI radar and also includes the new Zarechye (resulting in the Z in the aircraft's designation; the word 'zarechye' describes part of a town on the other side of the river) radio sonobuoy system instead of the Kayra-P. The Zarechye uses the new RGB-16 (passive omnidirectional; 9.5kg, 21lb), RGB-26 (passive omnidirectional; 13.9kg, 31lb) and RGB-36 (passive/active directional; 58kg, 128lb) sonobuoys capable of detecting quiet-running, new-generation submarines; older buoys from the Berkut-95 and Korshun-K systems can also be used. A new addition is the Nerchinsk system that is used to measure sound speed at depths as great as 200m (656ft), using RTB-91 telemetric buoys.

Avionics

The NPK VPMK navigation and piloting system is controlled by an Orbita-10TS-42 computer. The VPMK suite is based around the L14MA astro-inertial navigation device with standby DISS-7 Doppler radar supported by long-range A-711-03 and short-range RSBN-2S radio navigation, ARK-15M and ARK-U2 radio direction finders, and RV-18 and RV-5 radio altimeters. An AP-15 autopilot is fitted. The Groza-134VR weather radar is installed in the nose. The Strela-142M communication suite utilises two R-857G HF, single R-866 HF and two R-832M UHF radios, and a datalink. An SPU-14 intercom is also included.

Self-protection features

Tu-142MK: This version is protected by the SPS-100 Rezeda radar jammer and a pair of 23mm AM-23 cannon in a tail turret, provided with 1,200 rounds. Some aircraft based at Kipelovo received the Sayany-M electronic countermeasures (ECM) system that includes a characteristic thimble radome on the nose; as a result, they may be mistaken for the later Tu-142MZ version.

Tu-142MZ: In this aircraft the Sayany-M ECM system is joined by the Beryoza RWR, the L-083 Mak-UT infrared missile launch and approach warning sensor, Geran active electronic jammers and 50mm (1.9in) chaff/flare dispensers inside the main undercarriage fairings. Two twin-barrel 23mm GSh-23 cannon are carried in the tail turret.

The Tu-142MZ has a set of 50mm (1.9in) flare launchers fitted in the rear of the undercarriage nacelles. (Piotr Butowski)

RGB-75 buoys are loaded into the Tu-142MK's internal bay inside these cassettes, each of which contains 22 buoys. (Piotr Butowski)

Armament

Tu-142MK and **MZ**: A 9,000kg (19,842lb) maximum or 4,395kg (9,689lb) normal weapons load is located inside two fuselage weapons bays, with options including three torpedoes (the rocket-propelled APR-2/APR-3, or electric AT-2M or UMGT-1) or depth charges (including Zagon/Zagon-2 guided charges and nuclear depth charges), mines, and sonobuoys. One of the typical loading options for the Tu-142MK comprises three torpedoes and 66 RGB-75, 44 RGB-15, 10 RGB-25 and 15 RGB-55 sonobuoys.

History

A Soviet government resolution of 28 February 1963 tasked Tupolev with the creation of a submarine-hunting derivative of the Tu-95 strategic bomber able to patrol and destroy enemy submarines at a distance of 4,000km (2,485 miles) from its base. The aircraft was originally designated Tu-95PLO (Protivo-Lodochnoy Oborony, anti-submarine defence) and later Tu-142 and izdeliye VP (NATO reporting name Bear-F Mod 1) and made its maiden flight at Kuibyshev (later Samara) on 18 June 1968, piloted by Ivan Vedernikov. Series production was launched in Kuibyshev in the same year. The first 18 aircraft completed until 1972 were fitted with the Berkut-95 mission system, a derivative of the Berkut system as used in the smaller Il-38. In 1971, the factory at Kuibyshev was tasked with production of the Tu-154 airliner (see Chapter 4) and Tu-142 production was moved to another factory in Taganrog, which had recently completed production of Be-12 amphibians. A first Tu-142 from the Taganrog factory was flown on 4 November 1975, with Ivan Vedernikov at the controls. The first aircraft completed in Taganrog were of the upgraded Tu-142M version with a revised airframe that had already been adapted for the forthcoming Korshun ASW system. However, the system itself was not ready and the first 10 Tu-142M (izdeliye VPM, NATO reporting name Bear-F Mod 2) aircraft manufactured in 1975–76 were instead completed

IN317 is one of eight Tu-142ME versions that were delivered to India.
(Piotr Butowski)

with the Berkut-95. In 1977 the Tu-142MK entered production with Korshun system. On 19 November 1980 the aircraft was commissioned into service. Prototypes that never entered series production were the Tu-142MP of 1976 with the Atlantida ASW system (this being a mid-life upgrade of Berkut) and the Tu-142MRTs that appeared at the end of the 1980s as a reconnaissance and target acquisition aircraft with the Uspekh-1AV mission system. The final production version was the Tu-142MZ featuring the new Zarechye radio sonobuoy system and Sayany ECM system. It was flight tested in prototype form in April 1985, and underwent manufacture during 1993–94. In the early 2000s, two upgrade proposals were prepared, comprising the Tu-142MN with the Novella mission system for the Russian Navy and the export-optimised Tu-142MSD with the Sea Dragon system for India. However, neither of these upgrades has been implemented.

Production and operators

A total of over 100 Tu-142s of all versions were completed, including the first 18 aircraft in Samara (1968–72) and around 90 more in Taganrog (1975–94). The first of these entered service in May 1970 at Kipelovo-Fedotovo. In 1977 the first Tu-142s arrived at the Pacific Fleet's base of Khorol, from where they moved to Mongokhto (Kamennyi Ruchey) in 1978. Currently, Russia's Naval Aviation has two Tu-142 squadrons, one equipped with Tu-142MK aircraft at Kipelovo-Fedotovo and one with the Tu-142MZ version at Mongokhto. Combined, these provide for a total of a dozen airworthy aircraft (there are also around 10 Tu-142MR radio relay aircraft at the same bases; see Volume 1 for details).

Russia is still considering an equipment upgrade for its Tu-142s. The upgrade as currently planned differs from the previous Tu-142MN variant with the Novella system; instead, the upgraded Tu-142s would be fitted with the rival Kasatka mission system

A Tu-142MZ on approach to landing at Mongokhto air base in the Russian Far East. Mongokhto is the only base at which this version serves. (Russian MoD)

produced by the Radar-MMS company. According to reports in the Russian press, the aircraft could be upgraded during 2018–20.

Since April 1988, eight Tu-142ME aircraft have been used by the Indian Navy's INAS 312 based at Dabolim. From 2016, India plans to retire its Tu-142s due to their high operating costs, especially now that an alternative is available in the form of the Boeing P-8I Poseidon.

Variants in service

Tu-142MK (izdeliye VPMK, NATO reporting name Bear-F Mod 3) and **Tu-142MZ (izdeliye VPMZ**, NATO reporting name Bear-F Mod 4) are the current ASW versions of the Tu-142 in Russian Navy service, as described.

Tu-142ME (izdeliye VPMK-E, NATO reporting name Bear-F Mod 3) is an export version with downgraded 2Korshun-K-E mission system operated by the Indian Navy. More recently, the aircraft were upgraded with Israeli EL/M-2022A radar, Elbit AES-210 ELINT and Indian DRDO HOMI electronic support measures system.

Tu-142MR is a strategic radio relay aircraft; see separate entry in Volume 1.

FUTURE MARITIME PATROL AIRCRAFT

Russian companies are currently proposing several new designs for maritime aircraft and helicopters, but only two of these programmes – Apatit and Minoga – have been afforded a high priority and therefore have serious chances of implementation. In the Apatit programme, the Russian Ministry of Defence's contest for a large maritime patrol aircraft to replace the Il-38 and Tu-142, the Tupolev Tu-214P (based on the airframe of the Tu-214 airliner) is competing with the Beriev A-42 amphibian. The Minoga programme concerns a new ASW helicopter designed by Kamov to replace the Ka-27. Smaller patrol aircraft, based on the airframe of the Il-114 or Il-112 turboprop aircraft, the Be-200 amphibian discussed previously, as well as the Ka-62 helicopter, are not currently of interest to the Russian Ministry of Defence, since none of these is capable of carrying the entire suite of weapons and equipment required; instead, they will be offered for export. The new designs described below appear in order of their importance for the Russian Navy.

APK Apatit

The second Beriev A-40 prototype, 'Red 20', is no longer airworthy; the aircraft's development continues on paper only.
(Piotr Butowski)

Work on a new large aircraft for the maritime patrol, anti-submarine warfare, reconnaissance and target acquisition roles began in the USSR on 12 May 1982, when a government resolution ordered the Beriev Design Bureau of Taganrog to develop the **A-40** (or **izdeliye V**, popular name **Albatross**; NATO reporting name Mermaid) heavy ASW amphibian. The prototype, V-1 '10', flew on 8 December 1986 with a crew headed by Yevgeniy Lakhmastov. In June 1991 the second prototype, V-2 '20', was shown at the Paris Air Show (for this appearance, its original side number was changed to '378'). The third prototype was to be completed as a search and rescue version, known as the **A-42** (**izdeliye VPS**), but its construction was abandoned. Another version was to be the **A-44** (**izdeliye VPR**) surveillance aircraft. In subsequent years the design was evolved (on paper); in its current form it is known as the **A-42P** (**izdeliye VM**; **A-42PE** for export) and merges the functions of all three previous versions.

The A-40 prototype '20' is fitted with the Sova (owl) mission system made by the Leninets Company, and which is already obsolete. In later iterations of the design this was replaced by the Novella system and the aircraft is currently offered with the Kasatka-SB system. Similarly, the aircraft's engines have changed. The prototypes of the A-40 flew with Aviadvigatel D-30KPV turbofans (each rated at 117.7kN, 26,455lbf) fitted above the fuselage, aft of the wing, plus two Rybinsk RD-38K turbojet boosters (each rated at 27.0kN, 6,063lbf) installed below the main engines. Subsequent projects envisaged a powerplant of two Progress D-27A propfans (each rated at 10,440kW, 14,000hp) plus a single Klimov RD-33AS (rated at 51.0kN, 11,464lbf) turbofan take-off booster, and finally, two Aviadvigatel PS-90A-42 turbofans (each rated at 158.3kN, 35,583lbf). The A-42P's weapons options include up to six torpedoes, depth charges, mines, and other stores inside the fuselage bay, and anti-ship missiles carried on underwing pylons.

Somewhat after work had begun on the A-40, development of an alternative **Tu-204P** design was launched. This was to be a shore-based patrol aircraft derived from the Tu-204 airliner (first flown on 2 January 1989, piloted by Andrey Talalakin). The aircraft was to be equipped with the Leninets Novella-P mission system that combined a large nose radar, sonobuoy system, magnetic anomaly detector, electronic support measures, forward-looking infrared, and other equipment. Weapons and stores, including torpedoes, depth charges and sonobuoys, were to be carried inside a fuselage weapons bay; there was also provision for anti-ship missiles on four underwing pylons.

On 19 February 1996 a Russian government resolution halted the development of the A-40 amphibian and instead moved ahead with the Tu-204P project. However, despite official decisions, the Tu-204P programme remained at a standstill for many years. In the meantime, the Tu-214 airliner was developed (first flight on 21 March 1996, piloted by Aleksander Kosyrev), this being a derivative of Tu-204 with increased take-off weight. As a result, the Tu-204P project evolved into the **Tu-214P** (**izdeliye 312**). For more about the basic design of the Tu-214, see the Tu-214-ON section in Volume 1.

In early 2012 the designs for the large maritime patrol aircraft were revised yet again, with the launch of the **APK** (Aviatsionnyi Patrulnyji Kompleks, Airborne Patrol Complex), also known as **Apatit** (apatite). Once again, the Apatit programme saw the Beriev A-42P and Tupolev Tu-214P designs competing for the same requirement. According to the requirements of the 2012 contest, a prototype of the Apatit aircraft was to be ready in 2015 and then enter service in 2018. The intention of introducing the new patrol aircraft to service by 2018 was confirmed in the Russian press by the commander of Russian Naval Aviation, Major General Igor Kozhin in 2014. However, in June 2015 Kozhin provided revised, later dates: the ultimate choice of platform for the new patrol aircraft (i.e. the choice between the Tu-214 and A-42) was to be made in 2015–16, leading to a first flight 'by 2020'. Two mission systems that could be chosen for the Apatit aircraft are the Kasatka-SB produced by the Radar-MMS Company and a new system developed by the Leninets Company to replace the Novella.

Beriev A-42P specification (current project, with two PS-90A-42 engines)
Maximum length 47.16m (154ft 9in); wingspan 42.895m (140ft 9in); height 11.068m (36ft 4in); maximum take-off weight 96,000kg (211,644lb); normal mission load 4,000kg (8,818lb); maximum mission load 6,000kg (13,228lb); maximum speed 800km/h (497mph); cruising speed 680-740km/h (423-460mph); patrol speed 400-450km/h (249-280mph); ceiling 10,000-12,000m (32,808-39,370ft); patrol altitude 100-2,000m (328-

6,562ft); ferry range 8,000km (4,971 miles); operational radius with nominal weapons and 4-hour patrol duration 2,000km (1,243 miles) without in-flight refuelling.

Tupolev Tu-214P specification (estimated)
Length 47.5m (155ft 10in); wingspan 42.0m (137ft 10in); height 13.9m (45ft 7in); maximum take-off weight 110,750kg (244,162lb); maximum speed 850km/h (528mph); maximum range 8,000km (4,971 miles).

Kamov MPVK Minoga

The new maritime helicopter codenamed **Minoga** (lamprey), which is intended to be the successor to both the ship-based Ka-27 and the shore-based Mi-14, has been under development with the Kamov Company under the **MPVK** (Mnogovariantnyi Perspektivnyi Vertoliotnyi Kompleks, Multi-version Future Helicopter Complex) programme since around 2010. In July 2012, during a reorganisation of the Russian Helicopters Corporation, the Directorate of Special Duty and Maritime Helicopters was established, and among its tasks is the Minoga programme. According to a Russian Helicopters' presentation at that time, the prototype of the Minoga was to fly in 2018. Officially, the Minoga research and development programme was launched by an order of the Ministry of Defence dated 28 November 2014. In August 2015 the commander of Russian Naval Aviation, Major General Igor Kozhin confirmed that the new helicopter would be ready by 2018–20.

Kamov's MPVK Minoga project, which has the unconfirmed internal designation of izdeliye 450, is set to be a next-generation maritime helicopter to replace the Ka-27s. (Kamov)

The Minoga has two contra-rotating coaxial rotors and is powered by two Klimov TV7-117VK engines, each developing 2,088-2,237kW (2,800-3,000shp) of take-off power and 2,796kW (3,750shp) of emergency power. The helicopter is to be compatible with the same platforms, hangars and elevators aboard ships as the Ka-27. The Kasatka-VB (Vertoliot Bolshoi, for large helicopters) mission system for the Minoga was ordered from the Radar MMS Company in St Petersburg. According to a company representative, the contract has already been signed and related work is in progress. The complement of the Kasatka-VB system is typical for heavy maritime helicopters. The system is controlled by a KS-7 tactical-command and data presentation core that integrates the KS-1 radar, KS-10 sonobuoy system, KS-12 magnetic anomaly detector, KS-8 electronic support measures, KS-3 electro-optical turret, a dipping sonar, and the KS-2 communication suite with datalink. The helicopter's armament consists of two torpedoes, or up to eight depth charges and two anti-ship missiles.

The Minoga calls upon earlier work conducted by Kamov under the Ka-40 project; it remains unknown whether the Minoga will retain the Ka-40 designation, but it is probable. The preliminary design of the **Ka-40** (or **V-50**, or **Ka-27MF,** or **izdeliye 17D2**) helicopter was undertaken in 1990 within the **TKMV** (Tyazholyi Korabelnyi Mnogotselevoi Vertoliot, Heavy Ship-borne Multirole Helicopter) programme. Its powerplant was to consist of two Klimov TVA-3000 engines while the mission system was to be the Lira (lyre) developed by Leninets. The programme was officially stopped in the early 1990s but Kamov continued to work on it slowly, offering the new helicopter to various customers. In 2007 Gazprom showed an interest in a civil version, with a requirement for a large helicopter to service drill platforms in remote areas. For this purpose, Kamov revised the Ka-40 and offered it as the **Ka-32-10AG** (A denotes the

version certified in compliance with FAR 29 airworthiness standards and G stands for Gazprom), carrying 26 passengers and having a range of up to 1,200km (746 miles). Subsequent negotiations took place for some time with Iranian operator Navid Air, but no firm orders were placed.

Kamov MPVK Minoga specification (estimated)
Rotor diameter 16.3m (53ft 6in); take-off weight 13,000kg (28,660lb); maximum speed 300km/h (186mph); cruising speed 270km/h (168mph); service ceiling 5,000m (16,404ft), patrol endurance 2 hours at a range of 250km (155 miles) from base.

Ilyushin Il-114 maritime patrol variants

The Il-114 is a regional turboprop with accommodation for 64 passengers. The aircraft made its maiden flight at the very end of the Soviet Union, on 29 March 1990, piloted by Vyacheslav Belousov. After three test aircraft built by Ilyushin in Moscow, series production was launched in Tashkent, Uzbekistan. However, only 15 production aircraft were completed between 1992 and 2012. In May 2016, Russia decided to re-launch production of the extensively revised Il-114-300 variant at the Sokol factory in Nizhny Novgorod, a facility belonging to RSK MiG. A first Russian-made aircraft was scheduled to fly in 2019, which is unrealistic; subsequently, specialised military versions could be developed and fielded.

Alternatively, the mission systems described below may be installed in the new Il-112 transport aircraft (see Chapter 4), which shares the powerplant, wing structure and some systems with the Il-114. The launch of series production of the Il-112 is currently more likely than that of the Il-114.

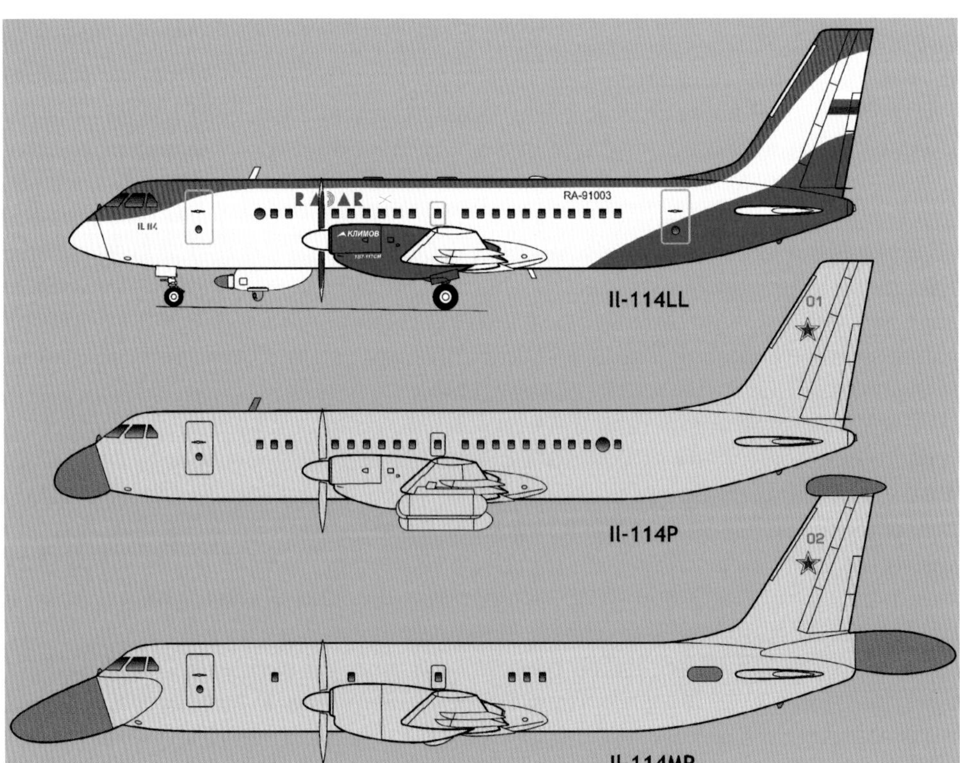

The current Il-114LL and 'paper projects' for the future Il-114P and Il-114MP maritime versions that feature progressively expanded mission systems. (Piotr Butowski)

This Il-114LL is the only example of the Il-114 currently still flying in Russia. It is used by the Radar MMS Company for trials of elements of the Kasatka mission system. (Piotr Butowski)

The only example of the Il-114 currently flying in Russia is the **Il-114LL** (Letayushchaya Laboratoriya, flying test-bed). Since April 2005 this has been used by the Radar MMS Company of St Petersburg for trials of elements of the Kasatka mission system. The Kasatka is planned to be fielded in various configurations and is expected to be used in possible future patrol versions of the Il-114.

Il-114P (Patrulnyi, patrol) is designed for patrolling the coast, sea border and 200-mile economic zone, as well as for ecological monitoring. The Kasatka mission system for the Il-114P includes two sensors only: a radar installed in the fuselage nose and an electro-optical turret with IR and TV cameras under the mid-fuselage. Two containers are carried under the fuselage: an SPPU-687 gun pod with a 30mm cannon and 150 rounds, and a pod with searchlight and loudspeakers; four other pods with rescue equipment are carried under the aircraft's wing. The passenger cabin has been subdivided into two compartments. The front part is used for carrying stretcher cases, survivors or a load of 3,000kg (6,614lb). The rear part of the cabin contains system equipment, stations for two operators, as well as positions for standby crew.

Il-114MP is a maritime patrol aircraft with a substantially expanded mission spectrum. The aircraft is designed for patrol, detection and tracking of surface ships and submarines, as well as for attacking them; the aircraft can also be used to lay mines. Therefore, the Kasatka system, besides the aforementioned radar and electro-optical turret, also includes a radio sonobuoy system, magnetic anomaly detector and electronic support measures. The Il-114MP can carry weapons including two Kh-35 anti-ship missiles. The Il-114MP weighs 30 tonnes, making it significantly heavier than the basic Il-114 (23.5 tonnes) or the Il-114P (26 tonnes). This requires more powerful engines and the Il-114MP is to be powered by two AI-20D turboprop with a take-off rating of 3,863kW (5,180hp) each. However, these are Ukrainian engines, which could present a problem in light of current relations between the two countries. Currently, Russia has no indigenous turboprop engines of equivalent power.

Patrol variants of the Il-114

	Il-114P	Il-114MP
Length	27.40m (89ft 10.75in)	29.654m (97ft 3.5in)
Wingspan	30.00m (98ft 5in)	30.00m (98ft 5in)
Height	9.186m (30ft 1.66in)	9.186m (30ft 1.66in)
Maximum take-off weight	26,000kg (57,320lb)	30,000kg (66,139lb)
Patrol speed	350-400km/h (217-249mph)	350-400km/h (217-249mph)
Patrol altitude	100-8,000m (328-26,247ft)	100-8,000m (328-26,247ft)
Patrol endurance at 300km (186 miles) from base	8-12 hours	9-12 hours
Engines	2 x TV7-117ST	2 x AI-20D series 5
Power	2 x 2,088kW (2,800hp)	2 x 3,863kW (5,180hp)
Flight crew	2	2
Mission crew	2-4	2-4

Apart from these two baseline versions, in July 1999 Ilyushin proposed the **Il-114PR** and **Il-114PRP** versions with signal intelligence and electronic warfare systems in various configurations, as well as well as the **Il-138** maritime patrol aircraft, the latter being a further development of the Il-114MP. The design of the **Il-140** airborne early warning aircraft, described in Volume 1, originates from the same period.

Kamov Ka-65 Okovka

For many years, Kamov continued design work on the naval **Ka-65** (**V-60K**) helicopter codenamed **Okovka** (binding), based on the Ka-62 medium general utility helicopter (see Volume 1 for details). The Okovka programme currently has a much lower priority than the Minoga programme and its prospects for success must be seen as unlikely, especially taking into account the serious delays suffered by the baseline Ka-62 helicopter. The Ka-62 prototype – at that time described as 'ready' – was presented in 2013; however, it only performed its first flight on 28 April 2016. Ultimately, considering its considerable percentage of foreign components, including engines and transmissions, the helicopter has little chance of entering military service in Russia in its current form.

The specifications of the Ka-65 are not known, but they are certainly close to those of the Ka-60, which has a take-off weight of 6,500kg (14,330lb), a maximum speed of 300km/h (186mph) and a range of 700km (435 miles). The ship-based Ka-65 was to be fitted with a radar and dipping sonar; new types of lightweight torpedo and guided depth charge were also to be developed for it.

STRATEGIC TRANSPORT AND TANKER AIRCRAFT

The legacy of Soviet strategic transports

The final few examples of the An-22 heavy transport aircraft still remain in Russian Air Force service. Although the An-22 was designed by the Antonov Design Bureau in Kiev, Ukrainian SSR, and was produced at the Chkalov plant at Tashkent, Uzbek SSR, its importance within Russia merits its inclusion in this chapter.

Antonov-operated An-22 UR-09307 prepares to land at Zurich Airport in 2016. Designed in Ukraine, the An-22 production run was completed at Tashkent, in Uzbekistan. (Alexander Golz)

Antonov An-22

NATO reporting name: Cock
Nickname: Antey

An-22 RA-09342 is one of the aircraft still on strength with the Russian Air Force. At the time of writing, five aircraft were in service at Migalovo air base, with another six aircraft non-operational. (Sergey Krivchikov)

Manufacturer

Developed by the Antonov Design Bureau in Kiev, Ukraine, series manufacture of the An-22 was undertaken in Tashkent (Uzbekistan), in the aircraft factory named after V. Chkalov.

Role

A heavy military transport and airborne assault aircraft with rear ramp, in terms of size the An-22 falls between Russia's standard Il-76 military transport and the 'super heavy' An-124. The An-22's cargo cabin is more capacious than that of the Il-76 while in terms of flight hours it is cheaper to operate than the An-124.

Details for An-22A

Crew

The flight crew of the An-22 consists of five, comprising two pilots, a flight engineer and a communications officer on the upper deck, and a navigator below them in the glazed nose.

Airframe and systems
The An-22 is of all-metal construction with a circular-section fuselage and high-mounted unswept wing fitted with double-slotted flaps on the trailing edge. The H-shaped tail unit has elevators and rudders on the dorsal/ventral sections. The control system is mechanical and is hydraulically actuated. The retractable undercarriage has steerable twin nosewheels. The main undercarriage units are accommodated within two long nacelles on the sides of the fuselage.

Each nacelle contains six pairs of braked wheels, in tandem. Thanks to the independent suspension on each pair of mainwheels, the aircraft can operate from semi-prepared runways. The undercarriage doors are opened only during the short period of lowering or raising the landing gear, in order to protect the inside of the bays against dust and mud.

Powerplant
The An-22 is powered by four Kuznetsov NK-12MA turboprops rated at 11,040kW (14,805shp) and driving eight-blade AV-90 propeller units. Each propeller unit consists of two four-blade coaxial contra-rotating reversible-pitch propellers, with a diameter of 6.2m (20ft 4in). A total of 96,000kg (211,644lb) of fuel is carried within 40 tanks located inside the wings and undercarriage nacelles; the aircraft has no in-flight refuelling capability.

Dimensions
Wingspan 64.40m (211ft 3.5in); length 57.31m (188ft 1 in); height 12.535m (41ft 1.5in); wing area 345m^2 (3,714 sq ft); cabin length 26.4m (86ft 7in) or 32.7m (107ft 3in) with ramp; cabin width 4.4m (14ft 5in); cabin height 4.4m (14ft 5in); cabin volume 640m^3 (22,601cu ft).

Weights
Empty operating 118,727kg (261,748lb); nominal take-off 205,000kg (451,947lb) at g-load of 2.3; maximum take-off 225,000kg (496,040lb) at g-load of 2.0.

Performance
Maximum speed 600km/h (373mph); maximum cruising speed 580km/h (360mph); approach speed 240km/h (149mph); range with full payload 3,700km (2,299 miles); range with full fuel 9,500km (5,903 miles); take-off run 1,460m (4,790ft); landing run 1,040m (3,412ft).

Transport capabilities
The aircraft can accommodate up to 60,000kg (132,277lb) of cargo, including large and heavy vehicles, missile systems, etc. Alternatively, the cargo hold can be configured to carry 151 paratroopers or 292 troops (in double-deck cabin configuration), or 202 casualties (however, the main cargo hold is not pressurised except for a forward cabin with capacity for 29 passengers). The freight hold is accessed via a loading ramp under the tail, with the fuselage door retracting upwards to leave unrestricted space for easy loading of vehicles or other cargoes. Cargo handling gear includes equipment for parachute landing of heavy items. Travelling cranes are suspended under the cargo hold ceiling, each with a 2,500kg (5,512lb) capacity winch.

The cockpit of the An-22 is provided with conventional instrumentation for the two pilots. Also seated on the upper deck are the flight engineer and a communications officer. The navigator's position is found in the glazed nose. (Stanislav Bazhenov)

Avionics

Early aircraft had the Initsiativa-4-100 radar targeting/navigation radar, later replaced by the Kupol-22 targeting/navigation system similar to that used in the Il-76. The Kupol-22 includes a KP-3 weather radar in the fuselage nose and a KP-2B ground mapping radar beneath. Other equipment includes RSBN-7S tactical and RSDN-3S long-range radio navigation units, DISS-013 Doppler radar, Kurs MP-2 instrument landing system, ARK-11 and ARK-U2 direction finders, RV-4 radio altimeter, 6202 IFF, R-847, R-862, R-802V and R-832M radios, and others.

Self-protection features

The aircraft is fitted with the Sirena S-3M radar warning receiver. Two KDS-16GM launchers with radar decoys are fitted inside the rear part of the starboard main undercarriage nacelle. Optionally, the aircraft may also be fitted with two packs of APP-50A countermeasures launchers at the main undercarriage nacelles, each pack being provided with 56 three-round 50mm (1.9in) decoy launchers.

Armament

The aircraft can carry four Shtyr-3 or Ogonyok-3 radio beacons or four 100kg (220lb) flare bombs. Alternative loads include three 250kg (551lb) or an unknown number – presumably one or two – 500kg (1,102lb) flare bombs. Flare bombs are used for illumination of the landing area; these are carried inside the rear part of the port main undercarriage nacelle. Bombs of up to 500kg can also be suspended under the wing.

History

Nicknamed Antey after a giant of Russian folklore, the Antonov An-22 (izdeliye 100; NATO reporting name Cock) made its first flight on 27 February 1965, piloted by Yuri Kurlin. At the time of its appearance it was the world's heaviest aircraft. Two months after its maiden flight the An-22 was exhibited at the Paris Air Show.

The cargo hold of the An-22 is provided with travelling cranes suspended under the ceiling, each of which supports a winch with a capacity of 2,500kg (5,512lb). (Stanislav Bazhenov)

Production and operators

The first series-production An-22 left the factory in Tashkent, Uzbek SSR, on 27 January 1966. Production of the An-22 continued until 1976 and amounted to 68 aircraft, including two prototypes built by Antonov and 38 An-22 and 28 improved An-22A versions built in Tashkent. Many problems were experienced at the beginning of An-22 operations. A first series of modifications were introduced in 1967–68 as a result of state acceptance tests. The next changes to the aircraft came in the wake of two fatal crashes in 1970. In the first of these accidents, which remains unexplained, aircraft CCCP-09303 crashed into the Atlantic on 10 July. In December 1970, the next aircraft crashed in India as the result of a manufacturing defect in the AV-90 propeller. As a consequence, many aircraft installations (mainly concerning the fuel system) were changed and the equipment improved; aircraft manufactured after these improvements were introduced are designated An-22A.

The first aircraft delivered to the Soviet Air Force in January 1969 were assigned to a regiment based at Ivanovo-Severnyi, followed in February 1974 by another regiment at Seshcha (in July 1975 this unit moved to Migalovo, near Tver). Between 1970 and 1989, An-22s completed numerous flights to Afghanistan, Algeria, Angola, Ethiopia, India, Syria, Vietnam and other countries. In 1971, they carried rescue equipment to Peru after that country was hit by an earthquake; similar actions were carried out in Armenia in December 1988. Between 1990 and 1992, An-22s evacuated military personnel and equipment from Georgia, East Germany, Poland and the Baltic States to Russia; it was an An-22 that was the last Russian military aircraft to depart a former Soviet air base in Germany, on 7 September 1994. Between 1994 and 1996, An-22s transported equipment and personnel to support the military campaign in Chechnya.

In the early 2000s there were 26 An-22s remaining in Russian military service, all of which were located at Migalovo. However, only nine of these aircraft were airworthy. At the time, the Russian Air Force planned to retain most of its An-22s with the inten-

Seen operating over Tver, Russian Air Force An-22 RA-09309 wears a unique camouflage scheme. (Sergey Krivchikov)

tion of carrying out restorative overhauls and modernisation to An-22-100 standard after 2010; however, these plans failed. At the time of writing, only five aircraft are still in service at Migalovo; a further six aircraft are preserved. One airworthy aircraft is operated by the Antonov Design Bureau in Kiev. Russia intends to keep its An-22s in service until at least 2020; they are currently undergoing overhauls at the ARZ-308 repair plant in Ivanovo.

Variants

The **An-22A** is the only version of this aircraft still in service.

Antonov An-124

NATO reporting name: Condor
Nickname: Ruslan

Recently, Russian Air Force An-124s, including this example, An-124-100 RF-82032 *Vladimir Gladinin*, have begun to receive red stars. For many years previously they flew with the Russian tricolour flag insignia. (Piotr Butowski)

Manufacturer

Developed by the Antonov Design Bureau in Kiev, Ukraine, series manufacture of the An-124 was undertaken by two factories: Antonov in Kiev and Aviastar-SP (SP for Samolotnoye Proizvodstvo, Aircraft Production) in Ulyanovsk, Russia.

Role

The An-124 is a very heavy, long-range military freighter. The An-124 remains the world's heaviest military transport aircraft.

Details for An-124-100

Crew

The An-124's flight crew of six comprises a pilot, co-pilot, navigator, two flight engineers and a communications officer; additionally, there are two loadmasters. For long-distance flights the aircraft can accommodate an alternate relief crew in a lounge compartment on the upper deck, just behind the cockpit, as well as up to 21 (or up to 88 when civilian certification is not required) cargo attendants in a cabin located on the upper deck behind the wings. The pressure differential in the cockpit and the additional crew compartments is 7.8psi (54kPa), reduced to 3.6psi (25kPa) in the cargo hold to allow structural weight savings. The transporting of personnel in the cargo compartment is not permitted under civilian certification.

Airframe and systems

The An-124 is a high-wing monoplane with moderately swept wings. The airframe is constructed mainly of light metal alloys, but with a titanium cargo hold floor and a certain amount of composites. In the double-deck fuselage, the upper deck has a diameter of 3.8m (12ft 5.5in) and the lower deck diameter is 7.2m (23ft 7in). The upper deck contains the crew cockpit and two compartments for the alternate crew and cargo attendants. The lower deck contains the cargo hold. The hold is accessed via a visor-type upward-hinging fuselage nose (the time to open is seven minutes) and a standard rear-door ramp, each of which are 6.4m (21ft) wide and 4.40m (14ft 5in) high.

Each wing trailing edge has three sections of extended-area single-slotted flaps, with differing deflection angles, and two sections of ailerons (with dampers). Twelve spoilers are fitted on the upper surface of each wing. There are six sections of leading-edge flaps. The fixed incidence tailplane carries elevators and a rudder. The de-icing system uses bleed air for the wing leading edges and electro-impulse for the tailplane leading edges and the fin. The aerodynamic configuration features near-zero static stability and is controlled by a quadruple-redundant fly-by-wire control (FBW) system with mechanical backup. The pilots have control wheels.

The retractable undercarriage has a steerable nose unit with a pair of two-wheel legs, with a tyre size of 1,120 x 450mm (44.1 x 17.7in). Each main unit comprises five tandem sets of twin wheels (1,270 x 510mm, 50 x 20in) housed inside nacelles on the fuselage sides; each set of twin wheels is independent of the others. The undercarriage height and slope can be adjusted.

Powerplant

The four Ivchenko Progress D-18T series 3 turbofans are each rated 229.8kN (51,654lbf) at take-off. Some aircraft are still powered by D-18T engines with the same rating but with a shorter service life and higher fuel consumption. Thrust reversers for the outer (cold) flow are standard for all engines. Two TA-12 auxiliary power units (APUs; each developing 291kW, 395ehp) are fitted in the main undercarriage nacelles. Ten integral tanks in the wing contain a total of 212,350kg (468,151lb) of fuel.

Dimensions

Wingspan 73.30m (240ft 6in); length 69.10m (226ft 8.5in); height 21.08m (69ft 2in); cargo hold length 36.48m (119ft 8in) at floor or 43.45m (142ft 7in) including front and rear ramps; cargo hold width 6.4m (21ft) at floor or 6.68m (21ft 11in) maximum; cargo hold height 4.40m (14ft 5in) maximum; cargo hold volume 1,160m^3 (40,965cu ft); wing area 628m^2 (6,760 sq ft); wing aspect ratio 8.556; wing sweepback at leading edge 33° root, 30° outer; wing incidence +3° 30'; wheel track 8.84m (29ft); wheelbase 22.9m (75ft 2in).

Weights

Empty, operating 178,400kg (393,305lb); maximum take-off 392,000kg (864,210lb); maximum allowable take-off for 10 per cent of cycles 402,000kg (886,258lb); maximum landing 330,000kg (727,525lb); maximum allowable landing for 3 per cent of cycles 387,000kg (853,190lb); maximum payload 120,000kg (264,554lb); maximum payload for 10 per cent of cycles 150,000kg (330,693lb).

Performance

Maximum Mach number 0.77; maximum speed 850km/h (528mph); maximum cruising speed 800km/h (497mph); approach speed 220-280km/h (137-174mph); required runway length 2,800m (9,186ft) at MTOW or 3,000m (9,843ft) at maximum allowable weight; ceiling 9,000-11,600m (29,528-38,058ft); range with 150,000kg (330,693lb) payload 2,650km (1,647 miles); range with 120,000kg (264,554lb) payload 4,650km (2,889 miles); range with 40,000kg (88,185lb) payload 11,350km (7,053 miles); maximum range 14,200km (8,823 miles).

Transport capabilities

The An-124-100 can carry up to 120,000kg (264,554lb), or 150,000kg (330,693lb) overload, including four platforms of the P-7 or P-16 type, which allow equipment or cargo to be paradropped. Alternatively, the aircraft can accommodate 12 ISO containers or other heavy/bulky cargoes including battle tanks, construction vehicles, heavy guns, missile systems, etc. Paratroop operations are limited by the limited pressurisation in the hold, but when conducted the paratroopers exit in two files via the rear hatch using D-5 parachutes of the forced opening type.

Loading facilities include two travelling cranes, of 10,000kg (22,046lb) capacity each, or a single 30,000kg (66,139lb) crane, installed on the cargo hold ceiling. Two electric winches each have a 3,000kg (6,614lb) pulling capacity. The floor height may be adjusted in order to make cargo handling easier: the main undercarriage unit oleos may be compressed to lower the cargo hold threshold; alternatively, the nose unit can retract after extendable 'rests' have been deployed, offering a sloping hold of 3° 30'. Thanks to the twin APUs, cargo handling can be carried out without ground power sources.

A Mi-24 helicopter is delivered to Kabul, Afghanistan by an Antonov-operated An-124, in December 2008. (US Air Force)

A view of the An-124 cockpit. The basic aircraft is operated by a pilot, co-pilot, navigator, two flight engineers and a communications officer. (Fyodor Borisov)

Avionics

The PNK-124M (A820M) flight-navigation complex produced by Kotlin-Novator of St Petersburg is controlled by an A821M computing system. The flight-control portion of the suite is the SAU-3-400 autopilot. The two main navigation systems within the complex are the I-21-1 (A826) inertial navigation and A829 astro navigation systems, supported by the Kupol-124 radar system, A723 long-range radio navigation (Omega and Loran compatible) system, A312 tactical radio navigation system, Kurs MP-70 instrument landing system, ShO-13V Doppler radar, ARK-22 (A318) radio direction finder, A-034 radio altimeter and GPS/Glonass receiver. The Kupol-124 (A822) radar system comprises two radars fitted under a common nose radome, with the A822-20 navigation and targeting unit below, and the smaller A822-10M weather unit above.

Additional instruments include the Honeywell TCAS-2000 traffic alert and collision avoidance system, Transas TTA-12 terrain awareness and warning system, BASK-124-01 data recorder as well as a SO-72M transponder and Parol-D (6202) IFF. The TIP-1B2 military communication suite includes an R-865GE HF radio, R887V receiver and an intercom. Alternatively, civilian Yadro-II-L1 HF and two Orlan-85ST UHF radios can be used. The cockpit instrumentation is conventional, with only one TV screen for the A822-20 radar indication and one LCD added later for weather radar indication.

Self-protection features

None.

History

On 2 February 1972 the Soviet government issued a resolution ordering a new strategic military transport aircraft from Oleg Antonov's design bureau in Kiev, Ukrainian SSR. The first project, known as the izdeliye 200 (since it was twice as heavy as the An-22, izdeliye 100, that preceded it), had reached the stage of full-scale mock-up, when the

Soviets realised that they required a more technologically advanced aircraft. A new governmental resolution dated 24 January 1977 launched the development programme for the izdeliye 400 design, which introduced a new supercritical wing and FBW control system. The prototype (serial number 01-01, civil registration CCCP-680125) made its first flight on 26 December 1982, with a crew under the command of Vladimir Tersky.

In the early 1980s the Western press published the first leaks concerning Antonov's giant new aircraft, attributing to it the designation An-40, and later An-400. The Soviets continued to suppress information about the new aircraft for several years. Only when the Lockheed C-5A Galaxy deprived the Soviet Union of a maximum load record set 17 years earlier by the An-22, was the An-124 was disclosed in May 1985. The new aircraft was shown at the Paris Air Show the following month (in the form of the second flying aircraft, serial number 01-03, civil registration CCCP-82002). On 26 July 1985, in the course of one flight, An-124 serial number 01-01 piloted by Vladimir Tersky set 21 world records for carrying capacity, including an absolute record: it carried a load of 171,219kg (377,473lb) to an altitude of 10,750m (35,269ft). From 6–7 May 1987, An-124 serial number 01-08 set a new record for range by a jet aircraft over a closed distance of 20,151km (12,521 miles), flying along the borders of the Soviet Union (the flight duration was 25.5 hours).

Production and operators

Production of the An-124 began at the Kiev aircraft plant, a neighbour of the Antonov Design Bureau, and a facility that today belongs to Antonov. The first series production aircraft, serial number 01-03, flew in December 1984. In parallel, a large aircraft factory (today named Aviastar-SP) was built in Ulyanovsk for the purpose of manufacturing An-124; the first aircraft completed in Ulyanovsk, serial number 01-07, made its first flight on 30 October 1985. Wings for 33 An-124s were manufactured in Tashkent, Uzbek SSR, and transported to Kiev or Ulyanovsk within the fuselage of an An-22 adapted for this purpose. In the 1980s the manufacture of 98 aircraft was planned, comprising 36 in Kiev and 60 in Ulyanovsk, plus two prototypes completed at the Antonov workshops. In fact, two prototypes (including one static example) and 54 series aircraft were completed, comprising 18 in Kiev (the penultimate of these was serial number 03-02 in February 1994, and the final example was serial number 03-03 on 6 October 2003) and 36 in Ulyanovsk (the final example was serial number 08-03 on 11 April 2004). Three incomplete airframes still remain at Ulyanovsk (serial numbers 08-04, 08-05 and 08-06).

On 10 February 1987 a first An-124, serial number 01-06, was delivered to the 566th Voyenno-Transportnyi Aviatsionnyi Polk (VTAP, Military Transport Aviation Regiment) stationed at Seshcha, near Bryansk, and already operating the An-22. In 1989, another unit, the 235th VTAP, was formed at Seshcha with two squadrons of An-124s and one of Il-76s. In February 1995 the 235th VTAP was moved to Ulyanovsk-Vostochnyi airfield where it was disbanded in 1999. The An-124 was officially commissioned into service with the Soviet armed forces on 28 March 1991. After 1991, no An-124s were supplied to the armed forces and all the aircraft manufactured after this date were delivered to civil operators. On 30 December 1992 a civil certification was awarded to the An-124-100 version by the Air Register of the Interstate Aviation Committee of the Commonwealth of Independent States (CIS).

As of early 2016, the Russian Air Force has a fleet of 26 An-124s, but only nine of these were airworthy. The non-flyable An-124 aircraft are being successively restored

and upgraded to An-124-100 standard at Ulyanovsk, at a rate of one or two aircraft per year. In 2008 the Ministry of Defence charged the Ulyanovsk facility with the restoration of 10 aircraft by 2015; thereafter, a contract was planned to cover restoration of a further 10 aircraft by 2020. The first aircraft returned to service after overhaul at Ulyanovsk was RA-82013 (serial number 05-02), on 21 September 2010, after more than 10 years spent on the ground. Most of the Russian Air Force's airworthy An-124-100s are assigned to the 224th Lotnyi Otryad (LO, Flight Detachment), which is registered as an airline company.

The largest civil operator of the An-124 is the Russian Volga-Dnepr Company with 12 aircraft; the Ukrainian Antonov Company operates seven aircraft and Maximus Air Cargo of the United Arab Emirates has one aircraft. Four more civilian aircraft are in storage and could be returned to service: two examples belonging to Polyot Airlines are stored in Ulyanovsk, two belonging to Libyan Air Cargo are stored in Tripoli and in Kiev, respectively.

Four aircraft have been lost during service. On 13 October 1992, CCCP-82002 (serial number 01-03) belonging to the Antonov Design Bureau crashed near Kiev. During

An An-124 with the front and rear cargo doors open for loading. (Piotr Butowski)

a test flight the nose radome disintegrated in a dive and its debris damaged three engines. Eight people were killed. On 15 November 1993, RA-82071 (serial number 07-04) of Aviastar Airlines crashed into the side of a mountain due to disorientation of the pilot on approach to Kerman airfield in Iran; 17 people were killed. On 8 October 1996, RA-82069 (serial number 07-02) of Aeroflot crashed on approach to land at Turin, Italy; two people on board were killed, together with two on the ground. The pilot was attempting to complete a go-around in heavy rain despite the fact that the thrust reversers were already engaged. The most recent crash occurred on 6 December 1997, when RA-82005 (serial number 01-07), leased from the Russian Air Force by Cargotrans, and carrying two Su-27UB fighters to Vietnam, crashed after take-off at Irkutsk. The aircraft hit a residential building; 23 people aboard the aircraft and 45 people on the ground were killed.

The most spectacular transport operation involving the An-124 took place during June–July 2001, when an An-124 of Polyot Airlines transported a US Navy Lockheed EP-3 surveillance aircraft, which had landed on the Chinese island of Hainan after a collision with a Chinese fighter on 1 April 2001. The EP-3 was flown from Hainan to Kadena Air Base, Okinawa and then to Marietta, Georgia, in the United States. In 1993 an An-124-100 carried the heaviest single load ever transported by air, a 124-tonne Siemens powerplant generator core secured on a load-spreading skid built for this purpose, totalling 135.2 tonnes. The generator was carried from Düsseldorf in Germany to New Delhi in India. In September 1990, 451 Bangladeshi refugees were emergency airlifted from Amman in Jordan to Dacca, Bangladesh in a single An-124, with only basic amenities hastily added to the cargo hold.

A considerable proportion of the civil An-124's services (according to Volga-Dnepr, two thirds) fulfil the orders of governmental customers, including the European Union, NATO and the United Nations. The first such governmental client was the United Kingdom, which leased an An-124 in 1992 to deliver equipment to the Falkland Islands. On 17 December 2001, Volga-Dnepr performed a first flight in support of the United Nations Assistance Mission in Afghanistan; Antonov began flights to Afghanistan in early 2002. In 2010 the 224th LO signed a four-year contract to provide transport for the French armed forces.

Since March 2006, Volga-Dnepr and Antonov, via Ruslan SALIS GmbH, have jointly participated in the NATO Strategic Airlift Interim Solution (SALIS) programme. The partners place up to six aircraft (two of which are available immediately, two more on six days' notice, and another two on nine days' notice) with crews, maintenance system and transport organisation at NATO's disposal. The first contract was completed at the end of 2012; Ruslan SALIS GmbH has since been rewarded with new contracts, the most recent of which is valid until December 2016, with an option to extend this until December 2017. At the time of writing, An-124s had flown over 3,000 missions within the SALIS programme. However, in September 2016 Ukraine announced that from 1 January 2017 it would cease further cooperation with Volga-Dnepr and offered to continue the SALIS programme on an independent basis, using Ukrainian An-124 and An-225 aircraft only. It is known that the Russian side also placed a separate offer for the tender.

Since autumn 2015, An-124s have been used to supply equipment for the Russian military contingent in Syria. For example, on 26 November 2015 they carried the S-400 surface-to-air missile (SAM) system to Syria.

An-124-100 UR-82029 is one of seven aircraft of this type operated by Antonov in Ukraine. (Piotr Butowski)

Variants in service

An-124 (**izdeliye 400**) is the basic military transport version. At the time of writing, none of the Russian Air Force's An-124s were airworthy and the aircraft were awaiting repair and upgrade to An-124-100 or An-124-100M(VTA) standard.

An-124-100 is the version adapted to fulfil the requirements of civilian customers. Due to stricter safety requirements, the aircraft is certified for reduced weights in comparison with the military An-124: the maximum take-off weight is 392,000kg (864,212lb) rather than 405,000kg (892,872lb), and the payload is 120,000kg (264,555lb) compared to 150,000kg (330,693lb).

An-124-100V is a sub-variant with noise-reducing covers on the engine nacelles to comply with Chapter 3 Appendix 16 of International Civil Aviation Organization (ICAO) standards. The noise covers were certified in 1996, and a first aircraft was converted in April 1997 (serial number 01-08). In service these aircraft are still designated An-124-100, without the V suffix.

An-124-100M has a crew reduced to four (with no communications operator or onboard engineer) thanks to the introduction of new Honeywell avionics. Two aircraft, serial numbers 01-06 (UR-82008) and 02-08 (UR-82027), are in use with Antonov.

An-124-100M-150 is as the -100M but with the maximum take-off weight increased to 402,000kg (886,258lb) and the maximum payload increased to 150,000kg (330,693lb). The range is increased to 3,200km (1,988 miles) with a payload of 150 tonnes, 5,200km (3,231 miles) with a payload of 120 tonnes, or 8,100km (5,033 miles) with a payload of 80 tonnes. The front ramp has been reinforced to allow quick and simple handling of 120-tonne mono-cargoes. Stronger tyres and improved brakes have been installed. One aircraft, serial number 01-08 (UR-82009), is operated by Antonov.

An-124-100-150 is capable of accommodating a 150-tonne payload but retains the original avionics and six crew.

An-225 (**izdeliye 402**, NATO reporting name Cossack, nicknamed **Mriya**, dream) is an increased-size An-124 originally designed for a single mission: the transport of large-size elements of the Soviet Buran space shuttle and Energiya rocket from the production plant to the launch facility. The An-225 was constructed on the basis of

The An-225 is the world's heaviest aircraft. While Antonov has held initial talks with Chinese partners with a view to manufacturing a second example, currently only one aircraft has been completed, and is in service with Antonov. (Pavel Vanka)

an An-124 by lengthening the fuselage, extending the wing centre section, installing two more D-18T engines, adding two pairs of wheels on each side and by redesigning the control surfaces. The An-225 flew for the first time on 21 December 1988, with Aleksandr Galunenko at the controls. It remains the world's heaviest aircraft, with a maximum take-off weight of 600,000kg (1,322,774lb); on 11 September 2001 an An-225 set an absolute record for lifting capacity, carrying a load of 253,820kg (559,577lb) to an altitude of 2,000m (6,562ft). Only one aircraft has been built. In 2001 it was restored and certified as the **An-225-100**; it is currently operated by Antonov.

Selected paper projects

An-124A was a project for a military version capable of operating from second-class airfields that featured a main undercarriage with six tandem sets of wheels rather than five.

An-124 SRT (Samolyot Retranslator, relay aircraft) was a project from the 1980s that was intended to replace the Tu-142MR (see Volume 1) in the role of communication with submerged submarines.

An-124FFR was a proposal of 1994 for a firefighting version, capable of delivering 200 tonnes of water plus retardants, using the cargo hold plus 70 tonnes stored in the wing centre section. A kit would have been provided to re-convert the aircraft to cargo carrying for off-season operations.

An-124VS (Vozdushniy Start) or **An-124AL** (Air Launch) was to be a launch platform for the 80-tonne Polyot rocket that could be used for delivering 3,500kg (7,716lb) satellites into Earth orbit. The origins of this project lay in a Soviet proposal for the air launch of the RSM-54 (Shtil-3A, NATO reporting name SS-N-23 Skiff) intercontinental ballistic missile, which was originally developed for submarines. At high altitude, the missile was to be ejected from the cargo hold by means of a parachute, and would have been stabilised in a vertical position before its engine started.

Oril (Eagle) was a Ukrainian project similar to the Russian An-124VS version, based on the Ukrainian 55-tonne Oril ballistic missile, able to deliver a 1,630kg (3,594lb) payload into a 200km (124-mile) orbit, or an 830kg (1,830lb) into a 1,000km (621-mile) orbit.

RA-82013 is the first An-124-100 aircraft to be restored at Ulyanovsk according to a Russian Air Force order of 2008. It returned to service on 21 September 2010, after more than 10 years spent on the ground.
(Piotr Butowski)

An-124-200 (first with this designation) and **An-124-210** were projects with Western engines, respectively the General Electric CF6-80C2 and Rolls-Royce RB211-524H-T.
An-124-102 was a concept with an increased-height fuselage; the cargo hold was to be 6.7m (22ft) high, 2.3m (7ft 6.5in) greater than in the standard version.
An-124-300 (first with this designation) was an Antonov concept of 2010 with insertions in the fuselage, wing centre section and tailfin increasing the aircraft's length to 75m (246ft), wingspan to 80m (262ft) and height to 24.9m (82ft). The take-off weight was to be 553,000kg (1,219,156lb). Due to a much increased fuel capacity (295,000kg, 650,364lb) and new 352kN (79,000lbf) turbofans (type not specified), the aircraft was expected to attain a range of 8,100km (5,033 miles) with the maximum payload of 150,000kg (330,693lb).

Koloss programme

In October 2006 a Russo-Ukrainian inter-governmental committee considered the matter of possible resumption of An-124 production for the first time. The greatest proponent of the resumption of An-124 production was Volga-Dnepr, the most important civil operator of the type; the airline promised to order 40 new An-124s by 2030. Assessments of total demand for new An-124s from other civil operators varied from 15 to 40 examples by 2030. The Russian Ministry of Defence declared an interest in purchasing of one aircraft per year starting from 2021, equivalent to 10 aircraft by 2030. However, none of the customers proceeded beyond declarations of intent, instead waiting for state funding to prepare for production. The question has been discussed at various levels in the following years, with joint talks with Ukraine continuing until early 2014, and thereafter only in Russia.

In late 2010 Russia launched a programme to upgrade the An-124 and resume production of the type, under the codename **Koloss** (colossus). The Ilyushin Company of Moscow was appointed as main contractor for the Koloss programme, which was accompanied by a change in the law in order to enable the further development of the aircraft without participation by the designer, i.e. Antonov. In February 2014, Ilyushin proposed that Antonov participate in the programme, but only as a subcontractor. The Koloss programme stipulates the upgrade of aircraft in Russian Air Force service to An-124-100M(VTA) standard and, in future, the launch of production of the new civil An-124-300 and military An-124-300V versions. Separately, and independent from the Koloss programme, Antonov was working on the An-124-111 mid-life upgrade for the Volga-Dnepr Company and also proposed a new An-124-200 version for production. New production is currently possible only in Ulyanovsk; the production rigging in Kiev has not survived, apart from that for the tail unit. According to statements from the Aviastar-SP CEO Sergey Dementyev in 2012, the Ulyanovsk plant retains rigging for An-124 production, but it requires servicing and overhaul. Dementyev claimed that the plant would require three-and-a-half years to resume production and to achieve a production rate of three aircraft per year.

Currently, due to the conflict between Russia and Ukraine and the economic crisis in Russia, resumption of An-124 production appears unrealistic, while the modernisation of existing aircraft will instead be conducted by each of the countries separately. For Russia, the key problem is the powerplant: the current D-18T engine is only manufactured by the Motor Sich plant in Zaporizhzhya, Ukraine and there is no Russian alternative. Sustaining the current operation of the aircraft is also problematic, since engine overhauls are conducted exclusively by Motor Sich; no Russian facility is currently capable of this work. As a result, Russian has begun to design new engines, which could be used on the An-124 in the future. The basic powerplant under consideration in the short term (a first An-124 with this engine is promised for 2019) is the three-spool NK-23D turbofan manufactured by Kuznetsov of Samara, rated at 235kN (52,900lbf), a similar output to the current D-18T. The engine is based on the core of the NK-32 series 02 engine as used in the Tu-160 bomber (the only engine core of this class currently available in Russia). According to calculations, at a cruising speed of Mach 0.75 at 11,000m (36,089ft) the NK-23D would have a bypass ratio of 5.4 (the current D-18T series 3 has a bypass ratio of 5.5), thrust of 5,000kg (11,032lb; compared to 4,860kg, 10,714lb for the D-18T) and a specific fuel consumption of 0.565kg/kGh (0.546kg/kGh for the D-18T). In the more distant future Russia is planning to produce new engines for heavy-lift transport aircraft (see Future strategic transport and tanker aircraft), including a potential new An-124-300 version, using both the core of the NK-32 series 02 (NK-65 engine) and the upgraded core of the new-generation Aviadvigatel PD-14 engine, which is currently being produced for the Irkut MC-21 airliner (the PD-24 is rated at 235.3kN, 52,911lb st, while the PD-28 is rated at 274.6kN, 61,729lb st). On the Ukrainian side, the problems concern expendable items for the An-124 that are supplied by Russia, including the tyres, brakes, and other components. Antonov is considering replacement of the aircraft's Russian avionics components with Western equipment during overhauls, for example, replacing the A822 radar with the Honeywell RDR-4000.

An-124-100M(VTA) is to be a considerably upgraded military version (VTA is Voyenno-Transportnaya Aviatsiya, Military Transport Aviation). In October 2013, Ilyushin

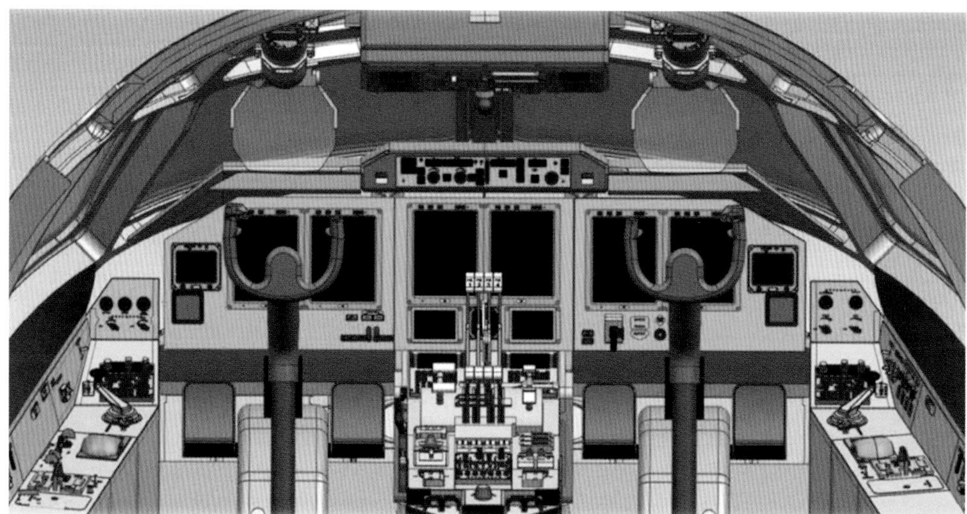

The proposed pilot's cockpit of the upgraded military An-124-100M(VTA) version with KSEIS-124 integrated displays. (UAC)

The navigator's and flight engineer's positions on the upgraded flightdeck of the An-124-100M(VTA). (UAC)

was charged with the related research and development work; the upgrade documentation and a mock-up of the new cockpit were prepared during 2014. The upgrade provides for new avionics including a fully 'glass' KSEIS-124 (Kompleksnaya Sistema Elektronnoy Indikatsii i Signalizatsii, integrated system of electronic indication and signalling) cockpit and a crew of four, a new digital EDSU-124 FBW control system, SAU-124 autopilot, new inertial navigation system, new S-801 communication suite, and other new items. For the time being the engines will remain unchanged, but in the future they may be replaced during overhauls by the Kuznetsov NK-23D, and later by the Aviadvigatel PD-24.

An-124-300 is to be a new-production aircraft with a take-off weight increased to 420-440 tonnes and a payload of 150 tonnes. The aircraft's range would by 6,000-7,000km (3,728-4,350 miles) with a 120-tonne load. New avionics would enable a reduction in crew complement to just two pilots. New, far more powerful engines rated at 28-30 tonnes of thrust are to be used. Previously, Ukrainian D-18T series 5 (take-off thrust 273.1kN, 61,399lb st) or Western General Electric GEnx, Roll-Royce Trent or Pratt & Whitney PW4000 engines were under consideration. Now, however, new Russian tur-

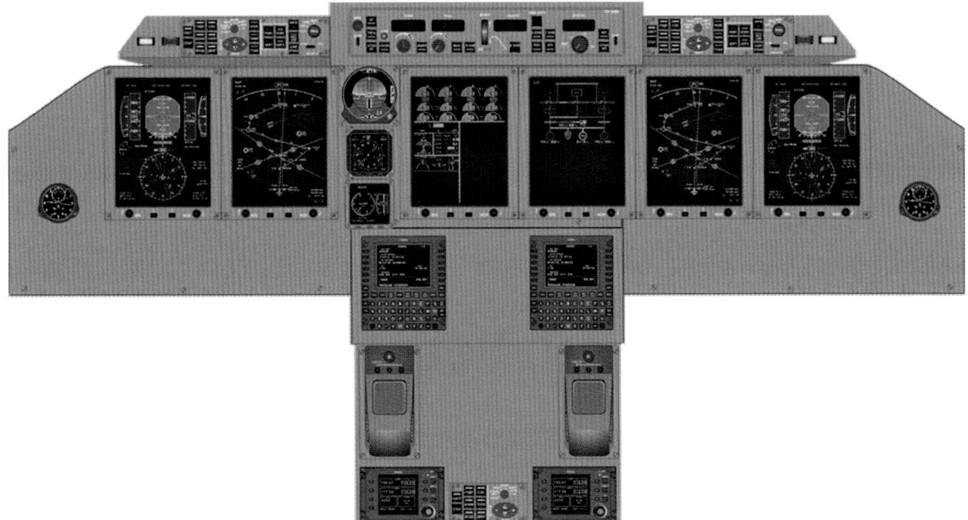

The new pilots' cockpit proposed by Antonov for the significantly upgraded An-124-200 version. (Antonov)

bofans engines represent the only viable option. A low-risk variant is the Kuznetsov NK-65 geared turbofan engine using the core of the NK-32 series 02 and rated at up to 289kN (65,036lbf) of thrust. In the more distant future the An-124-300 could be fitted with new-generation Aviadvigatel PD-28 engines.

An-124-300V is to be a new-production aircraft for the Russian Air Force.

An-124-111 is a civilian upgrade, guidelines for which were agreed between Antonov and Volga-Dnepr in August 2011 during the International Aviation and Space Salon (MAKS) in Moscow. The upgrade provided for new avionics including a fully 'glass' cockpit and a crew of four, new digital FBW flight control system and D-18T series 3M turbofans, differing from the current series 3 engines in their use of new ESU-18M full-authority digital engine control (FADEC); the engine's thrust will remain unchanged, but will be sustained at higher temperatures. However, Volga-Dnepr has recently begun to operate the Boeing 747-400/8F freighter and now aspires to modify the An-124 accordingly. Comparison shows that one flight hour for the An-124-100 is 40 per cent more expensive than that for the 747-400/8F; the Boeing aircraft carries 120 tonnes over twice the distance, has a crew of two instead of four to six, and has a serviceability rate of 95 per cent compared to 69 per cent for the An-124. Nevertheless, for certain tasks the An-124 remains irreplaceable: it is capable of hauling non-typical (very large) loads and operating from airfields without infrastructure, unlike the Boeing 747. Volga-Dnepr requested the **An-124-111-747** modification that incorporates avionics from the Boeing aircraft. When it comes to new production, Volga-Dnepr has expressed its desire to order the **An-124-300-747** version that uses the same engines as the 747-400/8F.

An-124-200 was the Antonov proposal for resumed production of the aircraft. This represented a relatively modest upgrade, similar to the An-124-111, with a strengthened airframe for a 150-tonne payload, modernised avionics for a crew of three to four, and D-18T series 3M engines. The aircraft was to be fitted with two TA18-200-124 APUs in place of the current TA12s. The service life was to be extended to 45 years (currently it is 25), or 10,000 cycles (currently, 6,000), or 50,000 hours (currently, 24,000). The An-124-200 would meet future ICAO requirements concerning noise and emissions as well as Eurocontrol's air-traffic requirements.

A pair of An-124s is seen flanking its predeccessor, the An-22, at Leipzig Airport in 2016.
(Alexander Golz)

Ilyushin Il-76

NATO reporting name: Candid-A (civil versions) and Candid-B (military versions)

The Il-76MD – this is RF-76764 – remains the backbone of the Russian Air Force's airlift capabilities. While around 120 Il-76s are assigned to five bases, plus a training centre, only around 80 of these aircraft are airworthy.
(Armen Gasparyan)

Manufacturer

Designed by the Ilyushin Company in Moscow, between 1973 and 2011 series manufacture of the Il-76 was undertaken in Tashkent, Uzbekistan, in the aircraft factory named after V. Chkalov. In 2012, production was re-launched at the Aviastar-SP factory in Ulyanovsk, Russia.

Role

Designed as a medium-/long-range military transport, the Il-76 was later converted for civil use, as well as medical evacuation, firefighting, astronaut training, electronic countermeasures and other duties.

Details for Il-76MD

Crew

The Il-76 is operated by a crew of six accommodated in a double-deck cockpit. The upper deck accommodates the two pilots, engineer, communications operator and air-landing operator (loadmaster); the lower deck accommodates the navigator. A rear gunner is included in the crew complement on some military aircraft.

Airframe and systems

To allow operations from unpaved runways, the Il-76 has a moderately swept wing with full-span leading-edge slats, two sections of triple-slotted trailing-edge flaps and ailerons with tabs. Forward of the flaps are four sections of spoilers (deflected differentially to support the ailerons or deflected together as airbrakes when landing) and four sections of airbrakes. The T-tail has a variable-incidence tailplane, elevators with tabs and a rudder with tab. The flight control system is of the mechanical, power operated type with manual control as standby. The multi-wheel retractable undercarriage consists of a four-wheel 1,100 x 330mm (43 x 13in) bogie at the front, and two main units of two four-wheel 1,300 x 480mm (51 x 19in) bogies in tandem.

Powerplant

The four Aviadvigatel/Perm D-30KP series 2 (izdeliye 53) turbofans are each rated 117.68kN (26,455lbf) for take-off, and are fitted with thrust reversers. A TA-6A auxiliary power unit is fitted in the starboard main undercarriage fairing. Up to 109,480 litres (28,915 gallons) of fuel, equivalent to 84,840kg (187,040lb) is carried in 12 tanks along the entire span of the wings.

Dimensions

Wingspan 50.5m (165ft 8in); maximum length 46.594m (152ft 10in); maximum height 14.76m (48ft 5in); cabin length excluding ramp 20.0m (65ft 7in); cabin length maximum 24.54m (80ft 6in); cabin width 3.45m (11ft 4in) at floor; cabin height maximum 3.4m (11ft 2in); wing area 301.2m^2 (3,242 sq ft); wing sweepback 25° at 25 per cent chord; wing anhedral 3°; tailplane span 17.4m (57ft 1in); wheelbase 14.17m (46ft 6in); wheel track 8.16m (26ft 9in).

Weights

Empty operating 89,000kg (196,211lb); maximum take-off 190,000kg (418,878lb); maximum permissible take-off 210,000kg (462,970lb) for no more than 15 per cent of take-offs; maximum take-off from unprepared runway 157,500kg (347,228lb); maximum landing 151,500kg (334,000lb); maximum payload 48,000kg (105,822lb).

Performance

Maximum permissible Mach number 0.77; maximum cruising speed 750-780km/h (466-485mph); ceiling 12,000m (39,370ft); range with maximum payload 3,800km (2,361 miles); range with 40,000kg (88,184lb) payload 4,760km (2,958 miles); range with 20,000kg (44,092lb) payload 7,400km (4,598 miles); range with maximum fuel 7,800km (4,847 miles); take-off run 1,700m (5,578ft); landing run 900-1,000m (2,953-3,281ft).

Transport capabilities

The Il-76MD can carry a load of up to 48,000kg (105,822lb) within a pressurised freight hold. Optionally, the aircraft's cargo compartment can seat 167 troops or 245 when the second deck is installed, or 126 paratroopers who are parachuted via the rear hatch in four rows, as well as via side doors on both sides of fuselage. Military equipment can be dropped from high altitude, as well as from an altitude of 3-5m (10-16ft) above the ground surface (the load, e.g. an armoured personnel carrier, is extracted from the cargo hold using a small parachute). Typical cargo loads include standard Russian con-

An Il-76MD of the People's Liberation Army Air Force delivers an armoured vehicle by parachute. Note the open side doors in the forward fuselage. (Archives)

Il-76TD RA-76445 operated by Volga-Dnepr unloads supplies for the US Army in Iraq in March 2008. (US Air Force)

tainers. Loading facilities include two LPG-3000A electrical winches on the floor, each with a capacity of 6,614lb (3,000kg), and four ET-2500 electrical telphers, each with a capacity of 5,512lb (2,500kg). Roller tracks are fitted on the floor. Four toe plates are used to load self-propelled and towed vehicles.

Avionics

The PNPK-76 Kupol-II-76 (cupola; II is the Roman numeral 2) targeting, navigation and piloting complex is produced by the Kotlin Novator company of St Petersburg, and is controlled by a KP1D-76 computing system (with Gnom-1A computer). The complex

Left: Cockpit of the Il-76MD. (Piotr Butowski)

Right: The slightly upgraded cockpit of the Il-76MF. (Piotr Butowski)

integrates KP2V (RLS-P, Radio-Lokatsionnaya Stantsiya – Panoramnaya, radar, panoramic) navigation radar in a radome below the nose (this is also used as a sight when paradropping), KP3A (RLS-N; N for Nosovaya, nose) weather radar in the nose tip, KP4 subsystem for formation flight navigation, KP5 optical sighting device, KP6 air-speed gauge and KP7 inspection system. The navigation system includes an INS-Il-76 inertial navigation system, DISS-013-S2M Doppler radar, A-711 long-range radio navigation, RSBN-7S tactical radio navigation, Kurs-MP-2 instrument landing system, ARK-15M and ARK-U2 automatic direction finders, RV-5 radio altimeters, and other items of equipment. The aircraft has an SAU-1T-2B autopilot. Communication devices include R-862, R-847T and R-861 radios as well as the R-099M for coded communication; an SPU-8 intercom is also included.

Self-protection features

Some military aircraft have SPO-10 Beryoza (or S-3M Sirena on older aircraft) radar warning receivers in large fairings on the sides of the nose as well as SPS-5 Fasol-1-I1 electronic noise jammers. Optionally, chaff/flare dispensers can be carried, including a 96-round 50mm (1.9in) APP-50R launcher on each side of the fuselage and/or two APP-50R launchers on the undercarriage fairings. Most military aircraft and some civil examples have a 9A-503 rear gun turret with two twin-barrel GSh-23 cannon and a 4DK Krypton radar sight.

The undernose KP2V panoramic radar of the Il-76MD's Kupol-Il-76 avionics complex is used for navigation and as a sight when paradropping. (Aleksey Mikheyev)

Armament

The aircraft can carry four 500kg (1,102lb) flare bombs for illumination of the landing area. For training purposes, smaller P-50 (50kg, 110lb) practice bombs are used.

History

In 1966 the Moscow team headed by Sergei Ilyushin was tasked with the design of a transport and air assault aircraft, known as the Il-76 (izdeliye 76), that would be capable of delivering 33,000kg (72,753lb) of cargo over a distance of 5,000km (3,107 miles) after taking off from an unprepared runway. The Lockheed C-141A StarLifter of 1963 proved to be a significant inspiration for the design of the Il-76. The first Il-76 prototype, CCCP-86712, recorded its first flight on 25 March 1971, piloted by Eduard Kuznetsov. Two months later the aircraft appeared at the Paris Air Show. On 8 May 1973 the first series-production aircraft, CCCP-76500, was flown, this having been built in Tashkent, Uzbek SSR. Approximately 80 examples of the initial version were built.

In 1978 production switched to the Il-76M (modernised) version with reinforced structure, increased wing fuel tanks and with a widened rear fuselage. The maximum take-off weight was increased from 157,000kg (346,126lb) to 170,000kg (374,786lb), while the maximum load was increased from 33,000kg (72,753lb) to 48,000kg (105,822lb). The Il-76T (transport) emerged as a civil derivative of the Il-76M with military equipment and tail gun position removed; thanks to this, the payload was increased to 50,000kg (110,231lb). In total, around 170 Il-76M/T airframes were completed at the Tashkent factory until 1981, when production switched to the military Il-76MD and civil Il-76TD, in which D stands for Dalniy, long range. The wing structure was further reinforced, and the maximum take-off weight was now increased to 190,000kg (418,878lb), allowing more fuel to be carried with the same payload (the fuel tanks have the same volume); range with a load of 20,000kg (44,092lb) was increased from 6,500km (4,039 miles) to 7,400km (4,598 miles).

The Il-76MD's tail turret with two twin-barrel GSh-23 cannon and 4DK Krypton radar sight. (Piotr Butowski)

On 1 August 1995 the lengthened Il-76MF was first flown. This was expected to be the next major production version. The essential requirement for this version was an increased cargo hold length, since it was originally intended to be used as a launch platform for the RSM-54 (Shtil-3A, NATO reporting name SS-N-23 Skiff) intercontinental ballistic missile, which was originally developed for submarines. The 45,600kg (100,531lb) missile was to be ejected from the cargo hold by means of parachutes, and would have been stabilised in a vertical position before its engine started. However, after the collapse of the Soviet Union, only one prototype Il-76MF was completed in 1995, followed by two production aircraft delivered to Jordan in June 2011.

In addition to these basic transport versions, dozens of other modifications have been built on the basis of the Il-76 as either short production series or single aircraft.

Il-76MF JY-JIC is one of only two production aircraft of this version; both were delivered to Jordan in 2011. (Piotr Butowski)

The Il-76MD Skalpel-MT military airborne hospital was equipped with three medical modules inside the cargo hold. Two aircraft (CCCP-86905 and 86906) were completed and were used during the war in Afghanistan in the 1980s, as well as for rescuing victims of the earthquake in Armenia in 1988. A civil Il-76TD-S (S for Sanitarnyi, medical) variant was built in 1991. The Il-76K, Il-76MDK and Il-76MDK-2 (K for Kosmos, space) were all built for cosmonaut training in simulated agravic (weightless) conditions, which could be generated for 22–24 seconds; several such manoeuvres (parabolas) can be performed during a single flight. The Il-76MD-PS (Poiskovo-Spasatelnyi, or Il-84 search and rescue aircraft, first flown on 18 December 1984, was capable of patrolling for three hours at a distance of 3,000km (1,864 miles) from its base with 40 rescue paratroopers and a large Gagara motor boat and life-rafts for 1,000 people; only one prototype was completed. The Il-76P (Pozharnyi) firefighting version of 1989 carries two tanks in its cargo hold for 44,000kg (97,003lb) of extinguishing agent that can be dropped within six or seven seconds, covering an areas measuring 500 x 100m (1,640 x 328ft). Several examples of the Il-76LL (Letayushchaya Laboratoriya, flying test-bed) aircraft are used for engine testing at Zhukovsky. The engine to be tested is installed in place of the standard inner engine under the port wing, leaving the aerodynamic configuration of the aircraft intact.

Il-76LL engine test-beds

Registration	Tested engines (year in which tests began)
86712	NK-86 (1975)
86891	D-18T (1982)
76492	PS-90A (1986), NK-93 (2005), Kaveri (2010)
76529	D-236T (1989), D-27 (1990), PD-14 (2015)
06188	TV7-117 (1989)
76454	SaM146 (2007)

Components developed for the Il-76MF, including the PS-90A76 turbofan and new avionics, were later integrated in a number of modernised, standard-fuselage aircraft. In September–October 2002 the Russian Air Force moved two Il-76MD aircraft to the Voronezh factory in order to upgrade them to Il-76MD-90 standard with PS-90A engines and new avionics. The first aircraft, RA-78854, flew after upgrade on 27 December 2005, and completed state trials in summer 2012. However, further upgrades were abandoned and RA-78854 remained the only Il-76MD-90 aircraft. In 2003, Russia's Volga-Dnepr Company ordered a newly built Il-76TD-90VD (VD for Volga-Dnepr) civilian version from Tashkent, powered by PS-90A76 engines; seven aircraft were completed.

On 20 December 2006 the Russian government decided to launch production of the Il-76 in Russia, at the Aviastar-SP factory in Ulyanovsk. At the same time, the aircraft was to be subject to an extensive update. The Ilyushin Design Bureau received more than 6 billion roubles (USD200 million at the then exchange rate) for the Kuznetsk-2 (named after a town in Russia) research and development programme that covered the design of the new Il-76MD-90A, also known as izdeliye 476. According to a government order of December 2006, aircraft '476' was to complete qualification trials by 2009. In fact, design of the aircraft only began in 2008. The first flying Il-76MD-90A, serial number 01-02 (serial number 01-01 is a static test airframe), registration RA-78650, first

Still retaining its original, Soviet-style national insignia, Russian Air Force Il-76MD '01 Red' carries the honorific name of Air Marshal Nikolay S. Skripko. The operating unit is the crew conversion centre based at Ivanovo. (Piotr Butowski)

flew at Ulyanovsk on 22 September 2012, with a crew commanded by Nikolai Kuimov. As of mid-2016 the aircraft had accomplished the first stage of acceptance tests and was being fitted with specific military systems (including a self-defence system and coded communication equipment). The second stage of tests was expected to begin in spring 2016 and to finish after a period of around six months, but had not commenced as of summer 2016. The next two aircraft were delivered to Beriev in Taganrog (serial number 01–03 on 21 November 2014 and serial number 01–04 on 29 April 2015) where they are being converted into prototypes of new special duty aircraft, one becoming the A-100 airborne early warning and control aircraft and the second, reportedly, the A-60 airborne laser gun (details of both are provided in Volume 1).

Production and operators

After two flying prototypes and a static test airframe had been completed at the Ilyushin facility in Moscow, production of the Il-76 began at Tashkent aircraft factory in the Uzbek SSR in 1973. The Soviet Air Force received its first Il-76 in June 1974. Commercial operations with Aeroflot began in December 1976. After the collapse of the USSR, production continued for a few years at a decreasing pace and had almost ceased entirely by 1995; only single airframes have been completed in the years since, making use of components completed earlier. The Tashkent factory completed a total of 944 airframes; this number includes 52 Il-78 aerial refuelling tankers and 30 A-50/EI early warning aircraft (see Volume 1). A new production line at Ulyanovsk began work in 2012 and had completed five aircraft by the end of 2015. Russia intends to manufacture 12 aircraft per year in Ulyanovsk; this rate is to be reached by 2020.

According to the best available estimates, around 360 aircraft remain in active service worldwide. The Russian Air Force is the largest operator with around 120 Il-76s (of which only around 80 are airworthy) based at Orenburg, Pskov, Seshcha, Taganrog and Tver operational bases, as well as the Ivanovo crew conversion centre. Other state operators in Russia have a total of around 20 aircraft, half of them flown by the Ministry of Interior. Additional military operators of the Il-76 comprise Algeria (17 aircraft), Angola (three), Armenia (three), Azerbaijan (three), Belarus (six), China (17), India (17), Iran (eight), Libya (17, present status unclear), North Korea (three), Syria (four), Ukraine (five) and Uzbekistan (three). The largest civilian operators include Aviakon (six aircraft), Abakan Air (five), SilkWay Airlines (six) and Volga-Dnepr (three).

The first and currently the only customer for the new Il-76MD-90A produced in Ulyanovsk is the Russian Ministry of Defence. On 4 October 2012 the Ministry of Defence signed a contract with United Aircraft Corporation – Transport Aircraft (UAC-TA) for the delivery of 39 new Il-76MD-90A to be manufactured by Aviastar-SP by 2018 (two prototypes, including one static example, and two airframes for Beriev were completed according to another, earlier contract). The value of the contract amounted to 139.42 billion roubles, which equates to 3.57 billion roubles or more than USD110 million (at the then exchange rate) for each aircraft. The first aircraft from this contract, serial number 01-05 (RF-78653), performed its maiden flight on 14 August 2015 and was been handed over to the Ministry of Defence in Ulyanovsk on 2 December 2015. The following day, the aircraft was flown to its permanent location at the 610th Transport Aviation Crew Conversion and Combat Training Centre at Ivanovo. The name *Victor Livanov* has been assigned to the aircraft, in recognition of the general manager of the Ilyushin Company between 1997 and 2014.

In 2015, Ilyushin reported that the final aircraft from the aforementioned contract for 39 Il-76MD-90As will be delivered in 2021, and not in 2018 as previously scheduled. Simultaneously, the company reduced the expected maximum output rate from 18 to 12 aircraft per year; this rate is to be reached by 2020. Russia claims that Algeria, Iran, Kazakhstan and South Africa could become the first foreign customers for the Il-76MD-90A.

The Russian Air Force also intends to order an upgrade for around 40 of the newest (latest built) Il-76MD aircraft, bringing them to Il-76MD-M standard. The Il-76MD-M project was ordered in December 2012 within the scope of the Kuznetsk research and development programme; the requirements were issued on 17 March 2013. The Minis-

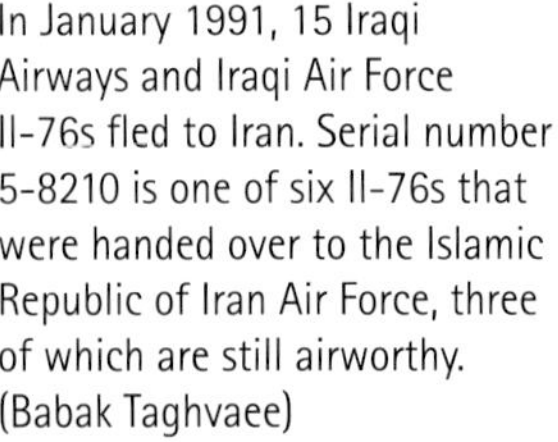

In January 1991, 15 Iraqi Airways and Iraqi Air Force Il-76s fled to Iran. Serial number 5-8210 is one of six Il-76s that were handed over to the Islamic Republic of Iran Air Force, three of which are still airworthy. (Babak Taghvaee)

This Il-76TD is operated by the Angolan Air Force, or Força Aérea Nacional de Angola. It is the only example of the type in Angolan service.
(Alex Rankin)

try of Defence has assigned two aircraft for the upgrade. The first of them, RF-76746, comes from the Taganrog regiment and was upgraded by Ilyushin at Zhukovsky. It first flew after the upgrade on 28 February 2016, with Nikolay Kuimov at the controls.

Ilyushin expected that Il-76MD-M series upgrades would be contracted in 2016 and that in the third quarter 2016 the first two aircraft would arrive at Zhukovsky for the upgrade. Series upgrades will take 12 years; they will be conducted by the Ilyushin facility in Zhukovsky.

Variants

Il-76M is the oldest version still in limited use; **Il-76T** is its civilian derivative.

Il-76MD, as described, is the main version in service with the Russian Air Force; **Il-76TD** is its civilian derivative.

Il-76MF (for Fuselage) is 6.6m (21ft 8in) longer thanks to two additional segments inserted into the fuselage. The Il-76MF can carry 186 paratroopers, or 305 troops in double-deck configuration, or four armoured personnel carriers. It is powered by four PS-90A76 turbofans and has the Kupol-III-76MF targeting, navigation and piloting system. The maximum take-off weight has been increased to 210,000kg (462,971lb), the maximum payload to 52,000kg (114,640lb), and the range with a 40,000kg (88,184lb) payload is increased to 5,800km (3,604 miles).

Il-76MD-90 is a mid-life upgrade with PS-90A-76 turbofans that can achieve a range of 4,500km (2,796 miles) with a maximum payload of 50,000kg (110,231lb). The aircraft is equipped with the modernised Kupol-III-76ME system and a 'glass' cockpit with five multifunction displays; the flight crew is reduced from six to five.

Il-76TD-90 and **Il-76TD-90VD** is a standard-fuselage civilian version with PS-90A-76 turbofans and new avionics; VD denotes the Volga-Dnepr airline. The aircraft features a flat undernose radome since the RLS-P navigation and targeting radar has been removed.

Il-76MD-90A (**izdeliye 476**) is a significantly improved version for Russian production, built according to new digital documentation (previous versions were made in Tashkent using paper documentation) and on new tooling. The most important novelty

Il-76MD-90A RF-78653, named *Viktor Livanov*, is the first aircraft completed under a contract for 39 Il-76MD-90As placed by the Russian Ministry of Defence on 4 October 2012. It flew on 14 August 2015 and was handed over to the military on 2 December 2015. (Piotr Butowski)

in terms of airframe design is an entirely new wing construction. The wing is 2,700kg (5,952lb) lighter than before but allows the take-off weight to be increased to 210,000kg (462,971lb) and the maximum payload to be increased to 60,000kg (132,277lb). The new PS-90A-76 engines are rated at 142.2kN (31,967lbf) of thrust for take-off and have 12 per cent lower specific fuel consumption compared to the previous D-30KP2s; when required, the pilot can set the engines from the cockpit for a maximum thrust of 156.9kN (35,274lbf). As a result, the Il-76MD-90A can attain a range of 4,000km (2,485 miles) with a payload of 60,000kg (132,277lb), or a range of 5,500km (3,418 miles) with a payload of 48,000kg (105,822lb), or a range of 6,500km (4,039 miles) with a payload of 40,000kg (88,184lb) of payload; maximum range is 9,700km (6,027 miles). The TA-6 APU is replaced with a new TA12A-76. The new avionics suite, including the Kupol-III-76M(A) digital targeting, navigation and piloting complex, and KSEIS-KN-76 'glass' cockpit with eight LCDs was developed by the Kotlin Novator Company of St Petersburg; however, some reports indicate that only three aircraft from the order for 39 will receive the new Kupol complex while the remaining 36 will be completed with the older suite. The aircraft is fitted with the SAU-76 digital autopilot, which enables it to land in ICAO Cat. II conditions. Another new feature is the BKS-76 communication suite as well as the Press self-protection suite provided by TsNIRTI, which includes warning sensors, an active infrared jammer and flare dispensers. The crew is reduced to five.

Il-76TD-90A it to be a civilian derivative of the Il-76MD-90A, with military self-protection and communications systems removed.

Above: Il-76MD-M RF-76746 is the first aircraft to undergo this modest mid-life upgrade; it flew on 28 February 2016. (Sergey Lysenko)

An Il-76MD-90A simulator reveals the considerably revised 'glass' cockpit. (Piotr Butowski)

Il-76MD-14 is a provisional designation for a further development, beyond the Il-76MD-90A version, powered by future PD-14M turbofans rated at 153.0kN (34,392lbf). It is planned to fit the PD-14M to the Il-76MD-14 some time after 2018. The Il-76MD-14 would have a range of 4,780km (2,970 miles) with a maximum load of 60,000kg (132,277lb). This represents an increase of 780km (485 miles) in comparison with the current Il-76MD-90A, and the maximum range of the new aircraft will be 10,800km (6,711 miles).

Il-76MD-M developed within **Kuznetsk** programme is a modest mid-life upgrade of the existing Il-76MD versions that incorporates some of the new avionics from the Il-76MD-90A; the traditional gauge-type cockpit remains unchanged. The aircraft also retains the current D-30KP2 engines. Externally, it can be easily distinguished by the electro-optical turret mounted under the nose, four windows for electro-optical missile-approach warning sensors in the end of the rear fuselage and in the nose, and seven 14-round 50mm (1.9in) decoy launchers in the rear of each main undercarriage nacelle. The service life of the upgraded aircraft is extended from 30 to 40 years.

The **Il-78** aerial refuelling tanker is described separately. The **A-50** and **A-100** early warning aircraft, **Il-82** radio-relay aircraft, and **A-60** experimental laser-gun aircraft are special derivatives of the Il-76 and are all described in Volume 1.

Ilyushin Il-78

NATO reporting name: Midas

The designated role of the Il-78 tanker in Russian Air Force service is support of the bomber force, in this case a Tu-95MS from the strategic aviation base at Engels.
(Evgeniy Kazennov)

Manufacturer

Designed by the Ilyushin Company in Moscow, series manufacture of the Il-78 was undertaken in Tashkent (Uzbekistan) between 1983 and 1993 by the aircraft factory named after V. Chkalov; later, in 2003–04, six aircraft were completed to meet an Indian order. At the time of writing, production was being re-launched at the Aviastar-SP factory in Ulyanovsk, Russia.

Role

An aerial tanker based on the Il-76MD transport, the Il-78 is currently the only tanker in service with the Russian Air Force.

Details for Il-78M

Crew

Compared to the basic Il-76MD transport, the crew of six includes a refuelling operator in the position usually occupied by the tail gunner.

Airframe and systems, powerplant and dimensions

As for the Il-76MD transport.

Weights

Maximum take-off 210,000kg (462,970lb).

Performance

Cruising speed 750km/h (466mph); speed during refuelling 430-590km/h (267-367mph); altitude during refuelling 2,000-9,000m (6,562-29,525ft); operational radius when 20,000kg (44,092lb) of fuel is delivered 5,050km (3,138 miles); operational radius when 30,000kg (66,139lb) of fuel is delivered 4,200km (2,610 miles); operational radius when 40,000kg (88,185lb) of fuel is delivered 3,450km (2,144 miles); operational radius when 50,000kg (110,231lb) of fuel is delivered 2,600km (1,616 miles); take-off distance 2,080m (6,824ft) at MTOW; landing distance 900m (2,953ft).

Avionics

As for Il-76, except that the RSBN-7S short-range radio navigation system has an added Vstrecha (rendezvous) mode for all-weather, day and night mutual detection and approach from a distance of 300km (186 miles). The system automatically controls the distance between the aircraft to be refuelled and generates a warning signal if the aircraft approaches too close (the closest permitted distance is 13m, 43ft).

Self-protection features and armament

None

Fuel transfer system

Two cylindrical fuel tanks are mounted inside the cabin (these are removable in the Il-78, but fixed in the Il-78M), providing a total capacity of 28,000kg (61,729lb) of fuel for the Il-78 and 36,000kg (79,366lb) for the Il-78M. Both versions can also transfer fuel from the standard wing torsion box tanks, which have a capacity of 84,840kg (187,040lb).

A removable additional fuel tank inside the Il-78's cabin. (Yevgeniy Yerokhin)

The fuel is transferred via three UPAZ-1 Sakhalin (Unifitsirovannyi Podvesnoy Agregat Zapravki, unified suspended refuelling gear) refuelling pods, designed by the Zvezda Company in Tomilino. Two pods are installed under the wing and the third pod is suspended on the port side of the rear fuselage. The central pod is designed for refuelling a single heavy aircraft, whereas the underwing pods are used to transfer fuel to two lighter aircraft (in combat conditions, three tactical aircraft can be refuelled simultaneously).

The UPAZ-1 has a transfer rate 2,300 litres (607 gallons) per minute; the internal hose diameter is 52mm (2in). The Il-78M can carry the PAZ-1M refuelling pod (for heavy aircraft) on the middle hardpoint; this has an increased transfer rate of 2,900 litres (766 gallons) per minute. For the Il-78M-90A and Il-78M2 the new UPAZ-1M refuelling pod with a transfer rate of 3,000 litres (792 gallons) per minute is being developed to replace the UPAZ-1.

The UPAZ pod houses a reeled hose and a fuel transfer pump. The pod operates autonomously (without external power), i.e. power for deploying and winding up the hose and the fuel transfer pump is provided by ram air turbine. At least 26m (85ft) of the UPAZ's hose has to be unwound prior to the initiation of refuelling, which begins automatically after the drogue has captured the probe and which is stopped after the pre-set volume of fuel has been transferred. The refuelling operation can also be stopped manually by the operator, or automatically after the entire hose length is unwound or when the difference in speed between the aircraft exceeds 3m/s (591ft/

The PAZ-1M pod fitted to the port side of the rear fuselage of the Il-78M is designed for refuelling a heavy aircraft and offers a transfer rate of 2,900 litres (766 gallons) per minute. The pod houses a reeled hose and a fuel transfer pump powered by ram air turbine. (Piotr Butowski)

min). Refuelling can only be carried out during direct visibility (for night operations, lights are used).

The aircraft may also be used for refuelling four aircraft on the ground, usually on advanced airfields. In this case the fuel is transferred via four fuel hoses connected directly to fuel tanks inside the fuselage.

History

Initial design work on a new Soviet tanker began around 1970, using the airframe of the Il-76 transport that was then under development. It turned out, however, that the limited take-off weight of the early Il-76s meant that the capacity of the fuel tanks was insufficient for fuelling other aircraft. Conversion of the Il-76 into an aerial tanker became a realistic proposition only with the arrival of the Il-76MD with reinforced structure and take-off weight increased to 190 tonnes. A prototype of the Il-78 aerial tanker, registration CCCP-76556, was tested in flight on 26 June 1983, with a crew led by Vyacheslav Belousov.

The aircraft was officially commissioned on 1 June 1987. A prototype Il-78M, CCCP-76701, with increased weight, flew for the first time on 7 March 1987, again with Belousov at the controls. A modified Il-78MK (Konvertiruyemyi, convertible) version, a derivative of the Il-78M that could be converted to serve as a transport aircraft, was designed in 1992–93, but did not enter production. Several years later, this latter project was realised as the Il-78MKI version for India. The Il-78MK-90 was to be powered by PS-90A turbofans; it took part in a tender in India but lost out to the Airbus Defence and Space A330 Multi-Role Tanker Transport.

However, when India put a stop on its A330 purchase in 2016, Russia restarted negotiations for the sale of Il-78MKIs to New Delhi. Another export version, the Il-78V using Mk 32B hose-and-drogue refuelling pods provided by Flight Refuelling Limited of the UK, remained a paper project.

Production and operators

A total of 46 tanker aircraft were completed at the Tashkent factory between 1983 and 1993, when production ceased. This total comprised 32 standard Il-78s, 13 Il-78Ms and one Il-78E for export to Algeria; subsequently, six Il-78MKI aircraft were assembled for India in 2003–04 using parts that had been manufactured earlier; this increased the total production to 52 aircraft.

The first five aircraft were delivered to the Soviet Air Force in 1985, arriving at the Ivanovo military transport aviation training centre. The first operational unit, the 409th Aviatsionnyi Polk Samolotov-Zapravshchikov (APSZ, Tanker Aviation Regiment) at Uzin, Ukrainian SSR gained initial operating capability in 1987 and remained at this base with 23 aircraft after the disintegration of the Soviet Union. The next unit, the 1230th APSZ at Engels, Russia, received 19 Il-78s between 1989 and 1993. In December 1994 the unit was renumbered as the 203rd OAPSZ (O for Otdelnyi, independent), and in September 2000 it moved to Ryazan-Dyagilevo air base where it remains today. Currently, the regiment operates around 15 aircraft and is the only aerial tanker unit in Russia. Operationally, the tankers serve exclusively to support Tu-160 and Tu-95MS strategic bombers (except during exercises when they also supply tactical aircraft with fuel); in terms of organisation, the tankers are under the command of Long-Range Aviation.

Some of the Ukrainian aircraft were later used as transports with their refuelling equipment removed. In December 2008, Ukraine sold four Il-78s to Pakistan, where they received the local designation of Il-78MP; the first aircraft was delivered in December 2009. In December 2011, Ukraine sold three previously stored Il-78s to China, with subsequent restorative maintenance performed by the Mykolayiv repair plant. The first aircraft was delivered to China in October 2014, the second in June 2015 and the third in June 2016. As of mid-2016, Ukraine has no operational Il-78s.

In order to fulfil an urgent requirement for aerial refuelling tankers, China acquired three Il-78s from Ukraine. After overhaul at Mykolayiv, deliveries to the People's Liberation Army Air Force began in October 2014.
(Jenyk)

In service with the Pakistan Air Force, the 'Midas' has the specific designation Il-78MP. Supplied from Ukrainian stocks, the four aircraft were delivered to Pakistan beginning in December 2009. (Paul Hodges)

In February 2001, India ordered six Il-78MKI (I for India) tankers to be delivered from at Tashkent between February 2003 and December 2004. In 2005, China ordered four Il-78s from Russia (together with 34 Il-76 transports); however, the contract was never realised since there were no more unfinished airframes available at Tashkent.

Along with the decision to resume production of the Il-76MD-90A transport aircraft at Ulyanovsk in Russia, it was decided to develop a new Il-78M-90A tanker on the basis of the same aircraft. Development of the new tanker within the Perspektyvnyi Samolot Zapravshchik (PSZ, Future Tanker Aircraft) or Kuznetsk-2 programme was contracted by the Ministry of Defence on 19 December 2012; at the time, the prototype was to fly in 2014. The project was accepted by the Russian Air Force in July 2013. However, the programme has been delayed; production of the first Il-78M-90A, s/n 02-01, began at Ulyanovsk on 16 January 2015, and its maiden flight was expected in May 2016, although this failed to happen. In 2017 the Russian Ministry of Defence is expected to place an order for 31 tankers to be delivered beginning in 2018. Potential export customers include Algeria. In August 2013, the Ministry of Defence ordered Ilyushin to upgrade the current tanker fleet to Il-78M2 standard (under the Kuznetsk programme; the programme's codename is the same as for the transport version).

Variants

Il-78 is the initial version with a maximum take-off weight of 190,000kg (418,878lb) and smaller cabin fuel tanks (for a total of 28,000kg, 61,729lb). It can deliver 20,000kg (44,092lb) of fuel at a range of 3,700km (2,299 miles) or 40,000kg (88,185lb) at a range of 2,100km (1,305 miles). The aircraft is convertible between transport and tanker configurations.

Il-78M is the main operational version, as described.

Il-78MP is a version operated by Pakistan.

New Il-78M-90A features the Il-76MD-90A's airframe and PS-90A engines, as well as new UPAZ-1M refueling pods with a transfer rate of 3,000 litres (792 gallons) per minute. (Ilyushin)

Il-78MKI is the convertible version used by India and fitted with Israeli fuel transfer systems.

Il-78M-90A (**izdeliye 478**) is a new version developed within the framework of the **PSZ** or **Kuznetsk-2** programme and based on the Il-76MD-90A (izdeliye 476) transport aircraft manufactured in Ulyanovsk, Russia. The aircraft's maximum take-off weight will be 220,000kg (485,017lb); it will be able to deliver 40,000kg (88,185lb) of fuel at a range of 5,000km (3,107 miles). The aircraft will be convertible between transport and tanker configurations.

Il-78M2 developed within the **Kuznetsk** programme is to be a mid-life upgrade of existing Il-78 and Il-78M aircraft, with some new avionics (the traditional gauge-type cockpit remains unchanged). The aircraft also retains the current D-30KP2 engines.

FUTURE STRATEGIC TRANSPORT AND TANKER AIRCRAFT

Ilyushin Il-96-400TZ

Il-96-400T RA-96101, here still in Polyot livery, is now being converted into an Il-96-400TZ tanker version. Two aircraft are to be ready by November 2018. (Piotr Butowski)

At the end of its existence, the USSR developed a long-range wide-body airliner, the Il-96, which failed to win popularity among airline operators. The initial version, the Il-96-300 with accommodation for 300 passengers, completed its maiden flight on 28 September 1988, piloted by Stanislav Bliznyuk. On 14 July 1993 an Il-96 operated by Aeroflot made the type's first commercial flight, from Moscow to New York. 6 April 1993 saw the first flight of the Il-96M version, powered by Pratt & Whitney PW2337 engines and fitted with Rockwell Collins avionics. Its fuselage was stretched by 9.35m (30ft 8in) to accommodate up to 436 passengers. On 26 April 1997 the Il-96T (Transportnyi) was first flown, this representing a freighter conversion of the Il-96M. However, the cooperation with American industry proved unsuccessful. The Il-96M prototype was abandoned and in 2007 the Il-96T was converted to become the Il-96-400T with Russian PS-90A1 engines.

Including the prototypes, 28 Il-96 aircraft of all versions had been built by 2016 (the newest of these is Il-96-300 RA-96022 that first flew on 23 November 2015), 17 of which were in service at the time of writing. The main operator of the Il-96 is the Presidential Administration of Russia, which operates nine Il-96-300 aircraft, including one Il-96-300PU (Punkt Upravleniya, command post) version, one Il-96-300PU(M) version and two Il-96-300PU(M1) versions with VIP interior, expanded communications suite, surgeon module, and other features. Five Il-96-300s are operated by Cubana de Aviacion, one Il-96-400VPU (Vozdushnyi Punkt Upravleniya, airborne command post) is operated by Russia's Federal Security Service, one Il-96-300 is operated by Ilyushin and one Il-96-400T is operated by the Voronezh Aircraft Production Association (VASO) (VASO). Three Il-96-400T aircraft, previously operated by Polyot Airlines of Russia, are currently being overhauled and converted to become military VVIP and TZ versions, as described below. A further four aircraft at the Voronezh production plant are in various stages of completion.

The question of converting the Il-96 to serve as an aerial tanker was raised for the first time as early as 2003, but the final stimulus was provided by the financial problems suffered by Polyot. In summer 2013 the airline ceased operations with its three Il-96-400T aircraft and did not collect a fourth example ordered from the production plant. One of these aircraft, RA-96104 (serial number 01004) was converted to become an **Il-96-400VPU** special passenger version for Russia's Federal Security Service; it was handed over to the FSB on 5 November 2015. Another aircraft, RA-96102 (serial number 01002), was acquired by the Ministry of Defence on 23 May 2014 and was converted to become an **Il-96-400 VVIP** version with SBUS-96-400 special communications suite; it made a first post-conversion flight on 8 April 2016 and was handed over to the MoD on 27 July 2016. On the strength of a contract signed on 6 January 2015 between the MoD and the United Aircraft Corporation, the two remaining aircraft, RA-96101 (serial number 01001) and RA-96103 (serial number 01003), will be converted to become **Il-96-400TZ** (Zapravshchik, tanker) versions. According to the contract, the VASO plant in Voronezh is to complete the conversion of both tankers and deliver them to the Russian Air Force by 25 November 2018. If operations by the two converted tankers prove to be successful, production might be continued.
Another military aircraft developed on the basis of the Il-96-400 aircraft will be the Il-96VKP Zvyeno-3S airborne command post, described in Volume 1.

Manufacturer
Designed by the Ilyushin Company in Moscow, the series manufacture of the Il-96 was undertaken by the Voronezh Aircraft Production Association (VASO) in Voronezh.

Role
An aerial tanker based on the Il-96-400T freighter, the Il-96-400TZ is convertible between tanker and freighter configurations.

Details for Il-96-400TZ

Crew
The Il-96-400TZ is operated by two pilots, an on-board engineer and a refuelling operator.

Airframe and systems
The Il-96 is a conventional all-metal low-wing wide-body freighter. The swept wing has complex high-lift devices with inner and outer ailerons (the latter to provide damping moment), double-slotted and two-section single-slotted trailing-edge flaps, multi-section full-span leading-edge slats, three-section airbrakes and multi-section spoilers. The wing features 3.1m (10ft 2in) high winglets. The tail control surfaces include a variable-incidence tailplane, elevators and an inset two-section rudder. The flight control system is triplex fly-by-wire, with manual back-up. The undercarriage consists of three four-wheel bogies under the wing centre section, and a front leg with two wheels. All 14 wheels are the same size of 1300 x 480mm (51.2 x 18.9in).

Powerplant
The four Aviadvigatel PS-90A1 turbofans are each rated at 170.6kN (38,360lbf) for take-off and 32.4kN (7,275lbf) for cruise (Mach 0.8). A total of 116,300kg (256,398lb) of fuel is carried in the wing tanks. The aircraft has an OMKB VSU-10-02 auxiliary power unit.

Dimensions
Wingspan 60.105m (197ft 2in); maximum length 64.694m (212ft 3in); maximum height 17.249m (56ft 7in); wheel track 10.40m (34ft 1in).

Weights
Maximum take-off 270,000kg (595,248lb); maximum landing 220,000kg (485,017lb); maximum payload 92,000kg (202,825lb).

Performance
Maximum cruising speed 850-870km/h (528-541mph); maximum ceiling 13,100m (42,979ft); operational radius when 65,000kg (143,300lb) of fuel is delivered 3,500km (2,175 miles); range with 92,000kg (202,825lb) payload 5,000km (3,107 miles); range with 40,000kg (88,185lb) payload 12,000km (7,456 miles); maximum range 14,500km (9,010 miles); take-off distance 2,550m (8,366ft); landing distance 1,700m (5,577ft).

Avionics
The Russian-made electronic flight deck is provided with six multifunction displays, an inertial navigation system, Traffic Collision Avoidance System (TCAS) II system, Enhanced Ground Proximity Warning System (EGPWS) system, Honeywell RDR-4B weather radar, satellite navigation receivers, etc.

Fuel transfer system
Four tanks for a total of 65,000kg (143,300lb) of fuel will be installed inside the fuselage. In the rear fuselage will be a single UPAZ pod for refuelling strategic bombers; in contrast with the Il-78 there will be no provision for underwing refuelling pods. Only the fuel from the additional fuselage tanks is transferred to receiver aircraft.

Ilyushin Il-106

In September 2015, within the framework of the **PAK VTA** (**Perspektivnyi Aviatsionnyi Kompleks Voyenno-Transportnoi Aviatsyi**) programme, the Ilyushin Design Bureau was tasked with conducting research and development work under the project name **Yermak** (named after a 16th-century Cossack, who conquered Siberia on behalf of Russia). This calls for the design of a heavy transport and troop-carrier aircraft with a load capacity of 80,000kg (176,370lb), placing it between the Il-76 and the An-124. Preliminary work on the general concept of the aircraft was conducted in 2013. The requirements for the aircraft include the capability to carry the entire suite of equipment utilised by an airborne division, and the ability to operate from short, unpaved airstrips. Thanks to multi-wheel low-pressure landing gear, the aircraft will be capable of unloading troops on a 1,200m (3,937ft) unpaved airstrip. The pilot project was to be ready by June 2016 and the preliminary design was to be finished in November 2017.

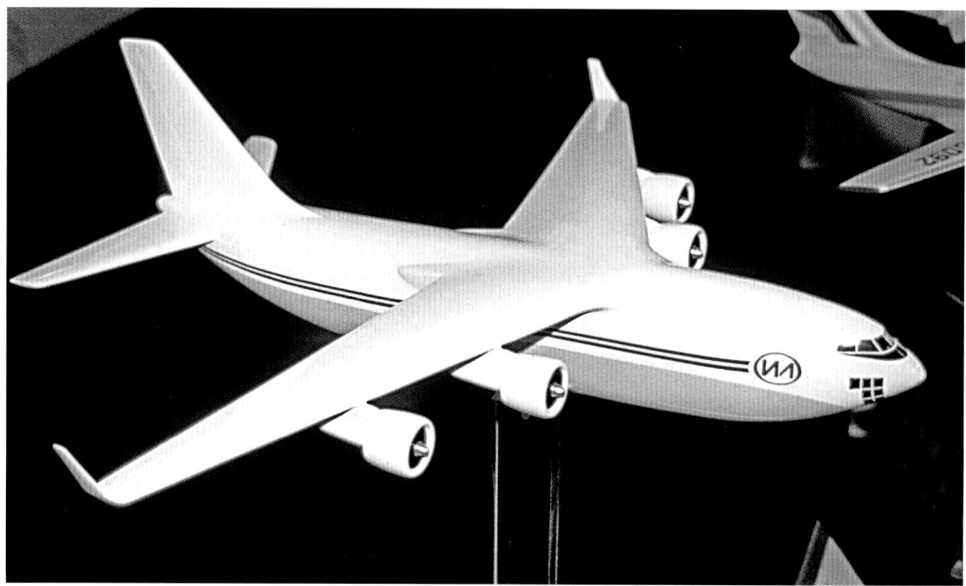

A scale model of the Il-106 in the form presented 25 years ago.
(Piotr Butowski)

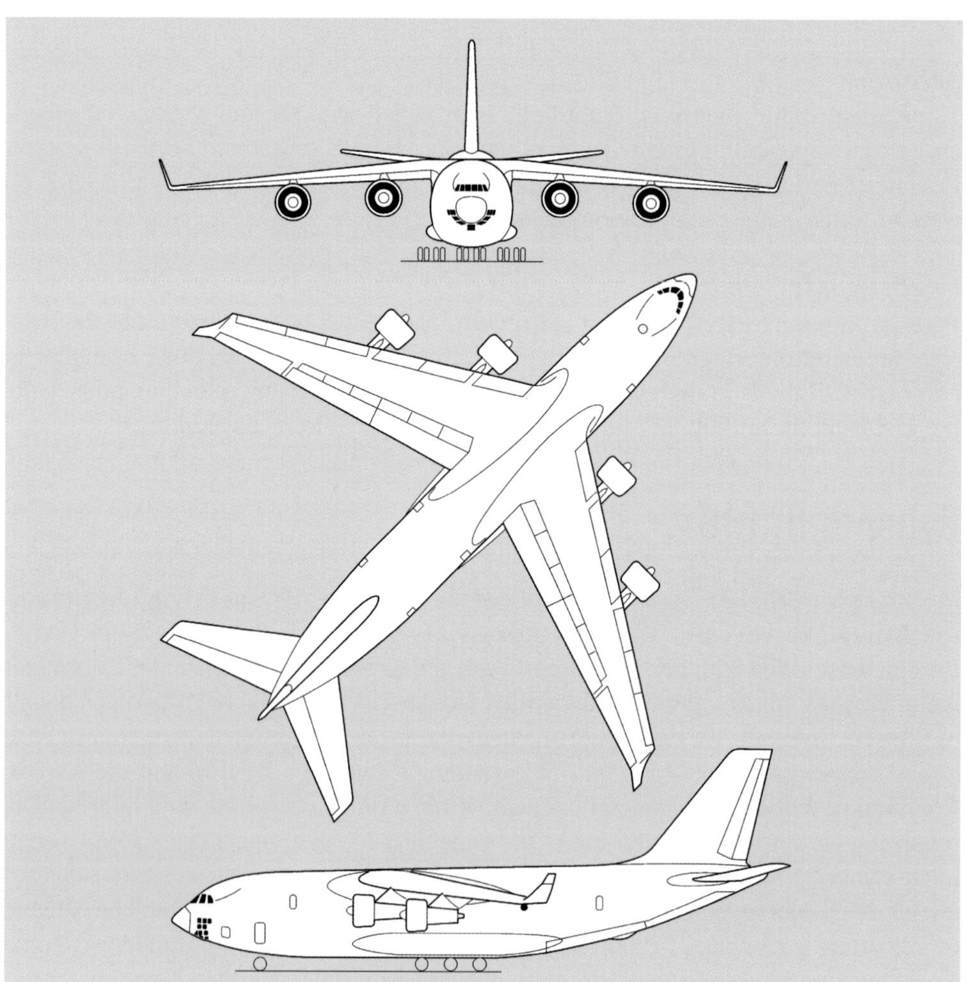

The super-heavy Il-106 transport aircraft project may be revived under the current PAK VTA programme.
(Piotr Butowski)

The PAK VTA programme is making use of the Il-106 design, first schemed by Ilyushin during 1987–92 as an equivalent to the American Boeing C-17 Globemaster III; the new aircraft will retain this original designation.

The Il-106 will be powered by four turbofan engines, initially employing the PS-90A1 rated at 170.6kN (38,360lbf) and later new engines of a similar class, probably the Aviadvigatel PD-14M. If Russia manages to develop new engines in the 35-tonne thrust class, the Il-106 will be built as a twin-engine aircraft. Based on the current, highly speculative designs, Russia has three engines available in this class: the Kuznetsov NK-65 (29.5 tonnes of thrust) and NK-35R-32 (35 tonnes) utilising the core of the NK-32 engine as used in the Tu-160, and the Aviadvigatel PD-35 (35 tonnes) based on the upgraded core of the PD-14 engine as used in the MC-21 airliner.

However, the Il-106 is at the bottom of the list as regards Ilyushin's current priorities, after the lightweight Il-112 and the medium Il-214 (see Chapter 4). As a result, a possible maiden flight of the Il-106 is not likely before 2025. In the meantime, the design will undoubtedly be significantly revised.

Ilyushin Il-106 specification (1992 design)
Powerplant: four Kuznetsov NK-92 turbofans, each rated at 176.5kN (39,683lbf).
Dimensions: wingspan 58.5m (191ft 11in); maximum length 57.6m (189ft); height 19.925m (65ft 4in); cabin length 34m (111ft 7in); cabin width 6m (19ft 8in); cabin height 4.6m (15ft 1in).
Weights: empty operating 126,250kg (278,334lb); maximum take-off 258,000kg (568,792lb); maximum take-off from rough runway 233,000kg (513,677lb); maximum payload 80,000kg (176,370lb).
Performance: cruising speed 820-850 km/h (510-528 mph); ceiling 9,000-12,000m (29,528-39,370ft); range with maximum payload 5,000km (3,107 miles); ferry range 17,750km (11,029 miles).

THEATRE AND SPECIAL-PURPOSE TRANSPORTS

The legacy of Soviet theatre transports

One of the assumptions behind the books in this series is that they should include only aircraft designed, or at least produced in Russia. However, there are several important types that were created within the USSR, but outside of Russia, the importance of which merits inclusion. Among them are the An-12, An-26 and An-72 theatre transports. These were created by a design team from Antonov in Kiev, in the Ukrainian SSR, and were produced in the Russian (An-12, in Irkutsk and Voronezh; An-72, in Omsk), Ukrainian (An-26, in Kiev; An-72, in Kharkiv) and Uzbek (An-12, in Tashkent) SSRs. However, as all of them still serve in significant quantities within Russia's air arms, they are included in this chapter.

The An-12 proved to be one of the most successful military transport aircraft of Soviet design, and as well as continued military use in Russia and elsewhere, derivatives of the 'Cub' remain in production in China to this day. (Avtor)

Antonov An-12

NATO reporting name: Cub

Seen landing with its port outboard AV-68 propeller feathered, An-12BK '17 Yellow' is operated by the Russian Navy. (Avtor)

Manufacturer

Developed by the Antonov Design Bureau in Kiev, Ukraine, series manufacture of the An-12 was undertaken by three factories: Irkutsk and Voronezh in Russia, and Tashkent in Uzbekistan.

Role

For many years the An-12 was used by the Soviet military as the standard aircraft for the transport of airborne troops and air assault missions. Today it has been replaced in these roles by the larger Il-76, but the An-12 still remains in service in Russia as an auxiliary transport, dispersed across various air bases. Electronic intelligence and electronic warfare versions are also in small-scale use.

Details for Antonov An-12BK

Crew

The An-12's crew of six comprises two pilots, a navigator, two flight technicians and a communications officer. A rear gunner is included on some aircraft.

The antiquated cockpit of the An-12. (Stanilav Bazhenov)

Airframe and systems

The An-12 is a four-engine shoulder-wing monoplane with unswept wing and conventional tail unit. The wing structure is of the double spar, box type. Double-slotted trailing-edge flaps are installed in the wing centre section; single-slotted flaps are fitted in each centre wing panel, and two-section ailerons (with tabs) are fitted on each outer panel. The tail unit has elevators (with tabs) and a rudder (with tab). The aircraft has a mechanical flight control system; the trailing-edge flaps are hydraulically actuated. The undercarriage has steerable twin nosewheels; each main unit consists of a four-wheel bogie, and these retract into the nacelles on the fuselage side.

Powerplant

The An-12 is powered by four Ivchenko Progress AI-20M turboprops each rated at 3,169ekW (4,250ehp) for take-off, driving 4.5m (14ft 9in) diameter four-blade variable-pitch AV-68 propellers; a TG-16M auxiliary power unit is fitted in the port undercarriage nacelle. The fuel volume is 29,600 litres (7,818 gallons), equivalent to (22,066kg, 48,633lb), carried in the wing and below the cabin floor. Auxiliary fuel tanks can be installed in the cargo hold for ferry flights.

Dimensions

Wingspan 38.028m (124ft 9in); length 33.11m (108ft 7.5in); wing area 121.73m^2 (1,310 sq ft); height 10.53m (34ft 7in); cabin length at floor 13.5m (44ft 3in); cabin width 3.1m (10ft 2in); cabin height 2.6m (8ft 6in); wheelbase 10.82m (35ft 6in); wheel track 4.92m (16ft 2in).

Weights

Empty, operating 35,140kg (77,470lb); maximum take-off 61,000kg (134,482lb); maximum landing 58,000kg (127,868lb); maximum payload 20,000kg (44,092lb).

Y-8C serial number 20143 is on strength with the People's Liberation Army Air Force's 13th Transport Division, and is based at Kaifeng.
(Top 81.cn)

Performance

Maximum speed 775km/h (482mph); cruising speed 550-600km/h (342-373mph); service ceiling 10,200m (33,465ft); range with full payload 2,000km (1,243 miles); range with full fuel 5,800km (3,604 miles); take-off distance 1,230m (4,035ft); landing distance 1,125m (3,691ft).

Transport capabilities

The aircraft can accommodate up to 20,000kg (44,092lb) of cargo or 91 troops when landing conventionally. Alternatively, military hardware of up to 16,000kg (35,274lb) or 60 paratroopers can be accommodated on two platforms when parachuting. The cargo hold is unpressurised except for the small front compartment for 14 persons of a reserve crew, which is pressurised to 7.1psi differential; a heating system and oxygen masks for troops are installed inside the cargo cabin. The freight hold is accessed via rear doors; the cargo is handled by 1,500kg (3,307lb) GL-1500DP remotely controlled winches and a 2,300kg (5,071lb) telpher.

Avionics

The aircraft has an RBP-3 navigation/targeting radar under the nose for precise air-landing; some aircraft have the more powerful Initsiativa-4 radar, distinguished by a much larger radome. Other items of avionics include the NAS-1B1-28 or DISS-013-12 Doppler navigation system, KS-SG heading system, AP-28D1 autopilot, ARK-11 radio direction finder, RV-2 or RV-5M radio altimeter, SP-50 instrument landing system, and RSBN-2S short-range radio navigation system (TACAN). R-832M or R-863 plus R-837 or R-856MA communications radios are also fitted.

Seen at Karaganda in 2015, this An-12 is operated by the Kazakhstan Air Force. Reportedly only a single example remained in active use with this operator in 2016.
(Alexander Golz)

Self-protection features

Some aircraft have a DB-65U tail turret with two flexible AM-23 23mm cannon, a KPS-53A optical sight and radio rangefinder. The Sirena radar warning receiver is fitted as standard. As an option, the aircraft can be fitted with KDS-155 chaff/flare launchers on the fuselage sides, for a total of 120 50mm (1.9in) decoys.

Armament

A small bomb rack (two on older aircraft) under each main undercarriage nacelle can be used to carry 100kg (220lb) FotAB-100-80 flare bombs in order to illuminate the landing area at night.

History

The An-12 was developed as the first Soviet military transport aircraft specialised for the air assault (air-landing) mission and equipped with equipment for dropping troops and equipment from the air. A crew headed by Yakov Vernikov tested the first An-12 (or izdeliye T) in flight on 16 December 1957.

Production and operators

A total of 1,253 aircraft were built in the Soviet Union including 155 in Irkutsk (1957–62), 258 in Voronezh (1960–65) and 840 in Tashkent (1962–72). The USSR exported 183 An-12s to 14 countries. Subsequently, many ex-Soviet aircraft were re-exported and An-12s remain popular in Africa, e.g. in Angola, Congo and Zimbabwe, where they are typically operated with Russian or Ukrainian crews. In the mid-1970s, China began series production of the An-12BK under the local designation Y-8 (Yunshuji-8).

The first An-12s entered service with the Voyenno-Transportnaya Aviatsiya (VTA, Military Transport Aviation) of the USSR in May 1959, and for almost 20 years the type

was the basic transport aircraft for the Soviet Air Force. During the large-scale exercise Dvina in 1970, a formation of approximately 200 An-12s dropped 8,000 paratroopers and heavy armaments within a space of 22 minutes. In its primary roles the An-12 was replaced by the larger Il-76 in the 1970 and 1980s. However, around 65 An-12s remain in Russian military service as auxiliary transports and can be found among various support units, normally being assigned to composite air regiments or squadrons together with other transport aircraft. Some An-12s (NATO reporting name Cub-C) are used as escort jamming aircraft, as described in Volume 1.

Variants

The basic transport versions of the An-12 (all of which received the NATO reporting name Cub-A) were the An-12A, An-12B and An-12BK, with the last of these currently being the most common version. In addition to the main versions presented below there were numerous prototypes and specialised variants.

An-12 was the early production model powered by four Kuznetsov NK-4 turboprops; maximum take-off weight was 54,000kg (119,050lb).

An-12A of 1962 received heavier but more reliable Ivchenko AI-20A turboprops; the maximum take-off weight was increased to 56,000kg (123,459lb) and was later raised to 61,000kg (134,481lb) when the wing centre-section was strengthened.

An-12B of 1963 was powered by AI-20M engines; it featured increased fuel capacity and a TG-16 APU was added for autonomous operations.

An-12P, **An-12AP** and **An-12BP** were similar to the An-12/A/B respectively, but with additional fuel below the cabin floor.

An-12BK became the most widely used version, with fuel capacity increased once again, a cargo cabin widened by 100mm (3.9in), and rear doors widened. A pressurised compartment was introduced for cargo personnel and spare crew aft of the flight deck. As described.

An-12RR (NATO reporting name Cub-B) was an electronic intelligence aircraft developed in the 1960s, and featuring numerous antennas, in many different configurations; this variant is no longer in service.

An-12PP (NATO reporting name Cub-C) and **An-12PPS** (NATO reporting name Cub-D) are standoff electronic countermeasures aircraft, described in detail in Volume 1.

Y-8 (**Yunshuji-8**) is a designation that applies to Chinese versions and derivatives of the An-12, some of which remain in production.

Ethiopia originally operated 16 An-12s, but numbers have since been greatly reduced. Serial number 1503 is one of the few aircraft to remain in service, and was overhauled locally by Dejen Aviation. (via Pit Weinert)

Antonov An-26

NATO reporting name: Curl

The An-26RT is a tactical radio relay aircraft used for extending tactical communication range. This versions features a large number of sword-type antennas dispersed around the fuselage. (Michael Mizikaev)

Manufacturer

Developed by the Antonov Design Bureau in Kiev, Ukraine, series manufacture of the An-26 was undertaken by the neighbouring factory in Kiev.

Role

A derivative of the An-24 short-haul passenger turboprop, the An-26 is a light auxiliary transport with a rear ramp. For other roles, see Versions.

Crew

The An-26's crew of three to five includes two pilots and a flight technician as standard, plus an optional navigator and communications operator.

Airframe and systems

The An-26 has a conventional configuration for a transport aircraft of its class, with shoulder wing, twin turboprop engines and a rear loading ramp. Single-slotted trailing-edge flaps are fitted on the wing centre section, with tracked double-slotted flaps on the centre panels and two-section ailerons on each wing outer panel. The flight control system is mechanical, with hydraulically actuated flaps.

Powerplant

The powerplant consists of two Ivchenko Progress AI-24VT turboprops, each rated at 2,103ekW (2,820ehp), driving 3.9m (12ft 9.5in) diameter four-blade AV-72T propellers. In the rear of the right engine nacelle is a Soyuz RU19A-300 turbojet, developing

8.83kN (1,984lbf) to provide additional thrust during take-off and climb, or in case of failure of one of the main engines. The turbojet is also used as an auxiliary power unit for starting the main engines and for driving the electric generators. A total of 7,100 litres (1,875 gallons) of fuel is carried in 14 wing tanks.

Dimensions

Wingspan 29.2m (95ft 9.5in); length 23.8m (78ft 1in); wing area 74.98m² (807.1 sq ft); height 8.575m (28ft 1.5in); cabin length 11.1m (36ft 5in) without ramp or 15.68m (51ft 5in) with ramp; cabin width 2.78m (9ft 1.5in) maximum; cabin height 1.91m (6ft 3in) maximum; wheelbase 7.651m (25ft 1in); wheel track 7.90m (25ft 11in).

Weights

Empty 15,850kg (34,943lb); maximum take-off 24,000kg (52,910lb); payload 5,500kg (12,125lb).

Performance

Maximum speed 540km/h (336mph); cruising speed 430-435km/h (267-270mph) at 6,000m (19,685ft); approach speed 195km/h (121mph); take-off distance over a 15m (50ft) obstacle 1,370m (4,495ft); landing distance from 15m (50ft) obstacle 3,806ft (1,160m); ceiling 9,000m (29,530ft); range with full fuel 2,700km (1,678 miles).

Transport capabilities

The aircraft can accommodate a load of up to 5,500kg (12,125lb) including small military vehicles up to a weight of 1,300kg (2,866lb), or 40 paratroopers, or 30 paratroopers on folding seats along the cabin sides; in rescue configuration, the An-26 can carry 24 litter patients and one to three litter-bearers. The rear loading ramp is opened hydraulically; when opened in the air, the ramp can slid back horizontally under the fuselage

The cockpit of the An-26 is provided with conventional flight and navigation instruments. (Andreas Zeitler)

for easy airdropping. The ramp entrance width is 2.40m (7ft 10.5in) at the floor and 2.10m (6ft 11in) at the top; height of the ramp entrance is 3.15m (10ft 4in) or 1.564m (5ft 2in) in a vertical line. A single cabin-top electrical telpher has a capacity of 1,500kg (3,306lb). On the floor are two roller tracks, tie-down positions and mats.

Avionics

The aircraft has an RPSN-3N Groza-26 navigation/weather radar in the nose, OPB-1R bombsight for airdropping operations and a conventional set of flight and navigation instruments that includes RSBN-2S tactical air navigation system (TACAN), ARK-11 direction finder, MRP-56P marker beacon receiver and SP-50M instrument landing system. R-802GM UHF and R-836/US-SK HF communication radios are also fitted.

Self-protection features

The aircraft is fitted with the S-3M Sirena radar warning receiver.

Armament

Two bomb racks installed on the sides of fuselage were originally intended for 100kg (220lb) flare bombs for illuminating the landing area at night. In many local conflicts, mainly in Africa (Angola 1967–84, Ethiopia 1977, Mozambique 1978–83), as well as in Peru (1981), Nicaragua (1980s) and Cambodia (1979–89), the racks were used for standard bombs and the An-26 was pressed into service as a makeshift bomber.

History

The An-26's first prototype flew on 21 May 1969, piloted by Yuri Ketov; a few weeks later the aircraft debuted at the Paris Air Show. The An-26 is a development of the 52-seat An-24 local passenger turboprop of 1959 with a new, wider fuselage and rear loading ramp.

An-26 '10 Yellow' of the Ukrainian Air Force, seen in 2016. This example is fitted with twin bomb racks on the sides of fuselage, originally used for carriage of flare bombs. (Giovanni Colla)

An-26 '02 White' is operated by the Kazakhstan Border Guard. (Alexander Golz)

Production and operators

The first series-production aircraft flew in September 1969 and large-scale production took place between 1970 and 1986 in Kiev, Ukrainian SSR. A total of 1,398 aircraft were been built for military and civil use, and 420 of these were exported to 27 countries outside the Soviet Union. Series production as the Y-7 (Yunshuji-7) was carried out by China. Approximately 140 aircraft currently serve with the Russian military including An-26 (NATO reporting name Curl-A) standard light transport versions, An-26Sh (Shturmanskiy) versions for training navigators, and An-26M (Meditsinskiy) medical evacuation aircraft with a cabin equipped for reanimation and surgery. Another widespread version is the An-26RT (Re-Translator; NATO reporting name Curl-B) tactical radio relay aircraft. Further An-26 transports – some equipped for bombing – serve with around 25 military operators around the world.

Variants in military service

An-26 is the standard light transport version, as described.

An-26 executive aircraft (it has no specific designation; it is popularly called **Shtabnoy**, staff, or **Salon**, lounge) has 12 armchairs in the front of the cargo cabin (the rear part remains unchanged) and additional communication equipment.

An-26RT (Re-Translator, relay; NATO reporting name Curl-B) has Inzhir (fig) radio relay equipment for extending tactical communication range; this version features a large number of sword-type antennas dispersed around the fuselage. A total of 42 aircraft were converted into An-26RT versions by the ARZ-308 repair plant at Ivanovo, Russia. The aircraft was widely used in the conflicts in Afghanistan and Chechnya.

An-26Sh (Shturmanskiy, navigator) is a trainer for navigators; a total of 36 aircraft of this version were manufactured in Kiev.

An-26M (Meditsinskiy, medical) is a medical evacuation aircraft with a reanimation and surgery cabin with accommodation for four wounded; two aircraft were in service with the Russian Air Force as of early 2016.

Y-7H serial number 71126 is operated by the 101st Air Regiment of the People's Liberation Army Air Force, a unit directly assigned to the PLAAF Headquarters.
(Eagle photo)

In 2016 the Hungarian Air Force was the last NATO air arm still operating the An-26, with a small number remaining in service.
(Istvan Topeczer)

Antonov An-72

NATO reporting name: Coaler

An-72 '08 Red' is one of two examples operated by the Kazakhstan Air Force. The unique configuration of this aircraft is a result of the requirement for short take-off and landing (STOL) performance. (Alexander Golz)

Manufacturer

Developed by the Antonov Design Bureau in Kiev, Ukraine, series manufacture of the An-72 was undertaken in Kharkiv, also in Ukraine. In the early 1990s a small batch was assembled in Omsk, Russia.

Role

Light short take-off and landing (STOL) military transport, mostly used as an executive aircraft. See also An-72P border patrol version in Variants.

Crew

The crew of three comprises a pilot, co-pilot and flight engineer.

Airframe and systems

The An-72 is a shoulder-wing monoplane constructed of aluminium alloys, with some use of composite materials (980kg, 2,161lb); the cargo cabin has a rear access ramp. The slightly swept (17°), high aspect ratio (10.32) wing has significant anhedral (10°). Two squat turbofan engines protrude ahead of the wing, with the exhaust nozzles located on the upper surface of the wing; thanks to this feature, a lifting force is generated even when the aircraft is at zero speed. The surface of the wings, flaps and spoilers in the exhaust gas zone is made of titanium alloys. Additional high-lift devices include double-slotted trailing-edge flaps on the wing centre section, triple-slotted flaps and four sections of spoilers on each centre panel (two of which are raised prior to landing and two of which open automatically on landing via an undercarriage sensor), and two-section ailerons (with tabs) on the outer panels. Three sections of slats occupy

the entire leading-edge span outboard of the engine nacelles. The T-tail has the tailplane located beyond the zone affected by exhaust gas and aerodynamic disturbances behind the wing; the tailplane has a unique inverted leading-edge slat coordinated with the wing flaps. The two-section rudder comprises a rear section subdivided into two parts, the lower (with tab) being activated manually by the pilot and used for directional control in normal flight, the other being adjusted by means of actuators. The upper part of the rear section is used for low-speed flights, whereas the front section is used only to compensate for thrust asymmetry in case of failure of one engine. The undercarriage has steerable twin nosewheels and low-pressure tandem mainwheels that retract into bays on the fuselage sides. The wheel bays are opened only during the opening and retracting process, being closed when taxiing and parking in order to protect the landing gear from dust and dirt encountered on semi-prepared airstrips.

Powerplant

The aircraft is powered by two Ivchenko Progress D-36 series 3A turbofans (1A or 2A in the early series), each of which is rated at 63.74kN (14,330lbf), with thrust reversers. Seven fuel tanks inside the wing torsion box contain 12,950kg (28,550lb) of fuel.

Dimensions

Wingspan 31.89m (104ft 7.5in); length 28.068m (92ft 1in); wing area 98.53m^2 (1,061 sq ft); height 8.75m (28ft 8.5in); cabin length 10.50m (34ft 5.5in) without or 14.30m (46ft 11in) with ramp; cabin width 2.15m (7ft 1in) at floor or 2.50m (8ft 2in) maximum; cabin height 2.20m (7ft 3in); wheelbase 8.12m (26ft 8in); wheel track 4.15m (13ft 7.5in).

Weights

Empty 20,200kg (44,533lb); maximum take-off 36,500kg (80,469lb); payload 5,000kg (11,023lb) standard or 10,000kg (22,046lb) maximum.

Performance

Maximum speed 705km/h (438mph); cruising speed 550-600km/h (342-373mph); approach speed 180km/h (112mph); take-off distance 930m (3,051ft) at 33,000kg (12,132lb) weight; landing distance 420-465m (1,378-1,526ft); ceiling 11,800m (38,715ft); range with full fuel 4,800km (2,983 miles); range with full payload 1,350km (839 miles).

Transport capabilities

As a standard transport, the An-72 can accommodate loads of up to 10,000kg (22,046lb) in a pressurised cargo hold or 68 troops, or 57 paratroopers, or 36 wounded (including 24 litter patients).

Avionics

A Buran-72 navigation/weather radar is carried in the nose; Malva-4 Doppler is also provided for navigation. The PK-72 flight complex provides flight along a programmed path and landing approach to an altitude of 30m (98ft).

Self-protection features

When used in a dangerous environment, the aircraft may be fitted with 12 32-round 26mm (1in) flare launchers on each side of the fuselage for self-defence.

History

The An-72 was originally intended as a jet-propelled successor to the An-26, capable of being operated from short (700m, 2,297ft) soil-surfaced airstrips thanks to its significant thrust margin, powerful high-lift devices and implementation of the Coanda effect, i.e. generating additional lifting force from the flow of airstream from the engine nozzles over the upper surface of the wing and flaps (similar to the Boeing YC-14 of 1976). The first An-72 prototype, CCCP-19774, (NATO reporting name Coaler-A) featured a shorter rear fuselage and smaller wing when compared to subsequent production aircraft. The prototype flew on 31 August 1977, with a crew led by Vladimir Terskiy. Series production began in 1985 in Kharkiv, Ukrainian SSR. A further civilian and military derivative for export, the An-74 (NATO reporting name Coaler-B) remains in low-rate production.

Production and operators

The first series-production An-72 performed its initial flight on 22 December 1985, in Kharkiv, Ukraine; 112 An-72s had been completed by the end of production in around 1991. The An-74 entered low-rate production in December 1989. After the disintegration of the USSR, a Russian factory in Omsk attempted to launch production of the An-74. An aircraft assembled in Omsk using parts supplied from Kharkiv took off on 25 December 1993. However, only five aircraft had been completed when production stopped.

Due to its STOL capability, the An-72 was originally intended for special forces as well as for other specific military tasks including supplying dispersed aircraft near the front-line (e.g. independent small units of vertical/short take-off and landing fighters). However, the An-72 has never played such role in the Soviet or Russian armed forces; indeed, the concept of attack aircraft deployed close to the front line has been abandoned. Currently, the An-72's most common role in the Russian military is as an executive transport; approximately 30 aircraft are in military use in Russia. The An-72 was not exported. Military operators of the An-74 comprise Egypt (three), Iran (10) and Laos (one).

An-72P RF-72020 is operated by the Russian Border Guard. The aircraft's UPK-23 gun pod is visible on the starboard side of the lower fuselage, in front of the undercarriage nacelle. (Dmitry Belov)

After Russia, the major military operator of the 'Coaler' is Iran's Islamic Revolutionary Guard of Corps Air and Space. The IRGCASF fleet includes six An-74-200s (cargo), including serial number 15-2257, and four An-74TK-200s (passenger). (Babak Taghvaee)

Variants

An-72 (izdeliye 72; NATO reporting name Coaler-C) is the standard production military transport aircraft, as described.

An-72S (Salon, lounge) is the military executive version with 38 passenger seats in the front compartment; the rear compartment is large enough to accommodate a small vehicle or other load.

An-72V is an export version with crew of two, sold to Peru.

An-72P (Patrulnyi) is an armed border surveillance version operated by Russia's Border Guard (subordinated to the Federal Security Service, FSB). Of the 17 aircraft manufactured in 1990–91, several are now in use at Yelizovo air base on the Pacific coast. The An-72P has its crew complement increased from three to five (with an additional navigator and radio officer), additional navigation and communication devices (including instrument target indication to assist supporting coast guard ships), an OTV-124 (Optiko-Televizyonnyi Vizir) optical-TV sight installed in the port nacelle of the main landing gear, and three photographic cameras. The cargo cabin is divided into two compartments with seats for two additional crewmembers in the front at convex windows (the navigator to port and the radio officer on the starboard side), and a 7.0m (23ft) long cargo hold at the rear. The aircraft is armed with a built-in UPK-23 gun pod housed in the starboard side of the lower fuselage, just in front of the undercarriage nacelle. Up to 650kg (1,433lb) of weapons can be suspended on two underwing pylons (bombs or rocket launchers). Four racks inside the cargo cabin above the ramp can carry 100kg (220lb) bombs, which can be used when the ramp is slid under the cabin. The An-72P is able to patrol for 6.3 hours.

An-74 (NATO reporting name Coaler-B) is a civilian (or export military) version, and until recently remained in low-rate production at Kharkiv in many sub-variants. It is not used by the Russian military.

Other versions of the 1980s that remained in prototype form include the **An-72P** electronic countermeasures aircraft (escort jammer), the **An-72R** battlefield reconnaissance aircraft and the **An-71** (NATO reporting name Madcap) airborne early warning and control aircraft.

Antonov An-140-100

RA-41254 is the first An-140-100 completed for the Russian Air Force. It performed its first flight on 6 August 2011 and was handed over to Chkalovsky air base in January 2012.
(Piotr Butowski)

Manufacturer

Developed by the Antonov Design Bureau in Kiev, Ukraine, series manufacture for the Russian Ministry of Defence is undertaken by Aviacor in Samara, Russia; production also takes place in Kharkiv, Ukraine and Shahin Shahr, Iran.

Role

The An-140-100 is a regional commercial turboprop used as a staff transport by the Russian military.

Crew

The An-140-100 has a standard crew of two pilots.

Airframe and systems

A high-wing monoplane, the An-140-100 is of conventional all-metal construction.

Powerplant

Two Motor Sich TV3-117VMA-SBM1 turboprops each provide 1,864kW (2,500ehp) at take-off. This engine is derived from the Klimov TV3-117 helicopter engine, but in this

The cockpit of the An-140 features conventional instrumentation. (Augustas Didzgalvis)

application each unit drives a six-blade 3.72m (12ft 2in) diameter AV-140 propeller; an AI-9-3B auxiliary power unit if fitted. Up to 4,640kg (10,229lb) of fuel can be carried.

Dimensions

Wingspan 25.505m (83ft 8in); length 22.605m (74ft 2in); height 8.225m (27ft); wheel-base 8.125m (26ft 8in); wheel track 3.18m (10ft 5in).

Weights

Maximum take-off 21,500kg (47,399lb), maximum landing 21,000kg (46,297lb).

Performance

Maximum cruising speed 540km/h (336mph); long-range cruising speed 475km/h (295mph); ceiling 7,200m (23,622ft); range with maximum payload 1,400km (870 miles); range with 52 passengers 2,400km (1,491 miles); range with full standard fuel and 43 passengers 3,050km (1,895 miles); ferry range 3,700km (2,299 miles); required runway length 1,350 m (4,429ft).

Transport capabilities

The An-140-100 can accommodate up to 52 passengers or 6,000kg (13,228lb) of cargo.

Avionics

The conventional instrumentation includes a Buran A-140 weather radar, Kurs-93M VOR/ILS navigation, ARK-25 radio direction finder, SN-3301 satellite navigation, TCAS-94 (Traffic Collision Avoidance System), and other items. An Orlan-85ST HF radio is provided for communication.

History

The An-140 short-haul regional airliner was intended to replace the An-24, offering twice as much fuel efficiency, longer range, higher speed and improved levels of comfort. The first of two prototypes built by Antonov, civil registration UR-NTO, flew on 17 September 1997 in Kiev. In addition to the two production versions, the An-140 and An-140-100, Antonov repeatedly offered further modifications, but none of these has progressed beyond the design stage – and none is likely to do so. Projected versions included the An-140-200 with accommodation for 68 passengers, the An-140C freighter, the An-140T (An-142) military transport with a rear ramp and the An-140MP maritime patrol aircraft with additional fuel to provide for an 11-hour endurance. Each of these was offered in several sub-variants with different engines and avionics. For example, the An-140-330T was a project for a military transport aircraft with enlarged fuselage, powered by 2,237ekW (3,000ehp) Ivchenko AI-30 turboprops. Within Antonov's designation system, the first digit in the additional index denotes significant changes to the airframe ('200' series aircraft have a stretched fuselages, '300' series aircraft have increased-diameter fuselages); the second digit denotes an engine option and the third indicates the avionics option.

Production and operators

Series production of the An-140 has been launched in three locations: in Kharkiv in Ukraine, Shahin Shahr (Isfahan province) in Iran, and Samara in Russia. The first production aircraft completed in Kharkiv flew on 11 October 1999; the first aircraft manufactured in Shahin Shahr flew on 7 February 2001; the first aircraft manufactured in Samara flew on 28 May 2005. After two prototypes manufactured by Antonov in Kiev, a total of around 37 aircraft were built, comprising 11 in Kharkiv, 12 in Samara and 14 (several of which remained unflown) in Isfahan. As of summer 2016, 13 or 14 examples were in operation, including nine in Russia and two in Ukraine (used by Antonov and Motor Sich). All Russian An-140s are operated by the military; the only commercial user, Yakutia Airlines, ceased operations with its four aircraft in 2015.

In 2009–13 the Russian Ministry of Defence placed orders with the Samara factory for a total of 14 An-140-100 aircraft (10 for the Russian Air Force and four for the Navy), for use as small staff transports. However, in 2014–15, due to the Russo-Ukrainian conflict, the cooperation broke down and production of the An-140 in Samara ceased. No aircraft were assembled in 2015, while on 16 March 2016 the most recent An-140 (RF-08021 for the Russian Navy) flew at Samara; Samara claims that one more aircraft will be completed. By summer 2016, the Russian Ministry of Defence had received nine aircraft, five of which belong to the Air Force and are based at Chkalovsky and Yekaterinburg; the remaining four belong to the Navy and are based at Yeysk.

Variants

An-140 was the initial version designed to deliver 52 passengers over a distance of 2,200km (1,367 miles).
An-140-100 is the standard production version with the wing extended in length by 1m (3ft 3in), more fuel, and take-off weight increased by 500kg (1,102lb) in order to carry 52 passengers over a distance of 2,400km (1,491 miles); as described.
IrAn-140 Faraz is the local name of the aircraft assembled in Iran.

This Iranian-built IrAn-140 was one of two delivered to the Iranian Police in 2008. After an accident suffered by a civilian IrAn-140 in 2014, the Iranian Civil Aviation Organisation placed a ban on flights by this type and the two Police aircraft (serial numbers 2201 and 2202) were grounded.
(Babak Taghvaee)

Antonov An-148

RA-61723 is an example of the An-148-100E, 15 of which were ordered by the Russian Ministry of Defence in May 2013. Although designed by Antonov, production is handled by VASO, based in Yoronezh, Russia. (Stanilav Bazhenov)

Manufacturer

Developed by the Antonov Design Bureau in Kiev, Ukraine and serially manufactured by Antonov in Kiev, Ukraine, and by the Voronezh Aircraft Production Association (VASO) in Voronezh, Russia.

Role

The An-148 was developed as a commercial regional jet and is used as an executive aircraft by the Russian military.

Details for An-148-100E

Crew

The An-148 has a standard crew of two pilots.

Airframe and systems

In the An-148, Antonov's classic high-mounted swept wing with anhedral carries two engines. The lower lip of the engine intake is 1.65m (5ft 5in) above the ground, to protect the engines against foreign object damage. The wing control surfaces include double-slotted flaps (deflected 20° for take-off and 40° for landing) and ailerons at the wing trailing edge, nose flaps (deflected 22°) between the fuselage and engines, three sections of slats (deflected 19°) that occupy the entire leading-edge span outboard of the engine nacelles, as well as five sections of spoilers on each half wing. The T-tail has a fixed tailplane, and single-section rudder and elevators. The flight control system is the EDSU-148 of the fly-by-wire type.

Powerplant
Two Ivchenko D-436-148 turbofans, each rated at 66.97kN (15,058lbf) for take-off; in lighter versions of the aircraft (A, B) the same engines are rated for 62.76kN (14,110lbf) of thrust. An Ivchenko AI-450MS auxiliary power unit is installed in the tail. A total of 11,700kg (25,794lb) of fuel is carried in one centre-section and two wing tanks.

Dimensions
Wingspan 28.91m (94ft 10in); length 29.13m (95ft 7in); height 8.19m (26ft 10in); wing area 87.32m^2 (940 sq ft).

Weights
Empty operating 25,170kg (55,490lb); maximum take-off 43,700kg (96,342lb); maximum landing 36,250kg (79,918lb).

Performance
Maximum cruising speed 870km/h (541mph); maximum allowable Mach 0.88; ceiling 12,200m (40,026ft); range with 85 passengers 3,800km (2,361 miles); range with 75 passengers 4,400km (2,734 miles); required runway length 1,900m (6,234ft).

Transport capabilities
Typically, the An-148 carries 75 passengers. The maximum load comprises 85 passengers; the maximum payload is 9,000kg (19,842lb).

Avionics
The An-148 has standard avionics for a regional aircraft. These allow for ICAO Cat. IIIA landing, RNR-1 navigation, Reduced Vertical Separation Minimum (RVSM) aircraft spacing, and Terrain Awareness and Warning System/Traffic Collision Avoidance System (TAWS/TCAS). The RDR-4B or Buran A-148 weather radar is fitted. The KSEIS-148 (Kompleksnaya Sistema Elektronnoy Indikatsii i Signalizatsii, integrated system of electronic indication and signalling) 'glass' cockpit features five IM-16-1 multifunction displays. Other items of avionics include an R-855A1 communication radio and SAU-148 autopilot.

History
The An-148 project was launched in 2001 as a replacement for the Tu-134 regional jet, the design of which dates back to the 1960s. A first flight of the new aircraft was performed in Kiev on 17 December 2004.

Production and operators
Two factories cooperate in production of the An-148: the Russian VASO plant in Voronezh and the Ukrainian Antonov plant in Kiev. Final assembly lines have been opened at both facilities. Currently, only the An-148-100B and E and An-158 versions are in production. The aircraft commenced operations on 2 June 2009. By autumn 2016, 42 aircraft had been flown; the most recent of these was serial number 43-07, registration 61730, flown on 26 September 2016. This total comprises 29 aircraft assembled in Voronezh, 11 in Kiev, and two prototypes built in Kiev.

Equipped with the KSEIS-148 suite, the cockpit of the An-148 includes five IM-16-1 multifunction displays for the two flight crew. (Mitya Aleshkovsky)

Although intended as a commercial aircraft, the An-148 has been ordered mainly by Russia's state structures (which purchase aircraft exclusively from the Russian production line). The largest operator is the Russian Ministry of Defence, which on 7 May 2013 ordered 15 An-148-100E aircraft to be delivered from VASO between 2013 and 2017 (comprising one aircraft in 2013, four each in 2014 and 2015, and three each in 2016 and 2017). The total value of the contract was 18,438 million roubles, which is equivalent to approximately USD35 million per aircraft at the then exchange rate. The first aircraft (RA-61718) was handed over to the Ministry of Defence on 6 December 2013, and nine examples had been delivered by September 2016. Other Russian state customers are the Federal Security Service (FSB; three An-148-100EA aircraft), SLO Rossiya (three An-148-100EA) and the Russian Ministry for Emergency Situations (EMERCOM; two An-148-100EM). Commercial operators comprise Air Koryo (two An-148-100B), Angara Airlines (five An-148-100E) and Cubana de Aviacion (six An-158); Antonov operates another two and Ukraine's governmental airline has one aircraft, all as of mid-2016.

The future of further production of the An-148 is unknown. Although production of the aircraft is not subject to mutual Ukrainian and Russian embargoes, the cooperation ties between the two sides are diminishing. In order to complete the manufacture of aircraft already at an advanced stage of completion at the Voronezh plant, Russia ordered landing gear from the Russian Hydromash plant (previously the landing gear was delivered by Ukraine). Ukraine is also able to produce the aircraft independently, after having replaced less critical Russian components with indigenous items; however, it is uncertain that Ukraine will find customers for the aircraft. In the meantime, there have been no new orders for the An-148.

Variants

An-148-100 is the basic version, which typically carries 75 passengers (the maximum is 85 passengers); the aircraft is offered in A, B and E subversions, described below.
An-148-100A has a maximum weight of 38,950kg (85,870lb) and can carry 75 passengers over a distance of 2,100km (1,305 miles).
An-148-100B has a maximum weight of 41,950kg (92,484lb) and can carry 75 passengers over a distance of 3,500km (2,175 miles).
An-148-100E (as described) has a maximum weight of 43,700kg (96,342lb) can carry carries 75 passengers over a distance of 4,400km (2,734 miles).
An-148-100EA is an executive 49-seat sub-variant with a forward VIP compartment for two persons and an economy-class cabin for 47 passengers.
An-148-100EM is a sub-variant operated by EMERCOM that can be configured in five convertible versions including two passenger configurations and three combined passenger/medical evacuation configurations with two to six medical modules.
An-148-200 is a proposed high-density version for 89 passengers; it is also intended to include A, B and E sub-variants.
An-148-300 (previously **An-168**) is a project for an executive jet with range extended to 7,000km (4,350 miles) and accommodation for 12 to 14 passengers.
An-148-300MP (**An-168MP**) is a proposed maritime patrol aircraft based on this airframe.
An-158 is an extended-fuselage version with accommodation for 99 passengers, and in production in Ukraine only; a first flight was recorded on 28 April 2010.
An-178 is a military transport derivative produced by Antonov without Russian participation, and therefore beyond the scope of this book. A first prototype flew in Kiev on 7 May 2015.

Ilyushin Il-18

NATO reporting name: Coot

The Il-18 is now a rarity in Russian military service. Just 10 examples of different transport versions remained in the Russian Ministry of Defence inventory in 2016. (Stanislav Bazhenov)

Manufacturer

Developed by the Ilyushin Company in Moscow, series manufacture of the Il-18 was undertaken by Moscow's Znamya Truda plant (which currently belongs to Russian Aircraft Corporation MiG, within which it is incorporated as the Production Centre No. 2).

Role

Medium airliner, also used as a military staff transport. In the past, the Il-18 was one of the most widespread Soviet commercial airliners. In the 1960s, Il-18s carried 40 per cent of all Aeroflot passengers.

Crew

The crew of five consists of two pilots, a navigator, a communications officer and an on-board technician.

Airframe and systems

The Il-18 is a conventional all-metal low-wing monoplane with four turboprop engines.

Powerplant

The Il-18D is powered by four Ivchenko AI-20M turboprops, each rated at 3,126kW (4,250ehp), and driving AV-68I propellers. The Il-18B/V/E versions are powered by AI-20K engines each rated at 2,942kW (4,000ehp). The fuel volume amounts to 23,550kg (51,919lb) for the Il-18D and 18,600kg (41,006lb) for other versions.

Dimensions

Wingspan 37.4m (122ft 8in); length 35.9m (117ft 9in); height 10.165m (33ft 4in); wing area 140m^2 (1,507 sq ft); wheelbase 12.755m (41ft 10in); wheel track 9.0m (29ft 6in).

Weights
Empty operating 32,245-33,760kg (71,088-74,428lb); maximum take-off, **Il-18B/V**: 61,200kg (134,923lb), **Il-18E**: 61,400kg (135,364lb), **Il-18D**: 64,000kg (141,096lb); maximum landing, **Il-18B/V/E**: 52,000kg (114,640lb), **Il-18D**: 52,600kg (115,963lb); payload 13,500kg (29,762 b).

Performance
Maximum speed 650km/h (404mph) at 8,000m (26,247ft); ceiling 9,200m (30,184ft); maximum range, **Il-18B/V/E**: 4,800km (2,983 miles), **Il-18D**: 6,500km (4,039 miles).

Transport capabilities
As a passenger transport, the Il-18 could accommodate various configurations from 80 to 122 passengers, later reduced to 100 passengers.

History
The prototype Il-18 first flew on 4 July 1957. The first production version was the Il-18A, which was not successful due to its use of very unreliable Kuznetsov NK-4 turboprop engines. After a crash of one of the aircraft on 7 May 1958, operations by the Il-18A were suspended and the aircraft were converted to the Il-18B version with more reliable (although less economic) Ivchenko AI-20 turboprops. All subsequent versions were powered by AI-20 engines.

Production and operators
Between 1957 and 1969 the No. 30 Znamya Truda production plant in Moscow built 564 Il-18 aircraft, including 335 of the most popular Il-18V version and 122 of the Il-18D version. Only a few of them still remain in military service, including one example in North Korea. In 2016 the Russian Ministry of Defence operated 10 Il-18s (seven D, two V and one E versions).

Variants in service
Il-18V was the most popular version, with accommodation for up to 110 passengers, and was powered by AI-20K engines.

Il-18E is similar to the Il-18V but with accommodation for a maximum of 122 passengers in more comfortable seats and with an improved air conditioning system. A small batch was produced during 1965–66.

Il-18D is a version with range extended to 6,500km (4,039 miles) thanks to increased fuel capacity and AI-20M engines. This was the final production passenger version of the Il-18, and was manufactured during 1965–69.

Il-20 reconnaissance aircraft and **Il-22** airborne command and relay aircraft are based on the Il-18 platform and are described in Chapters 3 and 4 of Volume 1 respectively.

Il-38 is a maritime patrol aircraft derived from the Il-18D and described in Chapter 2 of this volume.

Ilyushin Il-62M

NATO reporting name: Classic

RA-86495 is one of six examples of the Il-62M that were still operated by the Russian Air Force in 2016. The fleet resides at Chkalovsky, outside Moscow. (Stanislav Bazhenov)

Manufacturer

Designed by the Ilyushin Design Bureau in Moscow, series manufacture of the Il-62 was undertaken in Kazan.

Role

Intercontinental airliner used as an executive aircraft for the command staff of the Russian Ministry of Defence.

Crew

The Il-62 is operated by a crew of five, comprising two pilots, a navigator, a flight engineer and a communications operator.

Airframe and systems

The Il-62 is a low-wing monoplane with a 35° swept wing (at quarter chord) and a T-shaped tail with an adjustable tailplane (0 through -9°). The wing features single-slot trailing-edge flaps, deflected by 30° for landing, ailerons and spoilers. The aircraft features a flight control system that is unique for this class of aircraft, with push-pull rod controls without amplifiers. The nose landing gear features twin wheels and the main landing gear struts are fitted with four wheels. Due to the engines being mounted at the rear, the centre of gravity of the empty aircraft is shifted aft. The main landing gear struts are mounted forward of the centre of gravity (as a result of which the empen-

nage could be made smaller and lighter), hence the empty aircraft can sit on its tail. To prevent this happening, an additional rear supporting strut with two small wheels was introduced, this being deployed only on the ground.

Powerplant
The four Aviadvigatel D-30KU turbofans are each rated at 107.87kN (24,251lbf) for take-off, and are mounted in pairs on the rear fuselage. Up to 105,300 litres (27,811 gallons) of fuel can be carried, equivalent to 86,870kg (191,516lb). A TA-6A auxiliary power unit is fitted.

Dimensions
Wingspan 43.20m (141ft 9in); length 53.12m (174ft 3in); height 12.35m (40ft 6in); wing area 279.55m^2 (3,009 sq ft); wheelbase 24.488m (80ft 4in); wheel track 6.8m 22ft 4in).

Weights
Maximum take-off 167,000kg (368,172lb); maximum landing 107,000kg (235,895lb); payload 23,000kg (50,706lb).

Performance
Maximum cruising speed 870km/h (541mph); ceiling 11,000m (36,089ft); range with maximum payload 8,300km (5,157 miles); range with 100 passengers 10,000km (6,214 miles); take-off run 2,250m (7,382ft); landing run 1,000m (3,281ft).

Transport capabilities
Typical layouts provide accommodation for between 138 and 168 passengers; the maximum number of passengers is 192. In 'Salon' (lounge) configuration, as used by the highest officials, there is a luxury forward compartment for the 'main passenger' and a rear compartment for accompanying personnel.

Avionics
The Il-62 includes standard airliner avionics that comply with ICAO Cat. II. The 'Salon' aircraft used by the highest-ranking commanders have additional communications equipment, including satellite communications, which is indicated by a long, flat antenna along the spine of the fuselage.

History
Ordered in 1960 to connect Moscow with the most distant cities of the USSR without the requirement for an intermediate landing, the Il-62 was the Soviet analogue to the Vickers VC10 from the United Kingdom. The prototype Il-62, CCCP-06156 (temporarily powered by AL-7PB turbojets from a Sukhoi Su-7 fighter-bomber, later replaced with NK-8 turbofans), made the type's maiden flight on 2 January 1963, piloted by Vladimir Kokkinaki.

Production and operators
After three flying prototypes and two static airframes had been completed by Ilyushin in Moscow, a total of 287 aircraft were manufactured in Kazan between 1966 and 1996, including 94 Il-62 and 193 Il-62M versions. Some unfinished airframes remained at the

The VIP interior of Il-62M RA-86572. In 'Salon' (lounge) configuration, the aircraft features a luxury forward compartment for the highest-ranking passengers and a rear compartment for accompanying personnel.
(Alexey Ereshko)

factory, one of which was completed later, in 2004. The Il-62 began scheduled operations with Aeroflot on 8 September 1967. On 8 January 1974 the airline began scheduled operations using the considerably improved Il-62M with D-30KU turbofans and increased fuel. Thanks to these changes, the new aircraft could achieve a distance of 10,000km (6,214 miles) with 100 passengers, compared to 9,200km (5,717 miles) for the previous version. The high-lift devices on the wing, as well as other structural and avionics components, were also improved. In 1978 the Il-62M (designation unchanged) entered production with its take-off weight increased to 167,000kg (368,172lb).

As of 2016 it was reported that 12 aircraft were in use, including six examples operated by the Russian Air Force (all based at Chkalovsky, outside Moscow), two in North Korea and one in each of Belarus, Gambia, Sudan and Ukraine. All aircraft remaining in service are Il-62Ms with increased take-off weight.

Outside Russia, the Il-62M remains in limited military service, with single examples operated by Belarus, Gambia (C5-RTG seen here), Sudan and Ukraine.
(Bob Cornez)

Variants

Il-62 that entered operation in 1967 had NK-8-4 engines, a take-off weight of 161,000kg (354,944lb) and a range of 9,200km (5,717 miles) with 100 passengers.

Il-62M that entered operation in 1974 had D-30KU engines, a take-off weight of 165,000kg (363,763lb) and a range of 10,000km (6,214 miles) with 100 passengers.

Il-62M of 1978 has a reinforced wing (to extend service life) and weight increased to 167,000kg (368,172lb); it is the only version still in operation.

Tupolev Tu-134A Balkany

NATO reporting name: Crusty

A single Tu-134A Balkany, UN-65683, is operated by the Kazakhstan Air Force, and was photographed departing Astana in 2015. The aircraft was developed as an executive military transport in the mid-1980s. (Alexander Golz)

Manufacturer

Developed by the Tupolev Design Bureau in Moscow, series manufacture of the Tu-134 was undertaken in Kharkiv, Ukrainian SSR.

Role

The Tu-134A Balkany is an executive aircraft intended for the use of command staff of air armies and military districts. The aircraft was converted from existing Tu-134A or Tu-134A-3 regional commercial aircraft, and is popularly known as 'Salon' (lounge).

Crew

The Tu-134A Balkany is operated by a flight crew of five, comprising two pilots, a navigator, a flight engineer, and a communications officer, the last of which is absent on commercial versions of this aircraft.

Airframe and systems

The Tu-134 is a low-wing monoplane with a 35° swept wing. The wing includes two-section double-slotted trailing-edge flaps, ailerons (with trim tabs) and spoilers. The T-tail incorporates a variable-incidence tailplane, elevators (with trim tabs), and rudder (with trim tab).

Powerplant

The Tu-134A is powered by two Aviadvigatel D-30 series II turbofans with thrust reversers, each rated at 66.68kN (14,991lbf) for take-off. The Tu-134A-3 version is powered by D-30 series III engines rated at 67.96kN (15,278lbf). A TA-8 auxiliary power unit is fitted

in the rear fuselage. A maximum of 16,500 litres (4,358 gallons) of fuel, equivalent to 13,200kg (29,101lb) is carried in six integral wing tanks.

Dimensions

Wingspan 29.01m (95ft 2in); length 37.047m (121ft 6.5in); height 9.144m (30ft); wing area 127.3m^2 (1,370 sq ft); wheelbase 16.04m (52ft 7in); wheel track 9.45m (31ft).

Weights

Maximum take-off 47,000kg (103,617lb); maximum landing 43,000kg (94,799lb); payload 8,200kg (18,078lb).

Performance

Maximum cruising speed 850km/h (528mph); service ceiling 12,100m (39,698ft); range with maximum payload 2,100km (1,305 miles); required runway length 2,200m (7,218ft).

Transport capabilities

Two typical cabin configurations provide accommodation for 26 or 31 passengers, including a VIP compartment at the front, a communication system room and a standard 'economy' compartment at the rear. The military staff versions, comprising the previous Tu-134AK and the current Balkany, are distinguished by an additional door on the port side of the rear fuselage, just forward of the engine. This door is 87cm (34in) wide and 142cm (56in) high, and means the accompanying personnel do not pass through the main passenger's cabin (the standard door is located on the port side of the forward fuselage). The additional door is fitted with an autonomous electrically-actuated ladder.

This Tu-134A-3 Balkany is a Ukrainian Air Force aircraft and was seen at Borispol in 2015. (Alexander Golz)

Tu-134 RF-65573 is one of around 20 examples that remained in Russian military service in 2016. These aircraft were converted from previous Tu-134AK aircraft in Minsk, Belarusian SSR. (Avtor)

Mission systems

The Balkany (Balkans) is a powerful HF radio communications system featuring a long antenna 'sting' protruding from the rear fuselage.

Avionics

The flight/navigation system of the Tu-134A Balkany meets ICAO Cat. II requirements.

History

During his visit to France in spring 1960, the Soviet leader Nikita Khrushchev travelled in a Sud Aviation Caravelle airliner and was surprised by the low noise level in the passenger cabin. After his return to the Soviet Union he ordered Andrey Tupolev to relocate the engines of his then latest passenger aircraft, the Tu-124, to the aft fuselage, as in the Caravelle. On 29 July 1963 the prototype Tu-134 (Tu-124A) made its maiden flight in Kharkiv, with Alexander Kalina at the controls. On 9 September 1967 the Tu-134 made its first scheduled flight from Moscow to Adler on the Black Sea Coast.

Production and operators

Tu-134s were produced by a plant in Kharkiv, Ukrainian SSR, between 1966 and 1984; production totalled 852 aircraft. The three main passenger versions are the Tu-134 with accommodation for 72 passengers, the most numerous Tu-134A version with accommodation for 76 passengers and a fuselage stretched by 2.1m (6ft 11in), and the Tu-134B with accommodation for 80 passengers. Subsequently, many Tu-134A and Tu-134B aircraft had their engines replaced by D-30 series III units; thus modified, these aircraft were designated Tu-134A-3 and Tu-134B-3 respectively.

In 1970 the Tu-134K military staff version was developed, with a VIP compartment and additional door at the rear of the fuselage; in total around 180 examples of the Tu-134K and Tu-134AK versions were built. These featured several different cabin configurations, accommodating between 26 and 47 passengers, and various communications suites: Tatra, Tatra-M, Surgut-T, and Karpaty-ST.

In 1986, Tu-134AK CCCP-65980 was converted to serve as the prototype for the Tu-134A Balkany version; it made its maiden flight on 20 February 1986. During subsequent years, the repair facility at Minsk, Belarus converted around 40 Tu-134AK aircraft to the new Tu-134A Balkany configuration. Currently, the Russian Air Force and the Navy operate approximately 20 Tu-134A/A-3 Balkany aircraft. Two aircraft are operated by the Ukrainian Air Force. Around 50 standard Tu-134 airliners continue to fly throughout the world.

Variants in service

Tu-134A Balkany is a conversion of previous Tu-134AK staff aircraft powered by D-30 series II engines.

Tu-134A-3 Balkany is as Tu-134A, but has D-30 series III engines.

Tu-134A-4 is an executive aircraft (without the Balkany system) that was converted from a Tu-134UB-L trainer. A single aircraft exists, with the registration RF-12000, and is used as a transport by the commander of the Black Sea Fleet.

See also **Tu-134 trainer versions** in the following chapter.

Tupolev Tu-154

NATO reporting name: Careless

Tu-154M RA-85084 belonging to the SLO presidential air group is one of the last Tu-154s to be completed; it made its first flight in 2008. (Piotr Butowski)

Manufacturer

Designed by the Tupolev Company in Moscow, series manufacture of the Tu-154 was undertaken by the Aviacor aircraft plant in Samara.

Role

A medium airliner, the Tu-154 is used by the Russian military as a command staff transport.

Crew

Tu-154B-2: This version has a crew of four, comprising a pilot, co-pilot, navigator and flight engineer.
Tu-154M: While this version usually has a crew of four, as in the Tu-154B-2, some aircraft equipped with the Jasmine navigation complex have a crew reduced to three (without the navigator).

Airframe and systems

The Tu-154 is a low-wing monoplane with 35° sweep (at 25 per cent chord) and a T-shaped tail with variable-incidence tailplane, elevators and rudder. The wing control

surfaces include triple-slotted (Tu-154B-2) or double-slotted (Tu-154M) trailing-edge flaps (28° inner or 15° outer sections at take-off, 45° or 36° at landing), ailcrons (with tabs), leading-edge slats and spoilers (the outer spoilers are also used as ailerons); the aircraft has four overwing fences. The flight control system is hydraulic, but with electric slat, tailplane incidence and tab actuation. The undercarriage features steerable twin nosewheels and six-wheel main bogies.

Powerplant

Three turbofan engines are grouped together in the rear fuselage; the two side engines are equipped with thrust reversers. A total of 39,750kg (87,634lb) of fuel can be carried in six wing tanks; the fuel is routed via a collector tank. A TA-92 auxiliary power unit is fitted.

Tu-154B-2: This version is powered by three Kuznetsov NK-8-2U turbofans, each rated at 102.96kN (23,149lbf) for take-off.

Tu-154M: In this version, three Aviadvigatel D-30KU-154 II turbofans provide the same thrust as the NK-8-2Us, but with a 13 per cent reduction in fuel consumption.

Dimensions

Wingspan 37.55m (123ft 2in); length 47.925m (157ft 3in); height 11.40m (37ft 5in); wing area, **Tu-154B-2**: 201.45m² (2,168 sq ft), **Tu-154M**: 202m² (2,174 sq ft); wheelbase 18.92m (62ft 1in); wheel track 11.5 m (37ft 9in).

Weights

Tu-154B-2: Empty operating 50,700kg (111,774lb); maximum take-off 98,000kg (216,053lb); maximum landing 78,000kg (171,961lb); payload 18,000kg (39,683lb).

Tu-154M: Empty operating 55,300kg (121,915lb); maximum take-off 100,000kg (220,462lb); maximum landing 80,000kg (176,370lb); payload 18,000kg (39,683lb).

Tu-154M RA-85155 is an executive aircraft used by the commander-in-chief of the Russian Air Forces and based at Chkalovsky airfield. (Piotr Butowski)

Tu-154M UP-T5401 is operated by the Kazakhstan Air Force on behalf of the government in Astana. This is the only example of the aircraft remaining in Kazakh service. (Alexander Golz)

Performance

Tu-154B-2: Cruising speed 900km/h (559mph); ceiling 12,300m (40,354ft); range with maximum payload 2,650km (1,647 miles); range with full fuel 5,000km (3,107 miles); required runway length 2,200m (7,218 ft).
Tu-154M: Cruising speed 935km/h (581mph); ceiling 12,100m (39,698ft); range with maximum payload 3,900km (2,423 miles); range with full fuel 6,500km (4,039 miles); required runway length: 2,500m (8,202ft).

Transport capabilities

The Tu-154 can be configured in various layouts including 24 first class and 154 tourist class, 164 all-tourist class, and 180 all-economy class (six abreast seating).

Avionics

The flight avionics of the Tu-154 meet ICAO Cat. II requirements and include autopilot, triple inertial navigation system, ground proximity warning system, and HF/VHF communications. A Groza-154 weather radar is fitted in the nose. Some aircraft operated by the military have additional communications equipment, including satellite communication, which is indicated by a large flat dorsal antenna.

History

The Tu-154 was the most numerous Soviet/Russian jet airliner. The prototype, CCCP-85000, flew for the first time on 3 October 1968, piloted by Yuri Sukhov. The Tu-154 began scheduled services with Aeroflot on 9 February 1972.

Production and operators

A total of 1,026 Tu-154s of all versions were built at Samara (until 1991, Kuibyshev). The very last Tu-154M was flown on 5 December 2012 and handed over to the Russian Air Force on 19 February 2013. As of 2016, around 50 aircraft are still airworthy. The Russian military reportedly has 12 Tu-154B-2 and five Tu-154M versions with the Air

B-4022 is one of the few remaining Chinese military Tu-154Ms that serves in a pure passenger role, with most having been replaced by Western types. The majority of Chinese Tu-154Ms serve in the electronic warfare role. (Bruno Geiger)

Force and two Tu-154Ms assigned to Naval Aviation. Another major operator is the People's Liberation Army Air Force, which has 12 Tu-154Ms.

Variants in service

Tu-154B-2 became the most numerous production version. When compared to the earlier Tu-154 and Tu-154A, the Tu-154B version of 1975 introduced improved high-lift devices, more fuel, increased take-off weight and new avionics. The B-2 sub-variant of 1980, the only B-model currently in use, has accommodation for 180 passengers compared to 164 in the Tu-154B and B-1; it also introduced minor improvements. Many Tu-154Bs and B-1s have been upgraded to the B-2 standard.

Tu-154M is a completely upgraded version with new Aviadvigatel D-30KU-154 turbofans; it entered production in 1984.

See also the **Tu-154M-LK1** surveillance version for the Open Skies programme, described in Volume 1.

FUTURE THEATRE TRANSPORT AIRCRAFT

Ilyushin Il-112V

The latest model of the Il-112V tactical transport as presented at the Army-2016 exhibition held at Kubinka in September 2016.
(Piotr Butowski)

Following the resumption of Il-76 and Il-78 production, the next new transport aircraft programme to the implemented is the tactical Il-112 transport aircraft. This has been developed under the **LVTS** (Lyogkiy Voyenno-Transportnyi Samolyot, Lightweight Military Transport Aircraft) programme and is intended to replace the An-26 and, partly, the An-12. The Il-112 programme (as a regional passenger turboprop) received state backing for the first time according to a governmental resolution of 4 November 1994, but this was not followed by any funding. Subsequently, the Il-112 design was revised and modified on several occasions.

On 10 March 2000 the Russian Air Force announced a tender for the LVTS design, which was to be capable of carrying maximum load of 6,000kg (13,228lb) over a distance of 3,000km (1,864 miles) at a cruising speed of 650-700km/h (404-469mph). Other load variants included 60 troops or 37 paratroopers. The new aircraft was also required to be able to perform special missions including the landing of counter-insurgency teams; for this task, the LVTS was to be capable of accommodating 26 troops when taking off with a run of 280m (919ft). Other versions, including airborne command post, radio relay and, in the more distant future, electronic warfare and radio intelligence aircraft, were also to be developed on the basis of the LVTS.

On 8 April 2003 the **Il-112V** (Voyennyi, military) project won the LVTS competition. Beginning in 2004, the project received funding from the Ministry of Defence. In December 2004 the initial project was approved; the first flight was then announced by Ilyushin for 2006, and the first deliveries for 2008. Delays occurred from the very beginning, caused primarily by the Russian Ministry of Defence's general lack of interest in the aircraft. Indeed a rumour began to circulate that the then Russian Minister

of Defence Anatoly Serdyukov had said of the Il-112: 'I don't need an aircraft that will only fly the generals for fishing and hunting'.

The actual costs of the programme also turned out to be higher than planned. Vitaly Zubarev, CEO of the VASO plant, where the aircraft was to be constructed, said in September 2010 that the Ministry of Defence 'gave the contractors all the money specified in the contract, but it turned out that it was not enough'. The Ministry of Defence refused to grant additional money and broke the contract for the Il-112V on 14 May 2010. According to Ilyushin, by that time the documentation necessary for the construction of the prototype was 84 per cent ready and the VASO plant had completed 14.5 per cent of the production tooling. The Il-112V design has been included in the National Armament Programme 2011–20, which stipulates an optional purchase of 62 aircraft by 2020, but no firm contracts have followed.

Only on 14 November 2014 did the Ministry of Defence sign a contract with Ilyushin, renewing the Il-112V project in order to meet updated requirements. Following this, Ilyushin signed a series of further contracts with sub-contractors, including a 25 March 2015 contract with VASO for the construction of the prototypes. The order has been reduced from four to two prototypes (one for flight tests and the other for static and fatigue tests). The first flight is to be completed by 30 June 2017. The completion of the first stage of state trials and launch of series production is expected in 2019, initially in the baseline transport version and then with additional special equipment, including targeting equipment for precise parachute drops, a self-protection suite with infrared jammer, and other items. The design of the aircraft and a mock-up of the cockpit were approved by a Ministry of Defence commission on 11 June 2015. The first order for 48 Il-112V aircraft for the Russian Air Force is to be signed in 2016–17. A civilian Il-112T (Transportnyi, freighter) version is also planned.

The most serious technical difficulty facing the Il-112 project is the Klimov TV7-117ST turboprop engine, rated at 2,206ekW (3,000ehp) of take-off power. As the take-off weight of the aircraft has increased, this engine has become increasingly insufficient. However, this is still the most powerful turboprop engine available in Russia, and access to foreign engines is currently blocked. Alexander Vatagin, the head of Klimov, said in April 2010 that the engine had proven itself to be underpowered for the Il-112, and 'the increase of power output by a minor upgrade of the engine is now already impossible… From the outset, when the task was formulated, the 2,942ekW (4,000ehp) power should have been assumed.'

In the form in which the Il-112 project won the Ministry of Defence competition in 2003, the take-off weight amounted 19,700kg (43,431lb); now it has risen to 21,000kg (46,297lb). A further increase of the take-off weight with the current powerplant is impossible. As a result, in the latest version of the design the maximum payload has been reduced to 5,000kg (11,023lb) and range with this load has been reduced to 1,200km (746 miles); it is worth remembering that the original requirements of 2000 included the capability to carry a 6,000kg (13,228lb) payload over a distance of 3,000km (1,864 miles). Other payload options have also been reduced, including 50 troops or 26 paratroopers, or 23 casualties. The aircraft's crew consists of two pilots, a navigator and loadmaster.

Ilyushin Il-112V specification (design)
Powerplant: two Klimov TV7-117ST turboprops, each rated at 2,206ekW (3,000ehp) for take-off and 2,648ekW (3,600ehp) in an emergency, driving six-blade 3.9m (12ft 10in) diameter AV-112 propellers. An Aerosila TA-14 auxiliary power unit is fitted. A total of 7,900 litres (2,086 gallons) of fuel is carried in two separate wing tanks, one for each engine.
Dimensions: wingspan 25.740m (84ft 5in); overall length 23.492m (77ft 1in); height 8.903m (29ft 3in).
Weights: maximum take-off 21,000kg (46,297lb); payload 5,000kg (11,023lb).
Performance: cruising speed 500km/h (311mph); ceiling 7,600m (24,934ft); range with 5,000kg (11,023lb) payload 1,200km (746 miles); range with 2,000kg (4,409lb) payload 4,800km (2,983 miles); take-off run 800m (2,626ft); landing run 600m (1,969ft).

Ilyushin Il-214

The Il-214 is intended to replace An-12 medium transports and compete with the Lockheed Martin C-130J and Embraer KC-390. However, its introduction is unlikely before 2025. Ilyushin plans for production to take place in Ulyanovsk, alongside the Il-76 and Il-78.
(Piotr Butowski)

The **Il-214** is another Russian transport aircraft project, the preliminary development of which has dragged on for many years. This programme was launched in March 1999 with the signing the protocol of intent to create a joint venture for the development and production of the **MTA** (Multirole Transport Aircraft) by Ilyushin of Russia and Hindustan Aeronautics Limited (HAL) of India, based on Ilyushin's Il-214 pilot project; initially the aircraft was also called the **IRTA** (Indian-Russian Transport Aircraft). India had been working on the development of a medium transport aircraft several years in advance of this. Since 1996, India's Aeronautical Development Agency (ADA) had been researching the possible configuration of transport and passenger aircraft with a load capacity of 13,500kg (29,762lb) or 120 passengers. Entering cooperation with Ilyushin, HAL wanted to advance through the entire cycle of design and construction of a large aircraft with Russian assistance, in order to gain experience to pursue analogous indigenous programmes. Two versions of the aircraft were planned at that time, the **Il-214T** transport and **Il-214-100** passenger aircraft. Since the transport was

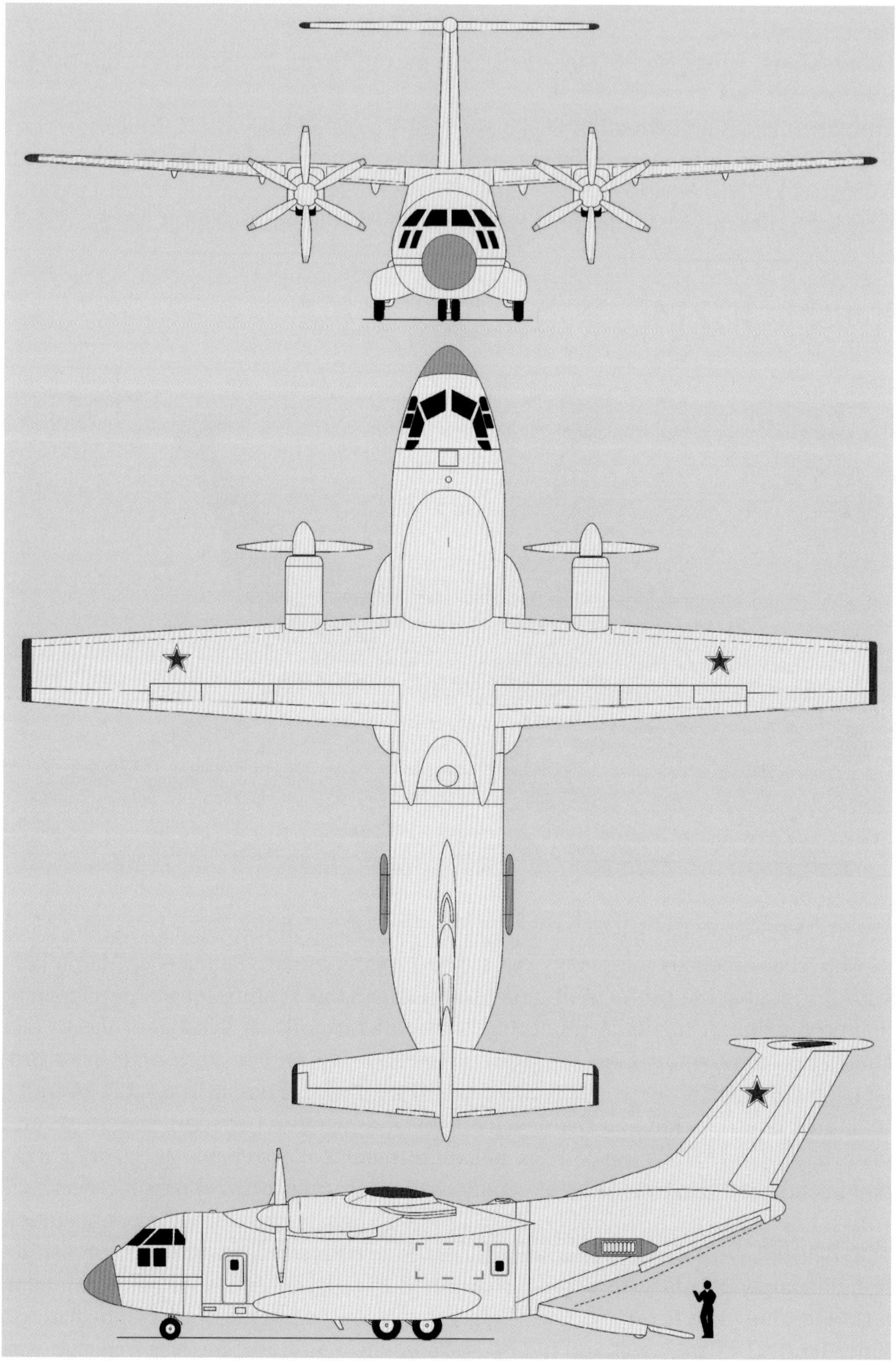

In its military version the Il-112V will receive specific systems for navigation, air dropping and self-protection. (Piotr Butowski)

to be the baseline version, the high-mounted wing configuration with super-critical moderate-sweep wings, T-shaped tail and rear loading ramp was chosen.

In February 2001, during the exhibition at Bangalore, Ilyushin and HAL were joined in the project by Irkut, which was to be the Russian manufacturer of the aircraft and would fund the development of the aircraft on the part of Russia. On 6 June 2001, Russia and India signed an inter-governmental protocol in Moscow confirming joint efforts on the MTA. On the part of India, HAL was to participate in the project (as a 50 per cent partner) and on the part of Russia, Irkut (40 per cent) and Ilyushin (10 per cent). The fourth partner, the Rosoboronexport arms trade company, did not invest money, but was required by Irkut and Ilyushin, who had no licenses for independent contracts with foreign customers. Parallel production of the aircraft was to be carried out on two production lines, in Irkutsk, Russia, and in Nasik, India. India agreed to purchase 45 aircraft, while the Russian side made no firm obligations, but estimated a demand for 60 aircraft for the Air Force, 15 for EMERCOM, 25 for civil operators in Russia, and 60 aircraft for other countries; a total of 205. Despite several difficulties within the programme, these numbers remained unchanged.

In 2004 the Russian Ministry of Defence intended to announce a tender for its own SVTS (Sredniy Voyenno-Transportnyi Samolyot, Medium Military Transport Aircraft) project, but since work on the Russo-Indian MTA was already advanced at that time, it was decided to order this aircraft without tender. In November 2004 a directive was issued by the Russian General Staff calling for the MTA to be utilised in the SVTS programme.

Only on 12 November 2007 did India and Russia sign an intergovernmental agreement providing for an investment of USD600.7 million in the MTA programme, divided evenly between both parties. Despite this, the work was still proceeding slowly. The Russian government assigned the first funding (2,156 million roubles, somewhat more than USD80 million) only in 2009. The Multirole Transport Aircraft Limited (MTAL) joint venture, announced in the protocol of intent in 1999, was finally formed on 1 December 2010 at Bangalore. The Russian participants are Rosoboronexport (25 per cent) and United Aircraft Corporation – Transport Aircraft (UAC-TA; 25 per cent), and the Indian participant is HAL (50 per cent); Irkut had now left the project. The parties confirmed the intention of investing USD300 million each into the joint venture. Series production was to be equally divided between Russia and India; the Russian plant responsible for producing the MTA was now changed from Irkutsk to Ulyanovsk. On 28 May 2012 the UAC-TA (which is actually the Ilyushin company), HAL and MTAL signed a general contract on the MTA programme, providing for the joint production of 205 aircraft. Then, on 12 October 2012, the same parties signed a contract for preliminary design of the aircraft.

Later, however, the MTA programme was stopped. Reportedly, India is dissatisfied with the aircraft's characteristics, and Russia is demanding more money to finance the project. In 2015, Russia confirmed that India was no longer planning to introduce the aircraft. In September 2015 the Russian Ministry of Defence ordered UAC-TA to adapt the MTA design to the requirements of the purely Russian SVTS programme. The contract with the Ministry of Defence for the SVTS design work and prototype is to be signed in 2017. The funds previously planned for the MTA programme will be reassigned to the SVTS project. Ilyushin is planning to fly the first Il-214 after 2020, and production will be located in Ulyanovsk.

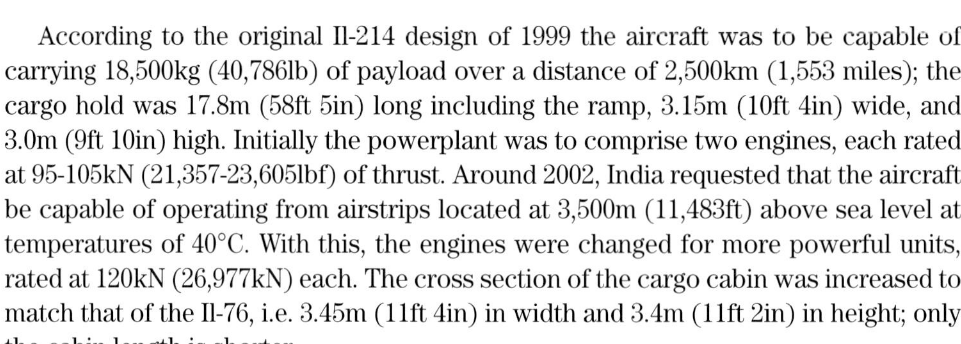

According to the original Il-214 design of 1999 the aircraft was to be capable of carrying 18,500kg (40,786lb) of payload over a distance of 2,500km (1,553 miles); the cargo hold was 17.8m (58ft 5in) long including the ramp, 3.15m (10ft 4in) wide, and 3.0m (9ft 10in) high. Initially the powerplant was to comprise two engines, each rated at 95-105kN (21,357-23,605lbf) of thrust. Around 2002, India requested that the aircraft be capable of operating from airstrips located at 3,500m (11,483ft) above sea level at temperatures of 40°C. With this, the engines were changed for more powerful units, rated at 120kN (26,977kN) each. The cross section of the cargo cabin was increased to match that of the Il-76, i.e. 3.45m (11ft 4in) in width and 3.4m (11ft 2in) in height; only the cabin length is shorter.

Later, a series of MTA designs of increasing size and weight was developed. The latest project, presented in February 2015 by MTAL at Bangalore, differs from the previous designs in the shape of its rear ramp and tail section, which are now very similar to those of the Il-76. The Il-214 has a moderately swept (24°) high-mounted wing, a T-shaped tail, rear loading ramp and low undercarriage carried in nacelles on the fuselage sides. The payload options include 20,000kg (44,092lb) of cargo or 140 troops in double-deck configuration (100 troops in single-deck configuration), or 90 paratroopers, or 80 casualties. Subsequent changes were made after the presentation of this design. In particular, Ilyushin's designer general Nikolay Talikov said in late 2015 that the Il-214 would be powered by two even more powerful Aviadvigatel PS-90A1 engines, as used in the Il-96-400.

Ilyushin Il-214 specification (design, 2015)
Powerplant: two Aviadvigatel PS-90A76 turbofans, each rated at 156.9kN (35,274lbf); or, in the latest design, two PS-90A1 turbofans, each rated at 170.6kN (38,360lbf).
Dimensions: wingspan 39.37m (128ft 2in); wing area 160m² (1,722 sq ft); overall length 40.235 m (132ft); length without refuelling probe 39.7m (130ft 3in); height 13.04m (42ft 9in); cabin length 14.0m (45ft 11in) without or 18.35m (60ft 2in) with ramp; cabin width at floor 3.45m (11ft 4in); cabin height 3.4m (11ft 2in).
Weights: maximum take-off 72,000kg (158,733lb); maximum payload 20,000kg (44,092lb).
Performance: maximum cruising speed 800km/h (497mph) at 11,000m (36,089ft); ceiling 12,200m (40,026ft); range 2,000km (1,243 miles) with 20,000kg (44,092lb), 3,150km (1,957 miles) with 16,000kg (35,274lb), 5,650km (3,511 miles) with 4,500kg (9,921lb), 6,500km (4,039 miles) maximum; required runway length 1,530m (5,020ft).

TRAINERS

The legacy of Soviet trainers

During the Soviet era the USSR's aircraft industry focused on larger programmes and many 'less important' designs were ordered from abroad, for instance from Czechoslovakia and Poland. As a result, the most popular jet trainer in the Soviet and Russian Air Force, the L-39C, was developed by Aero Vodochody in Czechoslovakia and thus does not fit within the remit of this book. Somewhat different are the Czech-made L-410 transport and the An-2 utility aircraft. The L-410 was originally developed and built by Let in Kunovice, Czechoslovakia. Today, the former Let is Russian owned, and limited production continues in the Czech Republic for the Russian military. The An-2 was designed by Antonov in Kiev and produced in Mielec, Poland. However, since it remains in Russian Air Force, and with other air arms around the world, it is described in this chapter.

L-39C jet trainers of Czechoslovakian design and manufacture still bear the brunt of military pilot training in Russia, despite the introduction of the Yak-130. Currently, the Russian Air Force operates around 150 L-39Cs. (Piotr Butowski)

Aircraft Industries L-410UVP

By the end of 2015 the Russian Air Force had received 15 new L-410UVP-E20 aircraft. Deliveries of this version began in February 2011. (Alexander Golz)

Manufacturer
The L-410 was developed and produced by the Let factory in Kunovice, in today's Czech Republic. The former Let is now known as Aircraft Industries, which is owned by Russia's Ural Mining and Metallurgical Company (UGMK) .

Role
A light general utility turboprop, the L-410 is used as a trainer and transport in Russian military service.

Details for Aircraft Industries L-410UVP-E20

Crew
The L-410 is operated by a crew of two pilots.

Airframe and systems
The L-410 is a conventional twin turboprop high-wing light passenger aircraft.

Powerplant
Two General Electric H80-200 turboprops, each rated at 597kW (800shp) for take-off and 522kW (700shp) continuous, driving metal five-blade 2.3m (7.5ft) diameter AV-725 propellers. Up to 1,300kg (2,866lb) of fuel can be carried, including in the wingtip tanks.

Dimensions
Length 14.424m (47ft 4in); wingspan 19.98m (65ft 7in); wing area 34.86m^2 (375 sq ft); height 5.829m (19ft 1.5in); wheelbase 3.666m (12ft 0.5in); wheel track 3.65m (12ft).

Weights
Empty 4,050kg (8,929lb); maximum take-off 6,600kg (14,551lb); maximum landing 6,400kg (14,110lb); maximum payload 1,800kg (3,968lb).

The 'semi-glass' EFI-890R cockpit of the L410-UVP-E20. (Kirill Skurikhin)

Performance

Maximum cruising speed 405km/h (252mph); maximum range 1,520km (944 miles); service ceiling 4,200m (13,780ft); take-off distance 510m (1,673ft) to 10.7m (35ft) at International Standard Atmosphere (ISA); landing distance 500m (1,640ft) from 15m (50ft) at ISA.

Transport capabilities

The L-410 can accommodate up to 19 passengers or 18 paratroopers, or 1,700kg (3,748lb) of cargo.

Avionics

The aircraft has a 'semi-glass' EFI-890R cockpit, RDR-2000 weather radar, GNS-430W satellite navigation receiver and Enhanced Ground Proximity Warning System (EGPWS). Optionally, the L-410 can be fitted with Traffic Collision Avoidance System (TCAS) II, KFC-325 autopilot, and other items.

History

The first L-410 prototype flew on 16 April 1969. The L-410UVP version was developed specifically to meet a requirement for Aeroflot of the USSR and received a wing that was extended by 2m (6.5ft) in length and new M-601B or D engines. The UVP (which means in Russian Ukorochennyi Vzlyot i Posadka, short take-off and landing) first flew on 1 November 1976. The Russian Air Force began purchases of the L-410 10 years later, initially in the L-410UVP-E version.

Production and operators

In the initial production period, which lasted until 1992, a total of 1,034 aircraft were completed, of which 872 were delivered to the USSR in the period from 1979 to 1992. This total comprised 642 for Aeroflot and 230 for the Soviet Air Force (the L-410UVP-E and -E3 versions only). In the post-Soviet era, production was reduced to a few aircraft each year. In June 2008, Aircraft Industries (the former Let Kunovice) was acquired by the Russian Ural Mining and Metallurgical Company (UGMK) in Yekaterinburg. Thereafter, additional Russian customers for the type appeared, including the Air Force. The production rate increased to 16 aircraft in 2014, and then reduced to eight in 2015, after a fall in demand from the Russian market. In total, over 1,100 aircraft of all versions had been manufactured by 2016; over 350 of these are in operation in more than 50 countries.

Deliveries of new L-410UVP-E20 aircraft to the Russian Air Force began in February 2011, and by the end of 2015 the service had received 15 aircraft. With the aim of circumventing possible sanctions, the aircraft are purchased in the Czech Republic by a Russian civilian company and then resold to the Ministry of Defence. Reportedly, in May 2016, Aircraft Industries received an order for four aircraft placed by the Ural Civil Aviation Plant (UZGA); it may be assumed that these aircraft are eventually intended for the Russian MoD.

The Russian Air Force's L-410 aircraft are used primarily as trainers within a training regiment based at Rtishchevo; this air base is home to around 65 aircraft from the 'legacy' production run (i.e. built until 1992), most of which are no longer airworthy, plus several new L-410UVP-E20 versions. Four new aircraft were delivered in 2015 to a composite transport regiment based at Koltsovo near Yekaterinburg, where they are used as staff transports.

The UGMK company, together with the UZGA, intends to move production of the L-410 to Russia. On 7 April 2016, UZGA began construction of a new production hall for the L-410 in Yekaterinburg; the first L-410UVP-E20 was due to be assembled here in 2017, and by 2019 the factory intends to reach an output rate of 12 aircraft per year. Initially, the aircraft will be assembled using parts delivered from the Czech Republic, before the full production cycle is launched in Russia. Finally, the aircraft is expected to receive Russian engines and avionics.

Outside Russia, current military operators of the L-410 include Bangladesh, Bulgaria (fleet currently grounded), the Czech Republic, Cape Verde, Djibouti (one new-production L-410UVP-E20), Honduras (L-410UVP-E20 versions), Lithuania, Slovakia (including four L-410UVP-E20s) and Tunisia (reportedly withdrawn from use).

Variants in Russian military service

L-410UVP-E (Ekonomicheskiy, economy) is a passenger version featuring 552kW (751shp) Czech Walter M601E turboprop engines driving five-blade V-510 propellers and with two wingtip fuel tanks; series production commenced in 1986.

L-410UVP-E3 is as the L-410UVP-E but in a transport/paradropping configuration.

L-410UVP-E20 is the current production version powered by General Electric engines and fitted with new avionics, as described.

Antonov An-2

NATO reporting name: Colt

An-2 '08 Yellow' is one the surviving examples of this classic utility biplane that continue in Russian military service for training duties. (Andreas Zeilter)

Manufacturer

Designed by Antonov in Kiev, Ukraine, series manufacture of the An-2 was undertaken in the Soviet Union, Poland and China.

Role

The world's most popular general utility aircraft, in Russian Air Force service the An-2 is today used for training parachute troops.

Crew

The An-2 is operated by a crew of two pilots.

Airframe and systems

The An-2 is a strutted biplane of mainly metal construction, but with partial fabric skinning. The upper wing has automatic slats, ailerons (including a port trim tab) and trailing-edge flaps; the lower wing has full-span trailing-edge flaps. The tail control surfaces are conventional with elevators (with a port trim tab) and rudder (trim tab). A cable-pushrod type flight control system is used, with the exception of electric flaps and trim tabs. The fixed undercarriage is of the tailwheel type.

Powerplant

The An-2 is powered by an ASz-62IR radial piston engine rated at a maximum of 735.5kW (1,000hp) (the ASz-62 is a distant descendent of the American Wright R-1820 Cyclone, a license for which was purchased by the USSR in 1934 together with the Douglas DC-3 transport). A total of 1,200 litres (317 gallons) of fuel is carried in six tanks inside the upper wing.

Dimensions
Length 12.735m (41ft 9in) tail up or 12.40m (40ft 8in) tail down; height 4.013m (13ft 2in) tail down; upper wingspan 18.176m (59ft 7.5in); lower wingspan 14.236m (46ft 8.5in); wheelbase 8.19m (26ft 10.5in); wheel track 3.454m (11ft 4in).

Weights
Normal take-off 5,250kg (11,574lb); maximum take-off 5,500kg (12,125lb); payload 1,500kg (3,307lb).

Performance
Maximum speed 253km/h (157mph); cruise speed 190km/h (118mph); approach speed 90km/h (56mph); service ceiling 4,160m (13,648ft); take-off run 180-220m (591-722ft); landing run 210-225m (689-738ft); range with maximum fuel 1,390km (864 miles).

Transport capabilities
The An-2 can accommodate 12 passengers or paratroopers.

Avionics
Equipment found on the An-2 comprises an RV-UM radio altimeter, ARK-19 radio direction finder, plus R-842 and R-860 communication radios.

History
The An-2 prototype first flew on 31 August 1947, with Pavel Volodin at the controls.

Production and operators
Within the USSR the An-2 was produced in Kiev (3,167 aircraft during 1950–62) and Dolgoprudny (429 An-2M versions during 1964–68). In 1960 mass production commenced in Mielec, Poland, where 11,911 aircraft were built (numbers differ slightly in various sources, even within the factory). In China a total of 727 An-2s were built in Nanchang (1957–68) together with around 275 in Shijiazhuang (beginning in 1970).

The An-2 is the oldest aircraft operated by the Russian Air Force. A few dozen examples are used to train parachute on behalf of the Airborne Troops (Vozdushno-Desantnye Voyska); operationally, the aircraft are subordinated to the Military Transport Aviation.

Outside of Russia, military operators of the An-2 comprise Armenia (six), Azerbaijan (three), Bulgaria (one), Cuba (15), Estonia (two), Georgia (two), Guinea (two), Kazakhstan (two), Latvia (four), Lithuania (seven), Macedonia (one), Mali (two), Moldova (five), Mongolia (10), Nicaragua (two), Tajikistan (one), Ukraine (four), the United States (one) and Vietnam (four).

Variants in Russian service
The only version in current Russian military service is the basic An-2.

Kamov Ka-226

NATO reporting name: Hoodlum

RF-13350, '416 Yellow', is one of 42 Ka-226V training helicopters acquired by the Russian military between March 2012 and April 2015. (Piotr Butowski)

Manufacturer

The Ka-226 was designed by the Kamov Company in Lyubertsy and is manufactured by the Kumertau Aircraft Production Enterprise (KumAPP); however, the first 10 helicopters were manufactured by the Strela factory in Orenburg.

Role

A general utility helicopter, the Ka-226 is used as a trainer by the Russian Air Force. A ship-borne version is under development.

Crew

The Ka-226 is operated a two pilots seated in the non-detachable cockpit. A detachable module provides accommodation for six passengers, or eight in a high-density configuration.

Airframe, rotor system and transmission

The helicopter features a modular fuselage with a 'skeleton' that incorporates the pilots' cockpit, the lifting section (engines and rotors), empennage and undercarriage, as well as interchangeable specialised cabins, including cargo, passenger, medical evacuation and others. The lifting section includes two coaxial contra-rotating three-blade rotors and VR-226 reduction gear (or the more robust VR-226T for the Ka-226T). The rotor blades are of glass/carbon-fibre and the composite/titanium rotor head has elastomeric bearings. The four-leg fixed undercarriage has single wheels on each unit.

Powerplant

Ka-226V: Two Rolls-Royce Allison 250-C20R/2 turboshafts, each developing 331kW (450shp) at take-off, with a continuous rating of 279kW (380shp). A total of 780 litres (206 gallons) of standard fuel can be supplemented by two 175-litre (46-gallon) auxiliary tanks.

Ka-226T: Two Turbomeca Arrius 2G1 turboshafts, each developing 427kW (580shp) at take-off; the emergency power rating is 519kW (705shp).

Dimensions

Ka-226V: Fuselage length 8.58m (28ft 2in); height 4.185m (13ft 9in); tail unit span 3.224m (10ft 7in); rotor diameter 13.0m (42ft 8in) each; wheelbase 3.44m (11ft 3in); wheel track 2.56m (8ft 5in) main and 0.99m (3ft 3in) nose.

Ka-226T: Fuselage length 8.88m (29ft 1in); height 4.265m (14ft); tail unit span 3.25m (10ft 8in); rotor diameter 13.0m (42ft 8in) each; wheelbase 3.44m (11ft 3in); wheel track 2.62m (8ft 7in) main and 1.06m (3ft 6in) nose.

Weights

Ka-226V: Empty, basic configuration 2,230kg (4,916lb); maximum take-off 3,400kg (7,496lb); maximum payload 1,050kg (2,315lb) internal or 1,300kg (2,866lb) on external sling.

Ka-226T: Maximum take-off 3,600kg (7,937lb) or 3,800kg (8,378lb) with external load; maximum payload 1,200kg (2,646lb) internal or 1,500kg (3,307lb) on external sling.

The cockpit of the Ka-226V features a pupil's seat on the left provided with an SEI-226 data indication system with a single large display. The instructor on the right has conventional instruments. (Piotr Butowski)

Performance

Ka-226V, all at maximum TOW: Maximum speed 210km/h (130mph); cruising speed 195km/h (121mph); OGE hovering ceiling 2,600m (8,530ft); service ceiling 5,750m (18,860ft); maximum climb rate 9.5m/s (1,870ft/min); range with standard fuel 500km (311 miles); range with maximum fuel 760km (472 miles).

Ka-226T: Maximum speed 250km/h (155mph); cruising speed 220km/h (137mph); climb rate 10m/s (1,969ft/min); OGE hovering ceiling 4,100m (13,451ft); service ceiling 5,700m (18,701ft); range with standard fuel 590km (367 miles); range with maximum fuel 870km (541 miles).

Avionics

Ka-226V: The instruments and navigation devices are of the conventional type; the SEI-226 data indication system includes a single IM-16-3 multifunction display (MFD). This version is fitted with SAU-32-226 autopilot.

Ka-226T: The helicopter has the KBO-226T avionics complex; this includes a fully 'glass' KSEIS-226 indication system with five MFDs.

History

The Ka-226 represents a refined development of the Ka-26 that dates from the 1960s (816 were built). The prototype, with Allison engines, made a first hovering flight on 4 September 1997, with Vladimir Lavrov at the controls. Two prototypes of the Ka-226T with Turbomeca engines were completed in 2009.

Production and operators

Series manufacture of the first Allison-powered versions was launched in 2001 at the Strela plant in Orenburg (production ceased at this location after 10 helicopters had been completed) and at the KumAPP plant in Kumertau, where production continues. Spring 2013 saw the production launch of the Ka-226T with Turbomeca engines. In recent years, the Kumertau facility has manufactured an average of 12 to 18 Ka-226s each year (in addition to other helicopters), mostly for Russian state structures (the Ministry of Defence, EMERCOM, Federal Border Service, and Home Office) as well as the gas giant Gazprom.

A first order from the Russian Ministry of Defence was placed on 1 March 2011, for 16 Ka-226V helicopters; this was later increased when another 26 helicopters were added to the order. All 42 aircraft were delivered to the Syzran air training base between March 2012 and April 2015. The helicopter completed state acceptance tests on 16 November 2011.

The Ka-226T version was originally developed for an Indian tender for 197 Reconnaissance and Surveillance Helicopters (RSH), in which it competed with the Eurocopter (now Airbus Helicopters) AS550C3 Fennec. However, in May 2015 the tender was cancelled. India is expected to order Ka-226T helicopters outside the tender procedure, these aircraft being co-produced by Russia and India.

An order for the future ship-borne Ka-226TM for the Russian Navy was planned but must be considered doubtful following the cancellation of the Mistral amphibious assault ships that were on order from France. The Federal Border Service has announced plans to acquire 10 Ka-226TM helicopters by 2020.

Variants

Ka-226 (modification **226.00**) refers to the early-production helicopters manufactured by the Orenburg factory, with Allison engines.

Ka-226A (**226.10**) is a specific model for EMERCOM. This has Allison engines and is a variant of the early version manufactured in Orenburg.

Ka-226AG (**226.50**) is the Gazprom-specific model with Allison engines, made in Kumertau.

Ka-226 (**226.55**) is the version with Alison engines delivered to Russia's Home Office (MVD) and Federal Security Service (FSB).

Ka-226V (**226.80**) is the trainer version for the Russian Ministry of Defence, as described.

Ka-226T has more powerful Turbomeca engines and strengthened VR-226N main gearbox. In addition it has a second hydraulic system (replacing the previous pneumatic

The Ka-226 features a modular fuselage with interchangeable specialised cabins, including cargo, passenger, medical evacuation and others. (Piotr Butowski)

system), a more powerful electric system, improved avionics, and other changes. The Ka-226T has been the standard production version since 2013.

Ka-226T (226.52) is a derivative for EMERCOM.

Ka-226T (226.57) is a version for the Federal Border Service of the FSB, intended to be based on small border patrol ships. It is fitted with Geofizika ONV-1-01 night-vision goggles, an SLG-300 electric winch and provision for 7.62mm (0.3in) calibre machine guns.

Ka-226TG is the Gazprom-specific version of the Ka-226T.

Ka-226TM is to be a derivative of the Ka-226T for the Russian Navy and the Federal Border Service that will utilise a conventional single-piece fuselage rather than the current modular airframe, and will have semi-retractable undercarriage. A first flight was scheduled for 2015 but the project has been subject to considerable delay, and has possibly been cancelled altogether.

Kazan Helicopters Ansat-U

RF-13354, '54 Yellow', is one of 40 Ansat-U training helicopters acquired by the Russian military between 2011 and 2016. Together with the Ka-226V, these aircraft are replacing Mi-2s at Army Aviation training bases in Saratov and Syzran. (Piotr Butowski)

Manufacturer

The Kazan Helicopters Company is responsible for both developing and manufacturing the Ansat-U helicopter.

Role

A lightweight general utility helicopter, the Ansat-U (Uchebnyi, training) version is used as a trainer by the Russian Air Force.

Details for Ansat-U

Crew

The pilot's seat is located on the starboard side with access via a door that opens forwards; the seat on the port side is for the student (or passenger in other versions) and has a similar door for access. Dual controls are provided in the training version. In civilian versions, four to six passengers can be carried as standard, with the option of a pilot plus nine passengers for short journeys. Access to the cabin is provided via horizontally divided (upward/downward opening) doors on both sides.

Airframe, rotor system and transmission

The Ansat is a helicopter of conventional construction that is built mainly of aluminium alloys. The non-load-bearing elements, such as the engine and transmission gear cowlings, doors and hatch covers, as well as the fuselage nose fairing, are manufactured using glass composites. The Ansat-U has fixed wheels while other versions have skids. A support to protect the tail rotor is fitted under the tail beam.

The main rotor has four blades with elastomeric bearings; the tail rotor has two blades. The blades of both rotors are made of fibreglass plastic. The VR-23A main transmission gear is of the two-stage type with a transmission ratio 16.4 and a rotor speed of 365rpm. The tail transmission gear is of the bevel single-stage type.

The Ansat is the first Russian helicopter to be equipped with a digital fly-by-wire (FBW) system, known as the KSU-A (KSU-A-U for Ansat-U); the electronic part of the system is quadruplex, while the hydraulic part is duplex. Thanks to the possibility to adjust the control system, the training version of the Ansat can imitate other types of helicopters, including the heavier Mi-8.

Powerplant

The Ansat is powered by two Pratt & Whitney Canada PW207K turboshaft engines fitted with a full-authority digital engine control (FADEC) system, each rated at 470kW (630shp) for take-off or 410kW (558shp) continuous; the emergency rating is 529kW (710shp). A total of 720 litres (190 gallons) of fuel can be carried in two tanks in the fuselage sides. In 2017, new, larger fuel tanks are to be installed. Currently, because of the Western embargo on deliveries of military equipment to Russia, the latter has accelerated the development of its own 588kW (800shp) class Klimov VK-800VA engine for the Ansat.

Dimensions

Main rotor diameter 11.5m (37ft 9in); tail rotor diameter 2.10m (6ft 11in); fuselage length 11.16m (36ft 7in), length with rotors turning 13.59m (44ft 7in); height 3.75m (12ft 4in); cabin length 3.25m (10ft 8in); cabin width 1.64m (5ft 5in); cabin height 1.3m (4ft 3in); undercarriage base 3.45m (11ft 4in), undercarriage track 2.60m (8ft 6in).

Weights

Empty 1,700kg (3,748lb); nominal take-off 3,000kg (6,614lb); maximum take-off 3,600kg (7,937lb); maximum payload 810kg (1,786lb).

Performance

Maximum speed 260km/h (162mph); maximum cruising speed 210km/h (130mph); service ceiling 4,600m (15,092ft); OGE hovering ceiling 2,900m (9,514ft); in-ground-effect (IGE) hovering ceiling 3,200m (10,499ft); climb rate 11.5m/s (2,264ft/min); maximum range 460km (286 miles).

Avionics

The NPKV-A piloting and navigation system provides for round-the-clock all-weather operation. Two IM-14 multifunction displays and a set of conventional instruments are provided in the cockpit. A weather radar (RDR-2000 or similar) can be optionally installed under the nose fairing.

The cockpit of the Ansat-U features a symmetrical instrument panel with a mix of two IM-14 MFDs and conventional analogue instruments. (Piotr Butowski)

History

In 1993, Kazan Helicopters – previously only a production facility – launched the design of a new lightweight twin-engine helicopter. With a take-off weight of 3,300kg (7,275lb), the helicopter can only be considered 'lightweight' according to Russian classification. While Kazan is the capital city of Tatarstan, an autonomous republic within the Russian Federation, Ansat means light or easy in the local Tartar language. The first prototype flew at Kazan on 17 August 1999, with Viktor Rusetsky at the controls.

In July 2006 one of six Ansats delivered to South Korea crashed, putting an end to flights by the type in that country. Kazan undertook additional testing and research, mainly concerning the FBW control system, introduced for the first time in a light helicopter application. Following modifications, the Ansat-K (Korean) version was developed, and in March 2010 this was granted a type certificate. However, it was limited to flights without passengers (South Koreans operates the Ansat on behalf of the forestry service and police). The main problem for the helicopter in terms of civilian applications is the impossibility of granting type certification for passenger flights with an FBW control system. To bypass this, in May 2012, Kazan began tests of the Ansat-GMSU version with a conventional mechanical flight control system. Currently, Kazan Helicopters is carrying out a programme for the extensive modernisation of the type, resulting in the Ansat-M, which is further divided into two stages: Ansat-1M and Ansat-2M. The company is also proposing a project for an enlarged version, known as the Ansat-3 Maximum (see Volume 1).

In 2005, Kazan Helicopters developed the Ansat-2RTs (Razvedchik-Tseleukazatel, reconnaissance-target indicator) helicopter that retained the engines, rotors and transmission of the standard Ansat but which has a new, narrow fuselage with tandem cockpits for the pilot and weapons system operator. The Russian TOES-521 forward-looking infrared turret was installed under the forward fuselage. The Ansat-2RTs is able

The Ansat-U features a conventional airframe and propulsion system but has an unconventional digital fly-by-wire flight control system. Thanks to the adjustment of this system, the Ansat-U can imitate heavy helicopters. (Piotr Butowski)

to carry 1,300kg (2,866lb) of weapons and stores on four pylons under short wings, including 80mm (3.1in) rockets and Igla anti-aircraft missiles. A fixed 12.7mm (0.5in) calibre machine gun is installed on the starboard side. UV-26 chaff/flare dispensers are installed on both sides of fuselage, while an L166V infrared jammer is located between the engines. The Ansat-2RTs (converted from the first Ansat prototype) made its maiden flight on 29 July 2005; however, it remains a one-off.

Production and operators

Series production began in 2004, initially for civilian customers. However, due to the aforementioned problems, the production of civilian Ansats was suspended after only 10 series helicopters (and six prototypes, including two Ansat-Us). At the end of 2015 there were only four helicopters in civil operation: two Ansat-Ks with the Russian Federal Security Service, one Ansat-K with the Russian Home Office, and one Ansat-LL with the Radar-MMS Company in St Petersburg. In 2016, civilian production was to be resumed in the form of the Ansat-GMSU (Ansat-1M) version. The factory has announced that it has six new orders for this variant.

On 14 September 2001 the Ansat-U (Uchebnyi, training) project won a tender from the Russian armed forces for a new helicopter that would be used for both basic and advanced training within the **Pervokursnik** (first-year student) program. On 15 May 2002 the Ministry of Defence charged Kazan Helicopters with the development of the helicopter. The state acceptance evaluation was completed on 29 October 2009. The first eight Ansat-U helicopters were delivered in 2010 to the Torzhok evaluation centre. On 1 March 2011 the Ministry of Defence ordered another batch of 32 helicopters to be delivered by 2018. On 9 October 2011 the first three helicopters of this order were delivered to the Sokol Army Aviation training base near Saratov, where they replaced the unit's Mi-2s. The contract was fulfilled in 2016, ahead of schedule; as a result, the

Russian military now operates a total of 40 Ansat-Us. Another Ministry of Defence contract for at least 20 helicopters, to be delivered in 2017–18, is expected. Above all, this latter order is intended to provide work to the Kazan plant, which otherwise lacks production orders.

Variants

Ansat is the initial civilian general-purpose version.
Ansat-K is the updated version for civilian use.
Ansat-LL (Letayushchaya Laboratoriya, flying test-bed) is used for testing equipment manufactured by the Radar-MMS Company, including sensors for the Kasatka maritime patrol system and missile seekers.
Ansat-U is the military training version, as described.
Ansat-1M (or **Ansat with GMSU**, Gidro-Mekhanicheskaya Sistema Upravleniya, hydro-mechanical control system) represents the first-stage upgrade, with conventional control system. It has the maximum take-off weight increased to 3,600kg (7,937lb) and the maximum internal payload increased to 1,185kg (2,612lb). It can attain a cruising speed of 240km/h (149mph), OGE hovering ceiling of 2,200m (7,218ft), and a normal range of 520km (323 miles). After two prototypes, the first of which flew in May 2012, the helicopter was certified on 28 August 2013 and entered production in 2016.
Ansat-2M is the project for the second stage of the Ansat-M upgrade, with new rotors, aerodynamic improvements and new KBO-226TA avionics (as used in the Ka-226TM). It was expected to fly in 2016.

KB SAT SR-10

The SR-10 takes off for its maiden flight on 25 December 2015. Currently, the aircraft is continuing flight tests at Kubinka air base. (KB SAT)

Manufacturer
The SR-10 was developed by KB SAT (Konstruktorskoye Byuro Sovremyennye Aviatsyonnye Tekhnologii, Modern Aircraft Technologies Design Bureau), a private design bureau, under a team led by Dmitry Kibyets.

Role
The SR-10 is a basic jet trainer.

Crew
The SR-10's student pilot and instructor pilot are seated in tandem.

Airframe and systems
The airframe of the SR-10 is made entirely of composites; the wing is manufactured by the Aviastar-SP plant in Ulyanovsk. A distinctive feature of the SR-10 is the wing, which incorporates moderate (10°) forward sweep.

Powerplant
The prototype SR-10 flies with a single Ukrainian Ivchenko AI-25TL turbofan rated at 16.87kN (3,792lbf), and taken from a Czech L-39C trainer. Production aircraft are to be powered by a Russian engine of similar class, e.g. the Saturn AL-55, Salyut SM-100 or Soyuz RD-2500.

Dimensions
Wingspan 8.40m (27ft 7in); length 9.59m (31ft 5.5in).

Weights
Nominal take-off 2,400kg (5,291lb); maximum take-off 2,700kg (5,952lb); normal landing 2,000kg (4,409lb).

The front (student pilot's) cockpit of the SR-10. (KB SAT)

Performance (design)

Maximum Mach number 0.85; maximum level speed 900km/h (559mph); maximum operational speed 700km/h (435mph); cruising speed 520km/h (323mph); approach speed 185km/h (115mph); ceiling 6,000m (19,685ft); maximum climb rate at sea level 60m/s (11,811ft/min); minimum sustained turn radius 290m (951ft); allowable g-load +10/-8; maximum range 1,500km (932 miles).

History

The SR-10 has been in development since 2007 and its full-scale mock-up was displayed at the International Aviation and Space Salon (MAKS) at Zhukovsky in August 2009. On 25 December 2015 the aircraft took off for its maiden flight from the abandoned military airfield of Oreshkovo, at Vorotinsk, near Kaluga, with test pilot Yuri Kabanov and Maksim Mironov (the owner of the aircraft) at the controls. As of summer 2016, the SR-10 was under evaluation at Kubinka air base. Before having completed the SR-10, the same team restored the historic Yak-30 '80' jet trainer to airworthy condition; it flew on 19 December 2007 after 45 years on the ground. On 20 February 2009 the restored single-seat Yak-32 variant, aircraft '70', was also flown.

Production and operators

In spring 2014 the SR-10 design was submitted to a competition held by the Russian Ministry of Defence for a new initial and basic training aircraft, but lost out to Yakovlev's Yak-152 design. Despite the defeat, KB SAT is still offering the aircraft to the Russian Air Force, this time as a transition trainer to 'fill the gap' between the propeller-driven Yak-152 and the twin-jet Yak-130. In July 2016, the Russian Ministry of Defence decided to accept the aircraft for state evaluation in 2017. However, a Russian military order for the SR-10 seems highly unlikely, since there is no need to introduce another aircraft between the Yak-152 and Yak-130. The SR-10 is also advertised as a sports aircraft and this is likely to represent its probable market niche. If it does enter series manufacture, production would take place at the Smolensk Aircraft Plant.

Mil/PZL Świdnik Mi-2

NATO reporting name: Hoplite

The Russian Air Force operates several dozen Mi-2 helicopters at the Army Aviation's training base in Syzran; the DOSAAF paramilitary organisation has a similar number. (Piotr Butowski)

Manufacturer

Designed by the Mil Design Bureau in Moscow, series manufacture, modification and modernisation of the Mi-2 was undertaken by PZL Świdnik in Poland.

Role

The Mi-2 is a twin-turboshaft general utility helicopter.

Crew

As well as one or two pilots, the Mi-2 has accommodation for seven to eight passengers.

Airframe, rotor system and transmission

The Mi-2 has a conventional three-blade metal main rotor with anti-flutter weights, balance plates and hydraulic dampers, as well as a two-blade tail rotor with its own gearbox.

Powerplant

The Mi-2 is powered by two PZL-Rzeszów GTD-350 turboshafts, each rated at 294kW (400shp). It can carry 600 litres (158 gallons) of standard fuel plus two optional 238-litre (63-gallon) auxiliary tanks on the fuselage sides.

Dimensions

Main rotor diameter 14.5m (47ft 7in); tail rotor diameter 2.7m (8ft 10in); length with rotors turning 17.42m (57ft 2in); fuselage length 11.4m (37ft 5in); height 3.75m (12ft 4in) to above rotor head; wheelbase 2.71m (8ft 11in); wheel track 3.05m (10ft).

Weights

Maximum take-off 3,550kg (7,826lb).

Performance

Maximum speed 210km/h (130.5mph); cruising speed 190km/h (118mph); OGE hovering ceiling 1,000m (3,281ft); service ceiling 4,000m (13,123ft); climb rate 4.5m/s (886ft/min); ferry range 796km (495 miles); range with maximum payload 170km (106 miles).

Avionics

The basic conventional instruments include a radio altimeter, radio direction finder and transceivers.

History

The Mi-2 (V-2) prototype first flew on 22 September 1961, with Herman Alfyorov at the controls.

Production and operators

After two prototypes had been built by Mil in 1961, subsequent series production was launched in Świdnik, Poland. After the Soviet Union transferred all development, production and marketing responsibilities for the Mi-2 to Poland in 1964, PZL Świdnik became the sole manufacturer of the Mi-2. The first Polish Mi-2 flew on 4 November 1965; by the time production came to an end in 1995 more than 5,450 units had been built, most of these going to the former Soviet Union. The Russian Air Force currently has several dozen Mi-2 helicopters that it uses for training at the air base in Syzran; the DOSAAF paramilitary organisation has several dozen more.

Other military operators of the Mi-2 comprise Algeria (28), Armenia (eight), Azerbaijan (seven), Congo-Brazzaville (three), the Czech Republic (five), Latvia (two), Libya (40, current status unclear), Mexico (three), Moldova (four), Myanmar (15), Poland (75), Senegal (two), Slovakia (two), Syria (20), Ukraine (21) and the United States (two).

Variants in Russian service

The only version in current Russian military service is the basic Mi-2.

Tupolev Tu-134 trainer versions

NATO reporting name: Crusty

The Tu-134Sh is used for training navigators and for bombing practice; it has a bomber radar in an undernose radome and bomb racks under the wing centre section. This particular aircraft, RF-66031, is based at Chelyabinsk. (Piotr Butowski)

Manufacturer

Training versions of the Tu-134 were developed by the Kharkiv factory's design section together with the Tupolev Design Bureau in Moscow, and series manufacture was undertaken in Kharkiv, Ukrainian SSR.

Role

The Tu-134 trainer versions comprise heavy trainers for bomber pilots and navigators. These aircraft were converted from Tu-134 regional commercial aircraft.

Crew

Tu-134 trainer versions are flown by a flight crew of four including two pilots, a navigator and a flight engineer. See individual variants for details of the students carried.

Airframe and systems

See Tu-134A Balkany in previous chapter.

Powerplant

Two Aviadvigatel D-30 series II turbofans rated at 68.0kN (15,278lbf) for take-off. Maximum fuel loads comprise 13,200kg (29,101lb) for the **Tu-134Sh**, or 14,400kg (31,747lb) for the **Tu-134UB-L**.

Dimensions

Tu-134Sh: Length 37.047m (121ft 6.5in); height 9.144m (30ft); wingspan 29.01m (95ft 2in); wing area 127.3m^2 (1,370 sq ft); wheelbase 16.04m (52ft 7in); wheel track 9.45m (31ft).
Tu-134UB-L: Length 41.918 m (137ft 6in); other dimensions unchanged.

Weights

Tu-134Sh: Empty operating 30,000kg (66,139lb); maximum take-off 47,000kg (103,617lb); maximum landing 43,000kg (94,799lb).

Tu-134UB-L: Empty operating 28,890kg (63,692lb); maximum take-off 44,250kg (97,555lb); maximum landing 43,000kg (94,799lb).

Performance

Tu-134Sh: Maximum cruising speed 860km/h (534mph) clean or 800km/h (497mph) with bombs; maximum range 3,400km (2,113 miles) with bombs dropped at halfway point; take-off run 1,400m (4,593ft); landing run 950m (3,117ft) at maximum landing weight.

Tu-134UB-L: Maximum cruising speed 860km/h (534mph); service ceiling 11,800m (38,714ft); maximum range 3,400km (2,113 miles).

Mission systems and avionics

See Variants.

Self-protection features

None.

Armament

Tu-134Sh: Two BD-360 bomb racks, each for the carriage of four 120kg (265lb) practice bombs, later replaced by two 'unified' (as used on the Tu-22M3, for example) MBD3-U6-68Sh bomb racks, each for six P-50 50kg (110lb) practice bombs.

Tu-134UB-L: None.

50kg (110lb) P-50 practice bombs on a rack under a Tu-134Sh. (Piotr Butowski)

The cockpit of the Tu-134UB-L bomber trainer, used for training Tu-22M3 and Tu-160 pilots. (Alexandr Shatsky)

History

The first Tu-134 trainer version, the Tu-134Sh, was developed by the Kharkiv aircraft plant's design team in 1971 with the intention of replacing the previous Tu-124Sh trainers used for bomber crews, and which were also manufactured in Kharkiv. The early Tu-134Sh received the same equipment as the Tu-124Sh-1.

Production and operators

The Kharkiv plant in Ukraine completed 852 Tu-134s, 199 of which were military trainer versions delivered to the Soviet Air Force. Currently, around 18 Tu-134Sh, 18 Tu-134UB-L and two Tu-134UB-KM training aircraft remain airworthy within the Russian Air Force's navigator school at Chelyabinsk, pilot school at Balashov and operational training centres at Ryazan and Yeysk. In the early 2000s at least seven Tu-134UB-L aircraft were converted by an aircraft repair plant in Minsk, Belarus, to become VIP transport versions for 10 to 15 passengers, with the new designation Tu-134B3-M. These conversions were attractive, since the Tu-134UB-Ls were the youngest Tu-134 airframes and had far completed far fewer cycles than comparable aircraft operated by airlines. In February 2013 the Russian Air Force applied for Ministry of Defence funding for the overhaul and restoration to airworthiness of around 50 Tu-134Sh and UB-L aircraft. Overhauls of these aircraft are being conducted in Minsk.

Variants

Tu-134Sh (Shturmanskiy, for navigators) is intended for training bomber aircraft navigators and for bombing practice. Externally it differs from the initial Tu-134A passenger version only in its enlarged radar radome under the glazed nose and the bomb racks fitted under the wing centre section (which has been strengthened for this purpose). The Tu-134Sh variant used for training navigators of long-range bombers and maritime patrol aircraft (informally referred to as the **Tu-134Sh1**) was fitted with the R-1A

RF-93938 is one of two Tu-134UB-KM conversions of Tu-134UB-L aircraft used for training Tu-22M weapons system operators.
The Tu-134UB-KM has the PNA radar and optical bombsight under the centre fuselage, both taken from the Tu-22M3. Note also the bomb racks.
(Avtor)

Rubin radar from the original Tu-22 bomber (NATO reporting name Blinder) installed within the undernose radome. The variant for training the navigators of tactical bombers (**Tu-134Sh2**) was equipped with the I-2 Initsiativa radar from the Yak-28 bomber. The OPB-15 bombsight from the Tu-22 was installed in the glazed nose, and two ventral windows were added for the BTs-63 sextant. In the cabin, 13 stations are installed for navigator trainees, but in practice only the two forward stations are important, one being equipped with the OPB-15 bombsight and the other with a radar sight. The remaining stations have only minimum equipment; as a result, there are typically no more than four trainees on board. The first Tu-134Sh flew in Kharkiv on 12 February 1971; production of this version totalled 90 aircraft.

Tu-134UB-L (Uchebno-Boyevoy dla Lyotchikov, combat trainer for pilots; NATO reporting name Crusty-B), derived from Tu-134B commercial airliner, is intended for training Tu-22M3 and Tu-160 bomber pilots. The Tu-134 was chosen for this role due to its thrust-to-weight ratio and take-off and landing characteristics being similar to those of the Tu-22M. The nose of the Tu-22M was 'mated' to a Tu-134B airframe, but inside the nose the standard ROZ-1 weather radar of the Tu-134 was installed. Because longitudinal and transverse stability are considerably worse at high angle of attacks, the permitted take-off weight had to be reduced to 44,250kg (97,554lb); the standard Tu-134B has a maximum take-off weight of 47,600kg (104,940lb). In the passenger cabin are seats for 12 trainees, who take turns occupying the co-pilot's seat during the flight. The first Tu-134UBL flew on 17 March 1981 in Kharkov; a total of 109 Tu-134UBL aircraft were built.

Tu-134UB-KM is a mid-life conversion of the Tu-134UB-L intended for training weapons system operators (WSOs) of the Tu-22M; two aircraft were converted in 1996 and 1999 by the ARZ-20 repair plant in Pushkin, near St Petersburg. The PNA radar from the Tu-22M3 was installed in the nose of the Tu-134UB-KM; the weather radar was moved to the lower fuselage. Under the centre section of the fuselage were installed the 015T optical bombsight from the Tu-22M, two MBD3-U6-68 bomb racks and a fairing for an AFA-BAF/40R photographic camera. The aircraft has equipment that can imitate the launch procedures of the Kh-22M anti-ship missile. Earlier, in 1983, a single Tu-134UB-L (CCCP-64728, the last UB-L to be built) belonging to the Leninets Company was converted by the Pushkin plant for training Tu-22M WSOs of the Soviet Navy, designated **Tu-134UB-K** (K for Komplex, complex). After the collapse of the USSR, this aircraft remained in Ukraine and was scrapped in the mid-1990s.

Yakovlev Yak-52

The Yak-52 is used for pilot selection and initial training aircraft and is operated by Russia's DOSAAF paramilitary organisation.
(Piotr Butowski)

Manufacturer

Developed by the Yakovlev Design Bureau in Moscow, series manufacture of the Yak-52 was undertaken by Aerostar in Bacau, Romania.

Role

The Yak-52 is a fully aerobatic trainer and pilot selection aircraft.

Crew

The Yak-52 accommodates two pilots in a tandem cockpit; there is no elevation provided for the (rear) instructor's position.

Airframe and systems

The Yak-52 is an all-metal low-wing monoplane. Its wing has pneumatically actuated split flaps and slotted ailerons with ground-adjustable tabs. The conventional tail unit has elevators and a rudder. The flight control system is mechanical with push-rods and cables, with the exception of pneumatic flaps. The semi-retractable landing gear is of the nosewheel type; the mainwheel legs retract forwards and the nosewheel retracts aft, leaving all three wheels exposed to prevent serious damage in a wheels-up landing. Skis are optional.

Powerplant

The single OKBM M-14P radial piston engine develops 268kW (360hp), driving a 2.4m (7ft 10in) V-530TA-D35 two-blade variable-pitch propeller. The aircraft has provision for 122 litres (32.2 gallons) of fuel.

Dimensions

Length 7.745m (25ft 5in); height 2.7m (8ft 10in); wingspan 9.3m (30ft 6in); wheelbase 1.86m (6ft 1in); wheel track 2.71m (8ft 11in).

Weights

Empty equipped 1,015kg (2,238lb); maximum take-off 1,305kg (2,877lb).

Performance

Never exceed speed 360km/h (224mph); maximum speed 285km/h (177mph); stall speed 90km/h (56mph) flaps down; take-off run 170m (560ft); landing run 300m (984ft); maximum climb rate 7m/s (1,378ft/min) at sea level; g limits +7/-5; ceiling 4,000m (13,125ft); range with maximum fuel 550km (342 miles).

Avionics

The Yak-52's instrumentation is very simple and includes a GMK-1A gyro and ARK-15M radio direction finders, Baklan-5 VHF communication radio, and SPU-9 intercom.

History

The prototype Yak-52 first flew on 8 August 1974, with Yuri Mitikov at the controls. During the early years of the Soviet war in Afghanistan, in May 1982 Yakovlev converted two Yak-52s into Yak-52B (Boyevoy, combat, or Yak-54) ground-attack versions armed with UPK-23 gun pods and UB-32 rocket pods on two pylons under the strengthened wing; an optical sight was fitted. The aircraft passed only preliminary tests. One of these aircraft is now on display at the aviation museum in Monino.

Production and operators

Series production of the Yak-52 was launched under an agreement within COMECON (the Soviet-led Council for Mutual Economic Assistance) at the Romanian Intreprinderea de Avioane plant in Bacau (now Aerostar SA). The first Romanian-built aircraft

A recently overhauled Romanian Air Force Yak-52 is seen at the Aerostar facility in Bacau. (Alexander Golz)

Non-Russian operators of the Yak-52 include the Vietnam People's Air Force, which is a recipient of recent-production aircraft from the Aerostar factory.
(VPAF-8AG via Grandolini)

flew in May 1978; the 1,500th aircraft was completed in spring 1990. After 1992 production dwindled due to a lack of further orders from Russia but continued on a small scale to meet orders from private Western users (Yak-52V version). Approximately 1,800 units have been to date, most of which were delivered to the USSR. In addition, 12 aircraft were delivered to Hungary in 1994, six of which were upgraded by Aerostar in 2003. A further 32 aircraft were delivered to Vietnam. Russia's DOSAAF aero clubs currently operate around 200 Yak-52s; however, the deputy head of the DOSAAF Viktor Chernov said in July 2014 that only 30 of these aircraft remained airworthy.

Variants

Yak-52, as described, is the only version used in Russia.
Yak-52B (Boyevoy, combat, or **Yak-54**) ground-attack version. See History.
Yak-52M is a prototype of an upgraded aircraft prepared in collaboration between Yakovlev and the ARZ-308 repair plant in Ivanovo. The M-14P engine has been upgraded to the M-14Kh version; the two-blade V-530 propeller was replaced by a three-blade MTV-9. Additional fuel tanks in the wing provided for an increase in range to 900km (559 miles). The most expensive part of the modernisation programme was the installation of the SKS-94MYa pilots' ejection system and a new cockpit canopy that was required as a result. The Yak-52M prototype performed its maiden flight on 16 April 2004, piloted by Oleg Kononenko. However, the Russian Air Force refused further orders.

Yakovlev Yak-130

NATO reporting name: Mitten

A pair of Russian Air Force Yak-130s executes a formation take-off, led by RF-44574 '59 White'. As of 2016 the aircraft were on strength with Russian Air Force units based at Armavir and Borisoglebsk. (Stanislav Bazhenov)

Manufacturer

Designed by the Yakovlev Design Bureau in Moscow, series manufacture of the Yak-130 is undertaken by the Irkutsk Aircraft Plant, both these entities belonging to the Irkut Corporation. Four pre-production aircraft, and the first 12 series-production aircraft, were completed by the Sokol factory in Nizhny Novgorod.

Role

The Yak-130 serves the Russian Air Force as an advanced trainer and lead-in fighter trainer (LIFT). Within pilots' schools, the Yak-130 is supplementing L-39C trainers (incapable of fulfilling the LIFT) as well as two-seat versions of the MiG-29UB and Su-27UB combat aircraft (which are too expensive in this role). Subsequently, within combat units the Yak-130 will provide a more economic supplement to two-seat versions of fighter aircraft in the role of sustaining pilots' skills.

Crew

The crew of two consists of a student pilot (in front) and an instructor seated in a tandem cockpit on Zvezda K36L-3.5Ya 'zero-zero' ejection seats; the front seat ensures 16° look-down visibility, while the rear seat ensures 6° look-down visibility. The original oxygen system was replaced by an on-board oxygen generator.

Airframe and systems

The Yak-130 is a mid-wing monoplane with the leading edge of the wing swept by 31°, while the trailing edge is perpendicular to the aircraft axis. The wing is fitted with automatic slats on the leading edges and ailerons and Fowler-type flaps on the trailing edges. The all-moving slab tailplane has dogtooth extended-chord leading edges. A door-type airbrake is incorporated in the upper fuselage. The airframe is built mainly of light alloys; carbon fibre-based composites are used for most of the control surfaces. Damage tolerance concepts are used throughout the airframe design. The aircraft is equipped with a KSU-130 quadruple digital fly-by-wire (FBW) flight control system.

Powerplant

The two Ukrainian Progress AI-222-25 turbofans with full-authority digital engine control (FADEC) are each rated at 24.5kN (5,510lbf). The engines were manufactured under a 50:50 cooperation agreement between the Ukrainian Motor Sich and Russian Salyut factories. In April 2015, Salyut declared that it was now producing the entire engine, including the 'hot' section that was previously delivered from Ukraine. Currently, and in order to circumvent licensing complications, Salyut is developing the SM-100 turbofan engine based on the AI-222-25 to power future Yak-130s.

Up to 1,700kg (3,747lb) of fuel can be carried in three internal tanks (one in the fuselage behind the cockpit and one inside each wing); the nominal fuel load is around 880kg (1,940lb). Two auxiliary drop tanks are fitted as standard under the wing; each contains 590 litres (156 gallons) of fuel, equivalent to 450kg (992lb). The main air intakes, located under the leading-edge root extensions (LERXes), are covered when the aircraft is on the ground and during take-off and landing, in order to protect the engines against foreign objects; in this configuration, air is provided to the engines via additional intakes installed on the upper surface of the wing-root extensions. The aircraft has a TA-14-130 auxiliary power unit.

Dimensions

Wingspan 9.84m (32ft 4in); length 11.493m (37ft 8.5in); height 4.76m (15ft 7in); wing area 23.52 m^2 (253 sq ft); wheelbase 3.949m (12ft 11in); wheel track 2.53m (8ft 4in).

Weights

Take-off, trainer configuration, no external stores 7,230kg (15,935lb); maximum take-off 10,290kg (22,679lb).

Performance

Maximum speed, sea level, 50 per cent internal fuel, clean 1,060km/h (659mph); maximum Mach number 0.93; approach speed, clean 190km/h (118mph); g limits +8/-3; sustained-turn g limit 5.4 at 5,000m (16,404ft); service ceiling 12,500m (41,013ft); climb to 9,000m (29,528ft) 3.0 minutes; operational radius with two 250kg (551lb) bombs, two flare pods, a gun pod and two drop tanks 680km (423 miles) in a hi-lo-hi profile or 380km (236 miles) in a lo-lo-lo profile; operational radius with two 500kg (1,102lb) bombs, two flare pods, two air-to-air missiles, a gun pod and two drop tanks 340km (211 miles) in a lo-lo-lo profile; maximum range, 10 per cent fuel reserves, clean 1,600km (994 miles); ferry range at 12,000m (39,372ft), with two auxiliary tanks 2,100km (1,305 miles); take-off run 550m (1,804ft); landing run 750m (2,461ft).

The front cockpit of the Yak-130 has three large MFTsI-0333M multifunction displays and an ILS-2-02 head-up display with PUI-130 data-input panel. (Piotr Butowski)

Avionics

The Electroavtomatika/St Petersburg K-130.01 (K-130.01E for export) equipment suite is controlled by a BTsVM90-604 computer and performs flight, navigation, targeting and training tasks. It integrates the RPKB/Sagem LINS-100RS-02 laser inertial navigation system (BINS-SP-1 in early aircraft) with the A737 satellite navigation receiver, RSBN-85 TACAN, ARK-40 direction finder, A-053-06 radio altimeter, SUO-130 weapons management system and izdeliye 4280 IFF. The data indication subsystem consists of three 152 x 203mm (6 x 8in) MFTsI-0333M multifunction displays in each cockpit; additionally, there is an ILS-2-02 head-up display with PUI-130 data-input panel in the front cockpit, and another PUI-130.01 panel in the rear cockpit. The pilot is provided with an NSTs-T helmet-mounted target indicator.

Self-protection features

Russian aircraft lack self-protection devices, while the export version for Algeria features two wingtip-mounted UV-26M decoy launchers, each with 64 26mm (1in) flares. The Belarusian Oboronnyye Initsiativy (Defence Initiatives) company offers Talisman electronic countermeasures (ECM) pods for the Yak-130; it is possible that they will be fitted to the aircraft purchased by Belarus.

Armament

The Yak-130 can carry up to a maximum load of 3,000kg (6,614lb), or a nominal load of 1,500kg (3,307lb) of stores including R-73 air-to-air missiles (AAMs), air-to-surface missiles (four Kh-25M), guided bombs (four KAB-500L/Kr), free-fall bombs (eight 250kg, 551lb), rockets, gun pods and fuel tanks. The aircraft has six underwing weapon

Left: Aircraft for Algeria and Belarus have wingtip-mounted UV-26M decoy launchers, each with 64 26mm (1in) flares. Other customers have not ordered this system. (Piotr Butowski)

Right: The centreline ventral NSPU-130 pod with twin-barrel 23-mm GSh-23 cannon is provided with 110 rounds. (Piotr Butowski)

pylons, plus two wingtip rails for close-air combat AAMs (or flare-launcher pods), and a centreline hardpoint under the fuselage that can accommodate an NSPU-130 gun pod (carrying a 23mm GSh-23 cannon with 110 rounds). Laser imitation of the cannon is provided for training purposes.

History

On 25 June 1990 the Soviet Military-Industrial Commission ordered a contest to select a new advanced jet trainer. According to requirements specified by the Soviet Air Force in January 1991 the new aircraft was to be powered by two engines providing a thrust-to-weight ratio of 0.6 to 0.7 at take-off, a normal take-off weight of 5,500kg (12,125lb), manoeuvring characteristics similar to modern fighters, a landing speed not higher than 170km/h (106mph) and annual operating costs 20 per cent lower than the then standard jet trainer in the USSR, the L-39. The competition was contested by the Sukhoi S-54, Myasishchev M-200, Mikoyan 821 (later designated MiG-AT) and Yakovlev Yak-UTS (later designated Yak-130, with reference to the Yak-30 training aircraft of 1960) projects. The first stage of the competition was concluded in January 1992; at the time the Sukhoi S-54 was deemed the best, but its design had to be disqualified, since a single-engine aircraft did not meet the requirements. Among the other designs, Yakovlev gained the highest score, but it was not a clear winner. During the next stage of the contest, on 15 July 1992, the Myasishchev M-200 design was rejected and the Air Force ordered more detailed designs of the aircraft submitted by the Yakovlev and MiG design bureaus. In May 1994 the Yak-130 project was deemed the better option, but the final choice was postponed again, and prototypes of both the Yak-130 and MiG-AT were ordered for testing. The Yak-130D demonstrator built according to the early design specification performed its maiden flight on 25 April 1996, with Andrey Sinitsin at the controls. A significant proportion of Yak-130D trials were conducted at the Aermacchi facility in Italy; in December 1998 the Yak-130D attained a 41° angle of attack during flight trials in Italy.

In 1993, Yakovlev and Aermacchi of Italy began cooperation on a common project under the name AEM/Yak-130. Under pressure from the Italian side, the design of the Yak-130 was significantly revised, primarily in order to reduce aerodynamic drag. In comparison with the original Russian design, the Russo-Italian AEM/Yak-130 was much more compact. The fuselage was 41cm (16in) shorter and the wingspan was

reduced by 94cm (37in). A digital fly-by-wire (FBW) flight control system replaced the previous analogue system. The avionics were developed entirely from scratch, and the gauge-type instruments in the cockpit were replaced by liquid-crystal displays. The configuration of the joint Russian-Italian design was frozen in February 1995.

While the AEM/Yak-130 design was taking shape, the Russian-Italian cooperation was increasingly hampered by both partners' actions. The Russian Air Force demanded that the aircraft had Russian engines and avionics while Italy preferred alternative systems. In December 1999, Yakovlev and Aermacchi ended their cooperation and since then each party has developed its own national version of the aircraft, the Yak-130 in Russia and the M-346 Master in Italy. With the handover of the aircraft's documentation to Aermacchi (today integrated within the Leonardo-Finmeccanica Group), Yakovlev was paid USD77 million; these funds allowed Russia to complete the project.

On 16 March 2002 the Yak-130 was finally approved by the Russian Air Force, beating the MiG-AT. Soon after, the Russian Ministry of Defence ordered three aircraft in the new configuration for tests, to be built at the Sokol plant at Nizhny Novgorod. The first of these aircraft, '01' made its maiden flight on 30 April 2004, with Roman Taskayev at the controls, followed by '02' on 5 April 2005 and '03' on 27 March 2006. When aircraft '03' crashed, it was replaced by '04' that first flew in July 2008.

In October 2005 the factory trials were completed. However, on 26 July 2006 aircraft '03' crashed because of a control system failure; the pilots ejected successfully. Flights of the two remaining aircraft were suspended for many months, while changes were made to the design and, primarily, the control system software. In November 2007 the Yak-130 completed the first stage of state evaluations, which formally provided the clearance for production of an initial batch of 12 aircraft, ordered as early as May 2005. On 22 December 2009 the Yak-130 completed state evaluations, which gave formal clearance for the aircraft to be operated within military units.

In the 1990s and early 2000s, Yakovlev prepared a series of preliminary designs for combat derivatives of the Yak-130. The Yak-131 was to be a Yak-130 with radar and expanded weapons options. The Yak-133 was to be a single-seat ground-attack aircraft (the rear seat replaced by an 850kg, 1,874lb fuel tank) powered by two more powerful AI-222-28 engines, each developing 27.46kN (6,173lbf). The Yak-133IB (Istrebitel-Bombardirovshchik) was to be a fighter-bomber, the Yak-133R (Razvedchik) a reconnaissance aircraft, and the Yak-133PP (Postanovshchik Pomekh) an escort jamming aircraft. The Yak-135 was to be a supersonic single-seat aircraft powered by two afterburning AI-222 engines, similar to the Chinese Hongdu L-15. Yakovlev also considered a modular family of heavy (with a take-off weight of around 10,000kg, 22,046lb) unmanned aerial vehicles (UAVs) known as Proryv (breakthrough); these were to be developed with the maximum utilisation of Yak-130 technology. UAVs included the Proryv-U (Udarnyi, strike) strike version capable of attaining a speed of 1,100km/h (684mph) with a 3,000kg (6,614lb) weapons load, as well as low-speed Proryv-R reconnaissance and Proryv-RLD (Radio-Lokatsyonnogo Dozora) early warning versions featuring long unswept wings.

Trials, and then operations, by Yak-130s were suspended several times due to accidents resulting from problems related to the aircraft's flight control system. In addition to the aforementioned '03', which crashed on 26 July 2006, on 29 May 2010 aircraft '93' crashed during take-off from Lipetsk airfield; the pilots survived. The crash was caused by the control system's vulnerability to maintenance faults by the ground crew:

The Belarusian fleet of Yak-130s includes a combat role, as demonstrated by this example armed with a pair of five-round B-13L launchers for 122mm (4.8in) rockets. (Stanislav Bazhenov)

during an inspection a technician zeroed the indications for all parameters, while in reality the parameters were not neutral. After take-off the control system interpreted the aircraft's position as exceeding the permissible envelope and attempted to 'correct' it, destroying the aircraft. As a result, flights were suspended again for many months. In the meantime, the flight control system software was completely rewritten. Another fatal crash occurred on 15 April 2014, near Akhtubinsk, killing one pilot. Flights by the Yak-130 were suspended again, until July 2014.

Production and operators

In May 2005 the Russian Air Force placed an order for 12 Yak-130 aircraft with the Sokol plant in Nizhny Novgorod. However, their production was delayed pending the completion of development flight trials. The first of these aircraft, '90', flew as early as 19 May 2009, but delivery was postponed until official certification was received in December 2009. Four aircraft, '90' to '93', were delivered to the crew conversion and military evaluation centre at Lipetsk between February and April 2010 (the first of these, '91', landed at Lipetsk on 18 February 2010); the remaining eight aircraft, '21' to '28', were deployed to the training air base at Borisoglebsk, near Voronezh, where the first example arrived on 6 April 2011.

In 2004 the Irkut Corporation bought the Yakovlev Design Bureau and decided to move Yak-130 production to the corporation's main factory in Irkutsk. The first Yak-130 made by the Irkutsk plant was '134', which flew on 21 August 2009; it is used by Yakovlev for tests. After the four pre-series and 12 series-production aircraft built in Nizhny Novgorod, all subsequent aircraft have been manufactured in Irkutsk.

On 7 December 2011 the Russian Ministry of Defence placed an order with Irkut for a batch of 55 aircraft valued at over 25 billion roubles (over USD800 million at the then exchange rate), with the delivery to be completed by 2015. The first aircraft from this order arrived at Borisoglebsk on 5 October 2012; on 8 November 2014, deliveries began

Russian Air Force Yak-130 RF-81689 '80 Red' carries underwing stores in the form of B-8 rocket pods for 80mm (3.1in) rockets and free-fall bombs.
(Stanislav Bazhenov)

to another air training base at Armavir. In December 2013 the Ministry of Defence ordered another 12 aircraft for a new aerobatic display team, with deliveries to be made in 2015 (in fact, these aircraft were not delivered; it is likely that the first Sokol-made aircraft will instead be adapted for the display role). The aerobatic version of the Yak-130 is lighter, being stripped of certain items of equipment, and has smoke generators for displays. Another order of December 2013 was for 10 aircraft for the Russian Navy's aviation training centre at Yeysk. An order for four aircraft for the cosmonauts' training centre at Chkalovskaya air base (Star City) is expected.

By early 2016 the Russian Ministry of Defence had received 79 aircraft from the total of 89 ordered; 44 of these were at Borisoglebsk, 32 at Armavir, one at Akhtubinsk, and two had been lost in accidents. Another four aircraft participate in the test programme with the Yakovlev Design Bureau; one further test aircraft crashed. The very first Yak-130D demonstrator has been handed over to the aviation museum at Monino. In 2016 the Russian Ministry of Defence intends to continue purchases; according to the Russian Defence Minister Sergey Shoygu, a total of 150 Yak-130s will be acquired between 2016 and 2020.

The first foreign contract for the Yak-130 came from Algeria, which in March 2006 ordered 16 aircraft to be supplied in 2008–09. In the event, deliveries began after a three-year delay. On 28 November 2011 the first three Yak-130s were transported by An-124 from Irkutsk to Algeria; they were joined by the 13 remaining aircraft within the following weeks. The Algerian version has instruments scaled in Imperial units and labels in French, an export variant of the IFF equipment as well as two 26mm (1in) UV-26M flare launchers installed at the wingtips as standard. A new order from Algeria is also possible; the previous contract includes a significant option for additional aircraft.

The next contract of January 2010 covered six aircraft (with an option for a further six) for Libya; this was subsequently cancelled. Another contract for 36 Yak-130s

Serial 104 is one of 16 Yak-130s ordered by Bangladesh in 2013. (Raihan Ahmed)

placed by Syria in December 2011 was suspended for a long time for political reasons; as early as 20 May 2008, Syrian pilots conducted familiarisation flights on the Yak-130 at Zhukovsky. However, since relations between the West and Russia have worsened, Russian officials have declared that they may begin deliveries to Syria.

On 18 December 2012, Belarus placed an order for four Yak-130s to be delivered in 2015. The initial Belarusian aircraft, '71', made a first flight at Irkutsk on 27 February 2015 and was delivered to Belarus on 14 April. All four aircraft ('71' to '74') were inducted into service at the Belarusian Air Force's 116th Attack Air Base at Lida on 27 April 2015. On 28 August 2015, Belarus ordered another four Yak-130s to be delivered in 2016; the first of these, '75', took to the air at Irkutsk on 28 May 2016 and the last, '78', flew on 2 July 2016. The Belarusian aircraft are also intended for combat missions. In 2015, Belarusian Yak-130s successfully launched guided bombs; on 4 February 2016 they fired R-73 AAMs for the first time.

Algerian Yak-130s feature some changes including export IFF equipment and wingtip flare launchers. (via Pit Weinert)

In 2013, Bangladesh ordered 16 aircraft to be delivered in 2015–16. The first of these flew in Irkutsk on 29 April 2015; the first six were induced into service in Bangladesh on 6 December 2015.

On 22 June 2015, Myanmar placed an order for an unknown number of Yak-130s.

The Rosoboronexport arms trade company and Irkut are conducting talks offering Yak-130s to a dozen Asian, African and South American countries as well as ex-Soviet states. In recent years, separate demonstrations of the aircraft and familiarisation flights have been made for delegations from Armenia, Azerbaijan, Iraq, Kazakhstan, Mongolia, Myanmar, Nicaragua, Uruguay and Vietnam. Russia has also offered the Yak-130 to Brazil, including an option to install Brazilian avionics and offer the aircraft to other Latin American countries.

Some years ago Yakovlev prepared studies of a series of single-seat Yak-133 combat aircraft based on the Yak-130 airframe. This is a fighter version with a radar and R-73 and R-77 air-to-air missiles. The aircraft are still within the company's portfolio. (Yakovlev)

Variants

Yak-130.01 is the initial production version made in Nizhny Novgorod; its internal factory designation is **izdeliye 62**.
Yak-130.11 are the aircraft built in Irkutsk for the Russian Air Force, as well as for Belarus.
Yak-130.12 are the aircraft for export.

Future variants

Yak-130M is the designation for a future aircraft to be developed within the **Ustupka** (concession) research and development programme, consisting of a modernisation of the equipment. The key element of the upgrade is a new mission computer. Other elements stipulated for the Yak-130M include improved inertial navigation, a new head-up display as well as the addition of a second radio. A new LD-130 laser rangefinder was first tested-fitted in front of the cockpit of Yak-130 '134', and was then built in to the nose of '01', both these aircraft belonging to Irkut. The LD-130, with built-in television camera for target identification, is aimed to improve the accuracy of cannon fire. The Yak-130 '01' with the LD-130 laser rangefinder, Belarusian Talisman-NT ECM pods mounted on the wingtips, as well as with a ventral gun pod, bombs and rockets, was displayed at the International Aviation and Space Salon (MAKS) at Zhukovsky in 2015. Range for ferry flights is to be extended by the addition of two (or a maximum of four) auxiliary drop tanks. An optional removable in-flight refuelling probe will meet MIL-A-87166 standard. Finally, the aircraft's undercarriage is to be strengthened.
LUS (Logkiy Udarnyi Samolyot, lightweight strike aircraft) is the codename for a further combat derivative of the Yak-130 with central computer, OEPrNK (Optiko-Elektronnyi Pritselno-Navigatsionnyi Kompleks) electro-optical targeting-navigation complex and a nose radar (the options for the radar are the FK-130 Kopyo-50 from Phazotron or Bars-130 from NIIP, or the Italian Grifo-200 from Leonardo-Finmeccanica). The targeting system will enable the use of the new Kh-38M air-to-ground guided missile, laser-guided bombs, Kh-31 anti-ship/anti-radiation missiles and beyond visual range AAMs.

Three views of another Yak-133 iteration, which in this version has a laser rangefinder and target designator in the nose instead of radar. (Yakovlev)

Yakovlev Yak-152

An artist's impression of the Yak-152, intended to serve as the Russian Air Force's future primary trainer and pilot screening aircraft. (Irkut)

Manufacturer
The Yak-152 was developed by the Yakovlev Design Bureau in Moscow, and series manufacture will be undertaken by the Irkutsk Aircraft Plant, both these entities belonging to the Irkut Corporation.

Role
The Yak-152 is a primary trainer and pilot selection aircraft for both civil and military use.

Crew
The Yak-152's student pilot and instructor (at the rear) are seated in tandem under a single bubble canopy; the crew are provided with SKS-94M2-152 ejection seats.

Airframe and systems
A low-wing monoplane with classic configuration and simple, reliable structure, the Yak-152 employs advanced aerodynamics to provide a high lifting force and in order to avoid spin. The retractable undercarriage is of the nosewheel type, with robust shock-absorbers and low-pressure tyres.

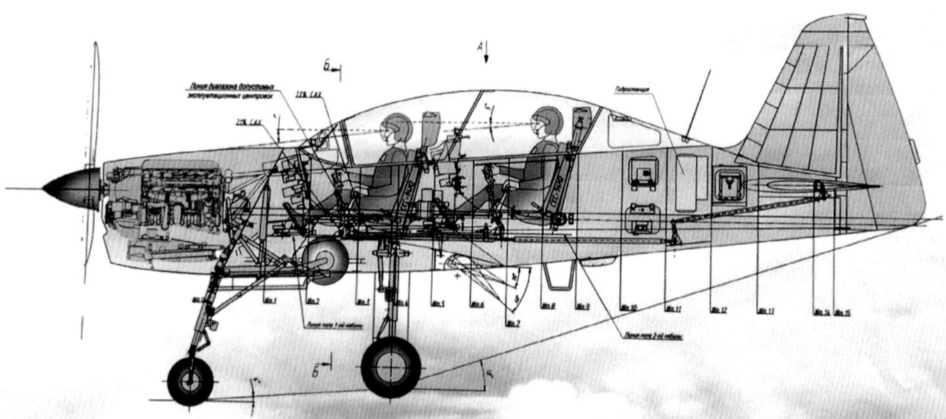
Yak-152 cutaway drawing (Irkut)

Powerplant

There are several engine options for the Yak-152. The baseline version for the Russian Air Force will be powered by an A03T six-cylinder Diesel engine rated at 368kW (500hp) at take-off, produced by RED (Raikhlin Aircraft Engine Development) GmbH, a company established in Germany by an emigrant from Russia, Vladimir Raikhlin; with this engine, the aircraft will have a three-blade MTV-9-E-C propeller. An alternative engine is the Russian OMKB M-14Kh piston engine rated at 265kW (360hp), as used in the Chinese Hongdu L-7. Further options are the RED A05 Diesel (221kW, 300hp) or Ukrainian Ivchenko turboprop AI-450 (331kW, 450shp). A total of 175kg (386lb) of fuel can be carried.

Dimensions

Wingspan 8.8m (28ft 10in); tailplane span 3.32m (10ft 11in); length 7.8m (25ft 7in); wing area 12.9 m^2 (138.9 sq ft), height 3.11m (10ft 2in).

Weights

Maximum take-off 1,490kg (3,285lb).

Performance (design, with A03T engine)

Maximum speed 500km/h (311mph); g limit +8/-6 (or +9/-7 with single pilot); climb rate 10m/s (1,969ft/min); ceiling 4,000m (13,123ft); range with maximum fuel 1,500km (932 miles); take-off distance 255m (771ft); landing distance 420m (1,378ft).

Avionics

Russia's Ministry of Defence requirement specifies that the aircraft's cockpit should be similar to that of modern tactical aircraft and that the Yak-152 is 'to provide continuity of skills for further mastering of the Yak-130 combat trainer'.

Armament

The version of the Yak-152 powered by the RED A03T engine is able to carry 550kg (1,213lb) of weapons and stores on four underwing pylons, including gun pods, rocket launchers, bombs and air-to-air missiles for close air combat.

The maiden flight of the Yak-152 took place at the airfield of the Irkutsk Aircraft Plant on 29 September 2016. The flight was performed by test pilot Vasiliy Sevastyanov. (Irkut)

History

The Yak-152 programme has been launched on several occasions. In the first instance, the Russian Air Force announced the tender for a successor to the Yak-52 as early as June 2001. From two proposals, the Yak-152 and Su-49, the Sukhoi project was selected in November 2001, but genuine work never began. The Ministry of Defence again announced a contest for an initial training aircraft in 2007, under the UTK PNP (Uchebno-Trenirovochnyi Kompleks Pervonachalnoi Podgotovki, Training Complex of Initial Training) programme, but this came to nothing. The rival to the Yak-152 was the Myasishchev M-107 design, based on the M-101T turboprop executive aircraft.

Meanwhile, the Yak-152 was eventually realised over a decade later, in order to meet a Chinese order. According to an agreement of June 2006, Yakovlev utilised the Yak-152 design as the basis for the AVIC (Aviation Industry Corporation of China) Hongdu L-7 (CJ-7) Kadet/Sokolik (cadet/brave young man) piston trainer. The L-7 prototype was presented at Airshow China in Zhuhai in November 2010. However, the exact state of the Chinese programme remains unknown; reportedly, the aircraft has only performed one flight and is now undergoing static tests.

Currently the UTK PNP programme is being implemented under the codename Ptichka-VVS (little bird). The design and mock-up of the Yak-152 were approved by a Russian Ministry of Defence commission during 23–25 September 2014. According to the contract, series manufacture and deliveries of the Yak-152 were to begin in November 2016. Previously, two flying prototypes and two static airframes for strength and fatigue tests were to be completed at the Irkutsk Aircraft Plant. As of June 2016, the first Yak-152 was under assembly in Irkutsk; finally, a maiden flight was recorded by the initial Yak-152 prototype on 29 September 2016.

Production and operators

Russia's Deputy Minister of Defence Yuri Borisov announced in September 2015 that the ministry would order around 150 examples of the Yak-152. Somewhat earlier, in June 2015, Andrey Lebyedyev, the chief of air operations of DOSAAF, said that his organisation was planning to purchase 105 Yak-152s by 2020.

FUTURE TRAINERS

Tupolev UTK DA

In order to replace the Tu-134 and An-26 aircraft used for training heavy bomber air-crew, a new aircraft, known as the **UTK DA** (Uchebno-Trenirovochnyi Kompleks Dal-ney Aviatsii, Training Complex of Long-Range Aviation) is planned. Reportedly, the UTK DA will be a variant of the Tu-214 airliner, although this seems to be an exces-sively expensive solution to this future requirement.

APPENDIX I: AIRCRAFT DESIGN AND PRODUCTION FACILITIES

Aero Vodochody

Antonov

Military aircraft in Russia are designed by nine long-established design teams named after their founders: Beriev, Ilyushin, Kamov, Myasishchev, Mikoyan, Mil, Sukhoi, Tupolev and Yakovlev; they are all located in Moscow or its vicinity, apart from Beriev, which is found at Taganrog on the Sea of Azov.

Entirely different to these major players is a new Russian design team, KB SAT (Konstruktorskoye Byuro Sovremyennye Aviatsyonnye Tekhnologii, Modern Aircraft Technologies Design Bureau), a private design bureau based in Moscow, and currently developing the SR-10 basic jet trainer.

One more well-established design team, Antonov, works in Kiev, the capital of Ukraine. Until recently, and despite the collapse of the Soviet Union nearly a quarter of a century ago, Antonov continued to cooperate closely with Russia.

Previously, in Soviet times, a number of military aircraft designs intended for Soviet military service were manufactured outside the Soviet Union, with production facilities including Aerostar in Romania, Aero Vodochody in Czechoslovakia and PZL Świdnik in Poland.

Today, the only such arrangement providing military aircraft to the Russian Ministry of Defence involves Aircraft Industries, a Russian-owned holding that produces the L-410 transport, originally developed and produced by the Let factory in Kunovice, based in what is now the Czech Republic.

Military aircraft production in Russia

As of 2016, military aircraft and helicopters are produced by the following factories in Russia:

① The Aviacor Aircraft Plant at Samara formerly manufactured Tu-95MS strategic bombers and Tu-154 airliners; by 2015 it was producing An-140 turboprop transports.

② Aviastar-SP at Ulyanovsk formerly produced An-124 heavy transport aircraft; it is now responsible for production of the Il-76 and Il-78, and associated variants including the A-100 airborne early warning and control (AEW&C) aircraft.

③ Beriev Aircraft at Taganrog formerly produced Be-12 and Tu-142 aircraft; it currently produces Be-200 amphibians and upgrades the A-50, Tu-142 and Tu-95MS.

④ The Irkutsk Aviation Plant (a subsidiary of the Irkut Corporation) manufactures Su-30 fighters and Yak-130 jet trainers and is preparing for production of the MC-21 airliner and Yak-152 primary trainer.

⑤ The Kazan Aviation Plant (a subsidiary of Tupolev) formerly produced Tu-22M and Tu-160 heavy bombers; it is currently upgrading these and producing special duty aircraft on the basis of the Tu-214 airliner airframe and is preparing to resume production of the Tu-160.

⑥ Kazan Helicopters produces Mi-8, Mi-17 and Ansat helicopters and is preparing for production of the Mi-38. Restarting production of the Mi-14 is also a possibility.

⑦ The Komsomolsk-on-Amur Aviation Plant (a subsidiary of the Sukhoi Company) produces Su-27, Su-30 and Su-35 fighters and is launching production of the T-50.

⑧ The Kumertau Aviation Production Enterprise (KumAPP) formerly produced Ka-27 and Ka-29 helicopters; it currently manufactures export Ka-28, Ka-31/Ka-35, civil Ka-32 and light Ka-226 helicopters.

⑨ The Lukhovitsy-based Production Centre No. 1 and Moscow-based Production Centre No. 2 are two subsidiaries of the Russian Aircraft Corporation (RAC) MiG, producing MiG-29 fighters; in the distant past the Moscow plant was responsible for building Il-18 airliners and the Il-20, Il-22 and Il-38 military versions based upon it.

⑩ The Nizhny Novgorod Aircraft Building Plant Sokol produced MiG-31s (and is currently upgrading them); after completing a small batch of Yak-130s it continues to manufacture MiG-29UBs. The plant is preparing for production of the Il-114 turboprop.

⑪ The Novosibirsk Aviation Plant (a subsidiary of the Sukhoi Company) formerly produced Su-24 tactical bombers and currently produces the Su-34.

⑫ The Progress Arsenyev Aviation Company formerly produced Mi-24 attack helicopters; it currently manufactures the Ka-52 and is preparing for production of the Ka-62.

⑬ Rostvertol at Rostov-on-Don manufactures Mi-35M (Mi-24) and Mi-28 attack helicopters, as well as Mi-26 transport helicopters.

⑭ The Ulan-Ude Aviation Plant produces various versions of the Mi-8 helicopter. It formerly produced Su-25UBs now intends to manufacture new Su-25UBM attack aircraft.

⑮ The Voronezh Aircraft Production Association (VASO) produces special duty aircraft on the basis of the Il-96 wide-body airliner and An-148 regional airliner; it is currently preparing for production of the Il-112 light transport aircraft.

All the above-mentioned fixed-wing aircraft companies (with the sole exception of the Samara-based Aviacor and KB SAT) are controlled by the United Aircraft Corporation. All helicopter design and production facilities are under the control of JSC Russian Helicopters.

Aviacor

Aviastar-SP

Beriev TANTK

Irkut Corporation

Kazan Helicopters

Komsomolsk-on-Amur

Kumertau

RAC MiG

Nizhny Novgorod

Novosibirsk

Progress Arsenyev

Rostvertol

Ulan-Ude

Voronzeh

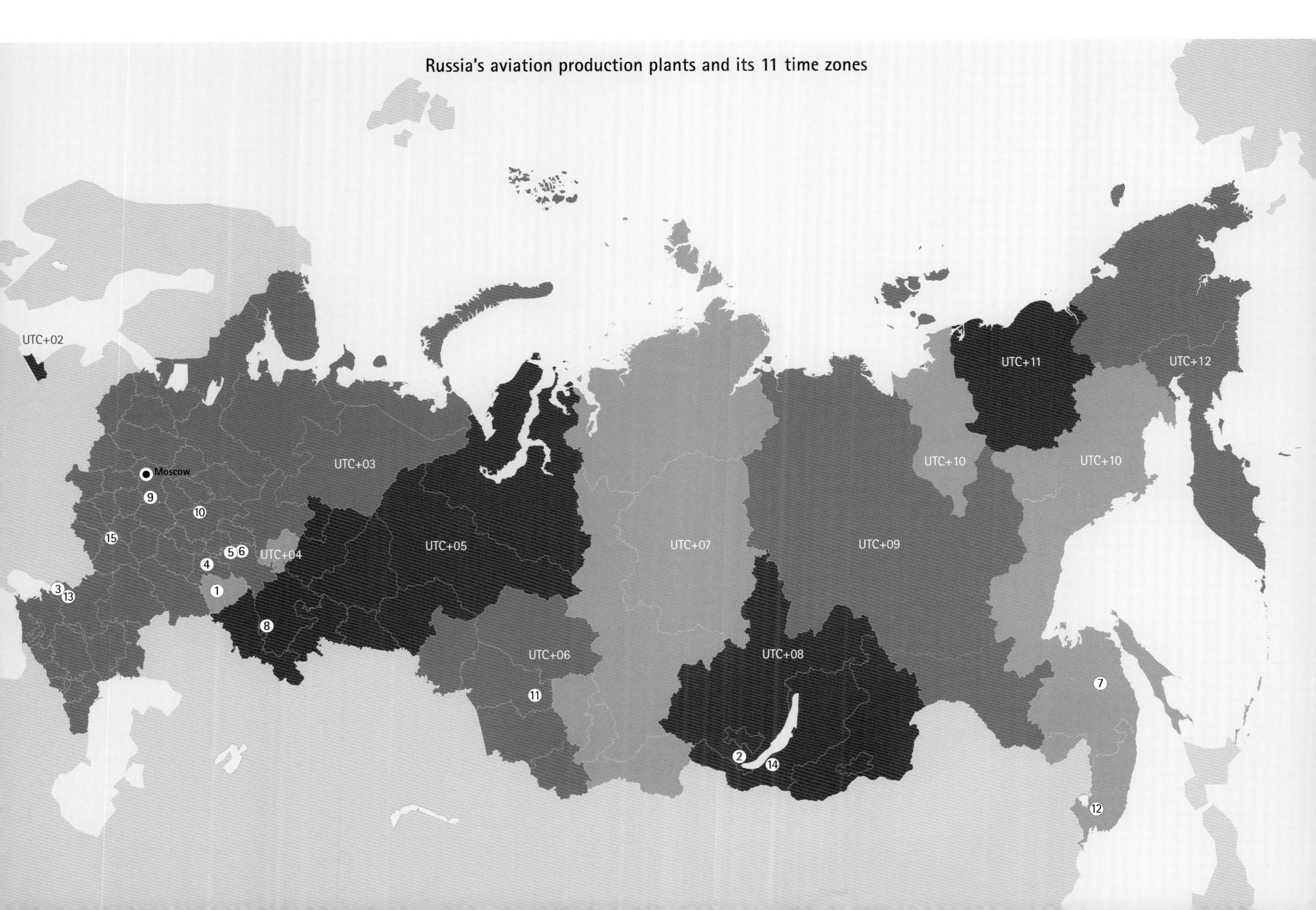
Russia's aviation production plants and its 11 time zones
UTC+02
UTC+03
UTC+04
UTC+05
UTC+06
UTC+07
UTC+08
UTC+09
UTC+10
UTC+10
UTC+11
UTC+12
Moscow
1
2
3
4
5
6
7
8
9
10
11
12
13
14
15